JORDAN'S PAWS ACROSS AMERICA

The True Story of a Dog and His Best Friend

Printed in the United States of America

ISBN 978-0-9821762-0-7

John Fredericks
www.paws-across-america.com

Cover Photos by John Fredericks
Cover and interior design by Gwyn Kennedy Snider

Fredericks, John.

Jordan's Paws Across America: The True Story of a Dog and His Best Friend

Disclaimer
I wrote this book in such a style and manner that it could be read by all age groups. It is
intentionally meant to be an easy read, and I went to great lengths to avoid using harsh
or inappropriate language, wherever possible.

DEDICATION

This book is dedicated to my mother, Eleanor,
who taught me to love the animals.
And, to Jordan, for teaching me everything else that matters.

FOREWORD

DOUG DUKE

EXECUTIVE DIRECTOR OF THE NEVADA SPCA

On a daily basis, and on a scale unmatched by any other media figure we are aware of, whether locally or nationally, John Fredericks and Jordan, both subtly and overtly, challenged countless people over more than a decade to re-think their relationship with companion animals.

Jordan and his life, and his dad's adoration for him, were celebrated during each newscast. Sometimes the messages from John were direct public pleas to not forget animals during times of extreme heat, while other times viewers just noticed that Jordan was at the studio and participating in tapings or brief segments. Regardless, the message was loud and clear—companion animals are loving beings, worthy and meant to be members of the family.

And beyond the helpful, lifesaving tips for animals, such as not leaving them in cars or tied up, John Fredericks and Jordan invited people to consider and support animal rescue on a constant basis. This blessing to animal rescue has been a godsend for those animals in emergency need, as more caring and compassionate people in the community considered helping save a life through a shelter or rescue, than contribute to more animal breeding and overpopulation. John called attention to the efforts of groups and shelters that were committed to making a difference and who were transforming animals without hope into sweethearts ready for adoption.

Jordan became a transformational figure for the community, for the reasons above. And as much as the community cherished him, it was his dad's publicly expressed loyal adoration and love for him that touched hearts and changed minds the most.

JORDAN'S PAWS ACROSS AMERICA

The True Story of a Dog and His Best Friend

JOHN FREDERICKS

with Donna Stidham, Esq.

and Michelle Danks

PROLOGUE

Many years ago, a co-worker of mine told me that four out of every five Americans will appear on TV at least once in his or her lifetime. Imagine that, four out of five. At the time I thought this was rather high. Now, I think the number might be low, especially given the explosion within the information and technology industries. At any rate, if you want to be on TV, you've got a pretty good shot at it.

When I think about it, the number of opportunities to get your face on TV is almost endless: standing behind the glass at the *Today Show*, appearing at a political rally, catching the winning touchdown pass in your high school football game, being interviewed by a local TV crew because you were the victim of a crime, or being deemed a hero because you've pulled someone from a burning house or car.

For some, being on TV is routine. Firefighters and police officers routinely appear in front of the cameras. Then there are the TV pitch people, celebrity spokespeople, reality TV contestants, game show contestants, and people hawking stuff on infomercials. Professional athletes, actors, and television news people appear on a daily or weekly basis. I fall into the latter category.

Again, four out of five Americans will appear on TV during their lifetime. That's an 80 percent chance at glory. Pretty good odds, unless you don't want your face to be seen. Take for example a convicted felon on the lam, or a deadbeat dad being made an example of, or a celebrity socialite who's been caught cheating on his famous model wife. In these cases, a TV crew is the last thing you want at your front door because then the odds are obviously stacked against you.

For one yellow Labrador Retriever, his odds ended up being much better: five out of five, or 100 percent. His name was Jordan. And, had he not been my companion, he would have probably ended up like the millions of other pets in our communities—a family member content to be loved, and in return, give unconditional love to his or her family.

Jordan's television fate was sealed on a spring day in 1994 in Santa Barbara, California. That was the day I rescued him from a "backyard" breeder and took him home with me. Little did I know at the time, but it was he who was rescuing me. I did not intend for Jordan to be on television. The only reason he ended up there, was because I had to take him with me everywhere I went. My living arrangement was ill equipped to handle the needs and living space of a puppy; we had no doggy door, no fenced yard and, because I adopted him on a whim, I had not made petsitter arrangements. So, wherever I went, he came with me. Hence, that included the radio and television stations where I was employed at the time.

As Jordan got older, and his confidence and need to investigate his surroundings grew, he sometimes wandered in front of the camera, making brief, comical, cameo appearances. What followed was far from what I ever imagined possible: Jordan went on to become one of the most popular on-air "personalities" in Las Vegas, Nevada television history. And, while you might not live in Las Vegas, there is still a good chance you've already met him, thanks to one of our on-air bloopers that has run on NBC for several years. I'll address more on this later.

My name is John Fredericks. As I write this, I am the chief meteorologist for the NBC affiliate in Las Vegas. I'm fairly well known by many of the viewers in the Las Vegas community for my on-air weather forecasts. However, I am probably best known for my work within the animal community, and for educating kids and adults not only about the weather, but also about the importance of loving and caring for our four-legged family members. I do believe pets are members of our families. As such, I believe they should be afforded all the care, comforts, and conveniences that any other family member receives.

I am on the board of directors of the Nevada Society for the Prevention of Cruelty to Animals. I work closely with most local rescue organizations and shelters. In the years Jordan accompanied me on television, he became a symbol of responsible pet ownership, proper obedience training, the importance of spaying and neutering pets, and promoting adoption from shelters, rescue organizations, and responsible, reputable breeders.

I initially intended to just write about our adventures on television. And, our cross-country trips together. However, in planning the book, it became clear that I had to tell my story too, because Jordan would not have become so well known had I not gone into broadcasting. Nor do I think I would have ever gained the level of popularity I had if Jordan had not been by my side.

Jordan was my on-air and off-air companion for thirteen and a half years. I was his best friend, and he my loyal sidekick. This is our story.

CHAPTER 1
My Start in Radio and Television Broadcasting

I grew up in Los Angeles, California in the 1960s, when radio meant everything to a young music-lover. The British invasion of The Beatles made this a revolutionary era in rock music. Prior to the British invasion, there were only doo-wop, big vocal groups, girl groups like the Shirelles and the Ronettes, Phil Spector's Wall of Sound, the Beach Boys, and then Elvis Presley. The Beatles invaded, and everything changed. The Fab Four opened the floodgates for other British groups like The Dave Clark Five and The Rolling Stones. The British invasion was followed by "The Motown Sound," the "Psychedelic Era," and, finally, classic rock. In the 1960s, individual radio stations played all types of music, not like it is today, where stations play a very distinctive format of music: Rock, Rap, Hip-Hop, Alternative, Country, and so on. In the sixties and most of the seventies, you would hear a Motown song followed by The Doors, The Beatles, The Supremes, etc., all on the same station. That is what radio listeners accepted, and liked, back in that era.

The radio personalities at that time had what was referred to as the

"Boss Jocks." Boss, as in Groovy, Far Out, Right On, and Bitchin'. With big, distinctive voices and names like Robert W. Morgan, The Real Don Steel, Sam Riddle and Casey Kasem—they were the god's of the airwaves. What they said became broadcasting gospel. And, if they said a song was destined to be a hit, by golly, it was going to be a smash hit. During my youth in the sixties, I came to worship these radio personalities, with hopes that someday I could be like one of them.

During that time, only two radio stations in Los Angeles played mainstream, contemporary, Top-40 hit music. Both were on the AM radio dial. FM radio didn't become widespread until the 1970s.

For Christmas, following my fourteenth birthday, my mother bought me a portable reel-to-reel tape recorder because I told her I wanted to practice being a disc jockey. I would sit at home at night with that tape recorder and record the disc jockeys—not the music—just the disc jockeys. They fascinated me for two reasons. First, they were famous, and most everyone, even secretly, would like to be famous. Second, I thought the disc jockeys played whatever songs they wanted. It wasn't until later I would find out that was the furthest thing from the truth. The music played on radio, for the most part, was pre-selected by the station's music director. So, when a disc jockey went into work, he or she played the songs that the music director had selected, based on popularity. It's no different today.

From a very early age I knew in my heart that one day I would be on the radio. Unfortunately, I was not blessed with a natural radio voice. I grew up with a fairly distinctive lisp and worked on my speech for years to get rid of it. When I eventually fulfilled my dream and became a disc jockey, I taught myself how to work the microphone in such a way that very few people noticed my speech impediment. However, I never did develop what we call in the trade "pipes"—that big, booming voice you hear from many of the best broadcasters.

I didn't become a disc jockey right out of high school. When I was eighteen years old, I had a job in corporate America, working in personnel administration, for a large farming corporation in central California. The job paid great, had good benefits, and suited me just fine at the time. It was during this period that I decided to take broadcasting classes at the local community college.

In the 1970s, disc jockeys had to have a Third Class Radio-Telephone Operators License to work in radio or television. To obtain the license, individuals were required to take a three-part test. Once an individual had their license, they could run everything in a radio station, a position known as the operator on duty. The operator on duty was responsible for all on-air functions of his or her respective radio or television station. Today, disc jockeys do not have this licensing requirement due to deregulation of the Federal Communications Commission (FCC) by President Reagan in the early 1980s.

By now I was married, working in corporate America, and living in Bakersfield, California. In other words, I was bored out of my mind and in need of a hobby. No offense to my beautiful ex-wife or to Bakersfield. The local community college was offering a class in preparation for the FCC Third Class License test. After completing this course in the fall of 1978, I took the test. Though difficult and technical in nature, I felt good about my performance but would have to wait weeks before the test results were released. I did my best to forget about it, and go on with my normal life, much like those who take the Bar Exam.

Several weeks after taking the FCC test, I received a phone call from a gentleman at a talk radio station in Bakersfield, asking me if I would like to work for his station. I told him I was awaiting the results of the FCC Third Class License test. To my surprise, he informed me that I had passed the test and been granted a license. He said the test results had been published, even before I was personally notified. He also said that out of everyone who took the test in Bakersfield, only two people passed, and I was one of them.

I jumped at the chance to work for the radio station. It was an old talk/

music format station, and they only needed me for the weekends. I worked from four p.m. to midnight on Saturday and Sunday evenings. This was a great opportunity for me to learn the radio business, and I could continue working at my corporate job during the week. I was hired to run the control room operating board. For the most part, I sat in the control room and put in tapes of pre-recorded programming, controlling the volume and the transition from one program to the next. Occasionally, the radio station would have live performances. At these times, there wasn't much for me to do after I cued the microphones, except wait for the live performance to end. Then, I'd play the next pre-recorded program.

The station's control mixing board, with all the volume controls and on/off switches, was the original from 1935. And it looked it. It was a big metal monstrosity, resembling an oversized breadbox, with a bunch of rotary volume knobs and toggle switches. The station employees' idea for bringing it up to date was to take a can of blue Krylon spray paint and give it a liberal coating—runs, drips, and all.

My first night of training was with a radio station employee who worked during the same shift I did. He was the one who was allowed to play records. Apparently, I was not trusted to do so during my first few weeks of employment there. One evening, I watched him set a bag of French fries on a record that was to be played next. When the time came, he took the French fries off the record, took out his handkerchief, blew his nose into it, wiped the record off with the dirty handkerchief, set the needle down on the record, and let it go. That was my introduction to the glamour of broadcasting.

After working at the radio station for a few weeks, I was allowed to read the news live on the air once every hour at the top of each hour. I was terrible at it. It seemed every time I spoke into the microphone, the phone lines would light up and I'd prepare for the worst. The callers never minced words. People would call and tell me to go back to work at the car wash, or whatever fast food joint I'd come from. They would say something like "you suck," which was followed by a dial tone. They'd ask me how on earth was I able to get a job at any radio station? The calls that hurt my feelings usually involved something about how I was, "the worst disc jockey on the planet." Or, "just do us a favor—either shut up, or quit." My favorite was when people called in to tell me that I stunk.

I later learned that many of the phone calls came from a salesperson who worked at the station. This individual, most likely having imbibed a few adult beverages, would call me to tell me what a terrible job I was doing. As the evening progressed, and our paltry listenership decreased, the calls decreased as well. By ten or eleven at night, I could say pretty much anything I wanted to, without recourse. Occasionally, I would just start talking about what my day had been like, send "shout-outs" to my wife and friends, or just make stuff up. Once I had a handle on the listening patterns of our viewers, it got to be a real fun gig.

Sadly, I admit, I was awful. But, there are no "naturally good" broadcasters. Disc jockeys aren't born with big booming professional radio voices or personalities. Sounding professional on the radio, takes time to develop. And, it takes years of practice. I may have been terrible, but I loved every second of it.

Every Sunday evening after leaving the radio station, I would drive home, sleep for a couple of hours, then get up to go work at the farming corporation. My co-workers would ask me why I worked at the radio station. They told me I was crazy. I didn't need the money, and they didn't understand why I took the job. My response was always the same. I wasn't doing it for the money—I was doing it because I wanted to be a disc jockey.

Even though I was working toward a dream, my first radio station was a nightmare in terms of conditions and location. There was no central air conditioning. The building's cooling system consisted of swamp coolers, which are useless during hot, humid conditions typical of summer months in Bakersfield. When it got really warm, the employees would simply open all the outside doors. With the doors wide open, there was no security, and the building was located in a terrible part of town. Bakersfield, like any city, had good sections and bad. This station was located in an area that was known as "east of the tracks," meaning on the wrong side of town. It was not uncommon to walk outside at the end of a shift only to find that your car had been vandalized. On other occasions, you were routinely accosted by panhandlers looking for a buck. I thought about bringing some form of personal protection with me to work each afternoon, but I hate guns and I'm not a fan of violence. Fortunately, the worst thing that ever happened was having the air let out of my tires one night.

The radio station only ran during the day. At midnight, I would power down the station transmitter and take it off the air. This was an FCC requirement. If the radio station didn't power down each night, anyone listening in would just hear static over the airwaves; additionally, the operator on duty (me) would have violated FCC regulations. The chief engineer, who happened to be an ordained warlock in a local coven—I told you the place was odd—would call on those occasions I failed to power down the transmitter and threaten me with a spell or curse. I'm not making this up. I'd drive home with visions of being turned into a pig or goat.

Working seven days a week took its toll on me. On many occasions, I fell asleep at the controls and dead air would broadcast over the airwaves long past midnight. Luckily for me, no one listened to the radio station past midnight other than the warlock.

One night, while a pre-recorded show was running, I went into the lobby to lie down on the couch. The next thing I knew it was 2:30 a.m. I failed to shut down the transmitter at midnight. When I walked back into the studio, all I could hear coming from the studio speakers was the transmitter trying to suck up sound over the airwaves. As quickly as I could, I powered down the transmitter and left. Fortunately, the warlock wasn't listening that night. And, since we had the lowest listening audience in town, no one else called either.

Another night I fell asleep during a live program. A gospel choir was in the studio adjacent to me. The studio and control booth where separated by a large glass window. I didn't have to do anything in the control booth during live segments other than sit back and relax. By the time the choir's program ended, I was sound asleep. The on-air light was still lit, so the choir stood silent. After about ten minutes, the minister started tapping on the glass to wake me up. I was sleeping so soundly, he then proceeded to bang on the glass. Finally I woke me up in a panic. I looked at the minister and he mouthed the words, "We're done." So, for ten long minutes all the radio audience had to listen to was silence. I quickly threw a record on and waited for the calls to begin flooding in. I think I received one.

Dead air is a disc jockey's worst nightmare. To this day, I have recurring nightmares from my radio days. It's always the same—the current song is ending and I'm frantically trying to find the next song to play. My arms are in the air reaching for a tape, and nothing's there. When I wake up, my arms are literally in the air reaching for non-existent tapes, I'm soaked in sweat, and often yelling out loud.

I worked for the warlock's talk-music station for seven months until I got my next job, working for the Buck Owens Corporation. Buck Owens had two very popular stations in Bakersfield—an FM rock station and an AM country station.

A friend of mine, who I worked with at the talk-radio station, had gotten a job working part-time for Buck Owens. When he was promoted, the station program director asked if he knew anyone who could take his position. My buddy gave him my name. The open position was on Buck Owens' country station Friday and Saturday nights, from midnight to six a.m. I interviewed with Buck's son, Buddy Alan. Because I was trained in personnel administration and human resource management, Buddy took an immediate liking to me. I had very little on-air experience, but Buddy decided to give me a try.

My on-air work still stunk, but I improved over time. Radio stations played actual records back then. Each record had to be "cued up" (the turntable needle had to be set in a precise location). There was an art to cuing records. First, you placed the record (either a 33 or 45 rpm) on the turntable, and then placed the needle on the record. In order to find the beginning of the song, you had to manually turn the record until you heard the first few notes. Professional turntables reached proper speed after turning a quarter revolution, so you'd back the record up one-quarter turn. This continual process of cuing each record over and over, led to what is known as "cue burn"—the needle would permanently scratch the grooves that preceded each song. These scratches were audible, even to the listener. Commercials were recorded on cartridges, similar to the old eight-track tapes.

Eventually, the station stopped playing music on records; songs were recorded on cartridges just like the commercials. Occasionally the cartridges would drag, which you could hear on-air. Years later, cartridges would make way for CDs and finally, computer hard drives. Compared to the warlock's station this one was state-of-the-art, and I was thrilled to be working there.

One of the duties at my new job was to read the news once an hour, at the top of the hour, over a pre-recorded Teletype sound effect. It was a recording that sounded like a short, quick, tapping sound. Once the news was read, I had to clear the Teletype machine located in the newsroom. This required pulling all of the Teletype wire news copy from the machine, and sorting it each hour. The Teletype included news, sports and weather, and was also the source of emergencies: a bombing, for example, or, god forbid, an assassination attempt on the president.

I would often wait several hours before clearing the Teletype wire copy. This would come back to bite me in the butt. I forgot to clear the Teletype one night, and the news director walked in to the newsroom at 6:00 a.m. He walked over to the Teletype and grabbed all of the copy that had come off the wires the last five or six hours. In other words, I had not monitored the news since the start of my shift. If something bad had happened, I would never have known unless someone called to alert me, and no one had.

Up until now, I had never met the news director. He was a rather gruff individual, highly uncommunicative. The few times I'd passed him in the hallway, he'd never acknowledged my existence, something not uncommon for rookie disc jockeys. I soon learned that many of the "old-timers" resented the "up-and-comers."

So, on this particular morning, the news director came into the studio with the copy, slammed it down in front of me and started screaming, "What the (insert four-letter word here) is wrong with you? The president could have died and nobody would have ever known." The guy went on a tirade: his veins were bulging out in his neck. Had he not been so serious, I would've probably laughed in his face. After all, this was Bakersfield radio, for goodness' sakes. But, he took his job very seriously. So, as I saw it, I had two choices. I could tell him where to go and walk out. Or, I could tell him I was very sorry and it would never happen again. I swallowed my pride and did the latter. It probably saved my job, and maybe even my career in broadcasting. I'll never know for sure. Regardless, I'm glad I decided to be contrite even though it was not in my nature. You have to understand that, at the time, I was in management for one of the largest corporations in California, and I really didn't need the radio station job, or the abuse. I was probably making two to three times as much as this guy, and I must admit, I had a pretty cocky attitude during those days, being young, making good money, and having such an important weekday job. But, by this time, radio was in my blood.

The news director didn't talk to me again for a very long time. Many years later, he became my news director when I was doing the morning radio show, and a friendship developed.

One of the most disturbing events that occurred during my tenure with the Buck Owens Corporation happened during my first day of orientation. It was a warm, late spring afternoon in 1979. The station was located on the main drag, Chester Avenue, in an unincorporated area of Bakersfield, known as Oildale. This area of town was known largely for honky-tonks that brought fame to the likes of Merle Haggard and Buck Owens; and sadly, for its racial segregation and ignorance.

I had just about reached the station's parking lot, and as I was about to pull in, when something across the street caught my attention. I was so shocked I slammed on the brakes, and was nearly rear-ended by the car behind me. Directly across the street from the radio station, on this warm summer afternoon in 1979, was a Ku Klux Klan rally. I'm not making this up. There were over two dozen people in white robes and those big pointed hoods, walking up the street carrying signs that spelled out racial epithets. I managed to pull into the parking lot, lock my car, and get into the station fast. Understandably in shock, I confronted a long-time employee about what I'd just seen, and to my horror and disgust, his response was, "Oh that happens all the time. You'll get used to it." I almost quit on the spot.

Fortunately, the KKK marches ended shortly thereafter. Unfortunately, I will never be able to exorcise those awful images from my head. What is wrong with people?

Several months into my tenure with the Buck Owens Corporation, management decided to discontinue the practice of overnight news reading. During the overnight hours, listenership was at its lowest, and management wanted the station to sound more like a jukebox for those in the listening audience working the graveyard shift.

I stayed on the weekend overnight shift, on and off, for about a year. I was working seven days a week. I would leave my job at the farming corporation on Friday, and go home to my wife. I'd try to get a few hours sleep, then go to work at the radio station at midnight. Then finally, I was offered a better shift—weekend mornings from 6:00 a.m. till noon.

I was so tired from working seven days each week that I once fell asleep at the Buck Owens station also. Luckily, it happened while I was still working the overnight shift, and management never found out. Not long after that incident, I did something even worse, and it almost cost me my job.

It was difficult for disc jockeys to take a bathroom break back then, while live on-air. Today, computers control most on-air programming. In

those days, disc jockeys could only be gone for as long as one song. In the sixties and seventies, songs were very short, lasting only two and a half minutes or less. One day I really had to go to the bathroom, and, I'm not talking "number one." I put on the longest

DJ for Buck Owens Corp Rock Station, Bakersfield, 1984

song I could find—Marty Robbins' "El Paso," which was just about four minutes and thirty seconds long. By the time I left the control room, did my business, and got back to the studio, Marty Robbins had left the building, and the airwaves. All that could be heard was the scratching of the needle at the end of the record.

Needless to say, all the phone lines were lit up, so I grabbed the most important one and answered, "Hotline."

"Son?" I heard on the other end of the line.

"Yes."

"Who is this?"

"This is John Fredericks."

"John, this is Buck Owens."

I remember thinking to myself, "Yeah, no kidding," because he had such a distinctive voice. I said, "Yes sir?"

"Is there something wrong?"

"Buck, I'm really sorry. I had to go to the bathroom, and the song ran out."

He replied: "Son, can you do me a favor next time? Can you put on a longer song?" Then, the phone line went dead.

I saw my radio career going up in flames. Fortunately, Buck must have been in a good mood that morning because I never heard another word about the incident. And, most importantly, I didn't lose my job.

My favorite Buck Owens story came several years later, after I'd made the jump from his AM country station to my morning gig on his FM rock station. Robert Palmer's "Addicted to Love" had become a huge hit, both on MTV and the radio. We played it constantly. Buck, becoming infatuated with the song, would call the hotline on many occasions to request we play it. I caught him in the hallway one day and asked him why he liked the song so much. He told me it had the most important two elements that were necessary for a good song to be great: "A simple melody, and a strong hook." Hook referred to the signature line of the song: "...might as well face it, you're addicted to love."

One morning while I was on air and had just played "Addicted to Love," the hotline light started blinking. I picked it up to hear Buck's voice on the other end of the line. He said he wanted to hear "Addicted to Love." I told him that I played it just five minutes before he called.

"Son, who owns this radio station?"

"You do, Buck."

The last thing I heard before the line went dead was: "Son, play the song." And I did, dedicating it to Buck Owens so my listeners would know exactly why the song was getting played, twice in ten minutes. Buck really knew his music. So much so he had dozens of number one country hits, in the 1960s, and 1970s.

Buck took quite a liking to me. So I did some research on him and found out just how big he really was in country music. I commented about this to him once during our chats and I'll never forget his response: "Son, when I was hot, I was white." In other words: "white hot."

I really liked Buck Owens. I was deeply saddened to learn of his death on March 25, 2006.

There were many times while I worked for Buck Owens I'd show up late to my job at the farming corporation. Each time I was late the manager became incensed, asking me how I could show up on time at my radio job making $5 an hour, but I couldn't make it on time to my full-time job. I didn't have an answer for him. That's when my priorities started to shift. I was making $30,000 a year working for a well-respected company, driving a company car and I had an expense account. And all I wanted to do was be a disc jockey on the radio.

I continued to work in radio part-time on the weekends for the next four years. By 1983 I had left my wife and my job at the farming corporation, and decided I was going to go back to school, and become a teacher. I really thought working in radio was just a fad that I would grow out of. I had no idea that once broadcasting gets in your system it stays there for the rest of your working life. Fortunately for me Buck Owens himself sealed my professional fate one afternoon shortly after I had returned to college. He was in the studio while I was on the air and asked me what I wanted to do when I "grew up." I told him I was studying to be a teacher. I'll never forget his response: "Son, you don't want to be a teacher. There's no money in teaching. You've found your calling. Son, you're a broadcaster."

To earn money while I was in school, in addition to working at the radio station I started working as a DJ at wedding receptions, parties, class reunions or whatever type of event I could get. Each weekend I had a gig, I would get to the venue a few hours early, set up the equipment by myself, change clothes and get ready for whatever was on tap for the evening. Some of these parties turned out to be quite eventful, eye opening and downright hilarious. I walked in on the groom cheating on his new bride with her maid of honor in the men's bathroom. I witnessed, and even helped break up numerous fights between the parents of the bride and groom. I watched in disgust as members of the wedding party threw up right there on the dance floor in front of me. And I saw guests hauling full plates of food out to their cars. I'll never forget being completely grossed-out standing next to and introducing a rather robust newlywed bride with enough nervous, newlywed gas to clear a stadium. I also learned a few valuable lessons playing wedding receptions. Any wedding for the most part is really a day for the mother of the bride. If mom's happy the day or evening usually goes off without a hitch. If she's having a bad time there's a good chance everyone else is miserable. And no matter what the bride and groom tell you they do or don't want you to play, in terms of dance music,

DJ Wedding Reception 1983

you just ignore their wishes and play whatever you feel will work with their guests. I can't count the number of times a bride or groom told me that "under no circumstances" was I to play the "Hokey Pokey," long a wedding reception favorite. And without fail, once I felt the mood was right; meaning people had enough to drink, I'd throw on the "Hokey Pokey" and the crowd would go nuts. I also learned there were songs that never failed to pack a dance floor. During the 1980s those songs included such classics as Rick James' "Superfreak," "Into the Groove," by Madonna, Michael Jackson's "Billie Jean," "Caribbean Queen," by Billie Ocean and, of course: "Shout," by Otis Day and the Knights, made famous in the movie *Animal House*.

I built a custom console with a mixing board, tape deck, power amplifiers and two turn tables. I bought an elaborate speaker system and had some guys from the metal shop at the farming corporation, where I still worked, build me speaker stands that would rise up and down. Having no way to transport all my new fancy deejay equipment, I bought a van. All my jobs came by word of mouth. In no time, I had DJ gigs every weekend, mostly for wedding receptions. It was great money. I made $200 to $300 dollars a night and it was easy money. I was getting paid a lot of money for playing music. The only downside was setting up and tearing down my equipment.

In 1981, MTV was launched over the television airwaves. Bit of trivia: MTV's first video was "Video Killed the Radio Star," by The Buggles. By 1983, Michael Jackson had released his *Thriller* video. People were obsessed with the video and who could blame them? It was one of the greatest videos ever made with one of the best songs ever written, directed by *Animal Houses'* own John Landis, costing a

Radio/Mobile DJ Days 1980's

reported $1 million. I had an ingenious idea. I was going to become the world's first mobile video jockey. I cashed out all the savings I made while working in corporate America, went to the Consumer Electronics Show in Las

Vegas and purchased a big-screen video projector.

I built a new console to house the projector and bought two Beta hi-fi decks. I also installed a five-inch television monitor with a video switching system so I could switch seamlessly from video to video and I purchased a $1,200 top-of-the-line camcorder and mounted it on top of my new console. With the camera I could project live video of people on the dance floor to the big screen. Everyone thought it was the coolest thing they'd ever seen up to that time.

I had to get even more creative, because at the time I couldn't just go down to the local music store and buy music videos. Music videos did not become consumer items until much later and they were very expense to buy when they were finally made available to the public. I would record videos off the television and then sync the music from the same record to match the video. This was a rather time-consuming process. I would cue the stereo record on the turntable and simultaneously cue the video I'd recorded from TV with reduced sound quality. Then I'd start both record and video. By using a manual pitch or speed control on the turntable I found I could sync the song to the video. However, it took between fifteen to thirty minutes per song. The newly dubbed and combined song with video and stereo music was re-recorded on a second Beta hi-fi tape. I ended up with several hundred songs in my library.

I got to the point where I could beat mix and spin records: the art of seamlessly mixing one song with another for continuous dance music. I started working the club circuit in Bakersfield. I got a job at the hottest nightclub in town as a club DJ a couple nights a week. It was a great way to earn a quick hundred dollars a night and meet women. For some bizarre reason, women are drawn to bartenders and DJ's. I think it has something to do with a perceived position of power. Plus, we were working so we must not be thinking about finding a date for later that evening. Right? You bet.

By 1987, during my Bakersfield radio heyday as a morning show host,

I was known as "JF of O," John Fredericks of Oildale. Think Fredericks of Hollywood without the underwear. Don't forget that the station was located in Oildale, home of those KKK rallies.

During my morning show I was allowed to let my creative side come

out and I developed a long list of funny characters that became regular members of my morning show "team."

My buddy who worked the morning shift on our AM radio station would do all the voices for the male characters I created. A few of my female co-workers handled all the voice work for the female characters. We would do some of the bits live on the air but most were pre-recorded. Most of the stuff we did with

Emcee for Fashion Show Night Club in Bakersfield circa 1987

the characters, was so stupid it was funny. And were we ever politically incorrect.

Captain Lavender, the drag queen, was an audience favorite. The Captain spoke with a lisp and would call up the radio station complaining about how upset he was about something that had recently happened in his life, like the time he went to the drag races and no one was dressed in drag. I don't think Captain Lavender would ever make it past today's radio station management, nor should he.

Then there was Harry, my apartment manager. Each time Harry called in he always had the same thing to say, "Hi John, this is Harry, your apartment manager." Then he'd ask me if I noticed what the date was. It didn't matter the time of the month. Before I could tell him the date he'd yell, "Where's the rent check deadbeat!?!!!" Then he'd hang up on me.

Babette, the morning weather girl character spoke in a high-pitched voice. She had an imaginary dog, Bootsie. Babette provided Bootsie's "bark. Her weather report was the same every day regardless of what was actually going on outside.

Buffy Farr-Farr, a name my college roommate came up with, was the morning show secretary. Her gag was having only one word to say, "No." No matter what question I asked her the response was always the same: "Buffy, can you bring me some coffee?" "No!"

Renee, from the dry cleaners, was one of my favorite characters. She spoke through her nose and every time she called she'd tell she found something disgusting in or on my pants. Her calls would always end the same way: "Mr. Fredericks, you're disgusting."

My morning radio show was like a three-ring circus. And I was the ringleader. The humor was lowbrow and sophomoric. But it was a hit with our listeners. Unfortunately, the show was not a hit with station management. After less than one year, despite high ratings, the show was scrapped and I was moved to the midday shift, a virtual radio jukebox for the office crowd.

My buddy, the same guy who did the male voices for the personalities I created on my morning radio show, got a job at the ABC television affiliate in Bakersfield doing the weekend weather. In those days, television station executives didn't care if an anchor knew anything about weather. All they cared about was if the person was able to ad-lib. Radio spawns broadcasters who can ad-lib. So my friend was soon promoted to the full-time weekday weather position. That reopened a spot on the weekends. My friend told the station managers he had just the man for the job. He called me up and asked me to consider meeting with the station's news director. I did.

The news director and I met over lunch a few days later. He had been a fan of my former morning radio show and offered me the weekend weather job on the spot. I told him I'd never appeared on television, save for some commercial work. He said I had to start somewhere. He then explained that we were in Bakersfield and people were a little more forgiving than in bigger cities. I saw it as a golden opportunity so I took the job. It was the spring of 1988 and I was about to embark on a new career: Television weather caster. Thankfully my new news director didn't immediately put me on-air.

I spent a couple of weeks shadowing my former radio station co-worker, learning the ropes. During my training period I hired a Mary Kay consultant to learn how to apply makeup. I already had suits from my previous career so I was ready to go on the air, or so I thought.

The night before I went live on the air for the first time I couldn't sleep. I was scared to death. The following afternoon I showed up to work four hours early. Many of the people in the television only knew me from radio and thought I'd be a natural on television since I'd become such an experienced radio broadcaster. Boy were they wrong. I was so nervous during my first on-air appearance, honest to God, I started doing the whole Albert Brooks bit; sweating profusely during his one and only anchor appearance in Broadcast News.

Before my first weather-cast, as we were going to a commercial break, the main news anchor announced: "Coming up next, weather with John Fredericks. You probably know him as 'JF of O' from radio." Everyone in the studio tried to reassure me that I was going to do fine and to just pretend I was talking to them and not to the camera.

Ten seconds before I was supposed to go on live for my very first weather report, the television station got knocked off the air. To this day I think it was a case of Divine Intervention. The television monitors went to snow. I was standing in front of the camera, thinking to myself: "Now what am I supposed to do?" The studio crew, reading my mind told me to do the weather report as if we were on-air in case power was restored.

We were still off the air when the commercial break ended. The floor director cued me and I stumbled and stammered my way through two or three minutes of weather. Then, as directed, I tossed it back to the news anchors. The station then went to another commercial break. The studio was dead silent. No one could even look me in the eye. I was that bad.

As soon as the station went to the commercial break after my weather-cast, we came back on the air. God must have been looking down on me saying: "I'm going to give this kid a break. I'm not going to let anyone see him live on-air for his first time." By the 6:00 p.m. newscast I had calmed down a bit and managed to get through my weather-cast without any significant, embarrassing moments. By the 11:00 p.m. newscast, I was a little better. By Sunday, the sweat stains under my arms were considerably smaller.

The following Monday the news director called me in and told me that he didn't see "it" in me yet. Fortunately, he thought I had what it took to do the job. That made one of us. He told me despite how hard it was to watch me that previous weekend he was going to stick with me. And he did. If it weren't for him I wouldn't be where I am today. My first television news director saw something in me I didn't see myself. It took a while but eventually I got to the point where I was comfortable and a lot of my humor and personality began coming out during my weather casts. I even started getting phone calls from viewers who told me how much they enjoyed my easy-going style and sense of humor.

Later that year, during the holiday season of 1988, the station held a cartoon drawing contest for kids. Each week it was my job to announce the weekly winner on-air following my weather-cast. After I would finish my weather report, I'd hold up the winning entry and announce the winner's name. On one occasion, while I was showing a drawing on-air, the floor director was frantically trying to get my attention. Eventually I realized what he was trying to tell me: the picture was upside down. I turned the picture right side up and everyone in the newsroom started laughing. I said to my co-anchor: "It will be okay. We'll have the crew edit this out and nobody will ever see it." The news anchor, who thought I was serious, turned to me and said: "John this IS live television." I froze like a deer in headlights and said: "We're live, right now?" I paused for a few seconds then started busting into laughter. Everyone in the studio started laughing as well. The sports anchor called me up later and said, "Dude, you had me crying! That was one of the funniest things I'd ever seen." I use that old "we'll edit that out later" gag to this day. Sadly, a few years later I accidentally recorded over the only copy of that on-air incident.

By early 1989 I was working three jobs: my radio job five days, weather on the weekends, and I was still a deejay two nights during the week at a local nightclub. I was exhausted. And I was on the verge of self-imploding. I was worn down and simply couldn't continue at that pace. I told myself something had to give. I still loved radio and since I considered it my full-time career I quit my TV weather job.

By early fall of that year I starting getting restless and was growing tired of living in Bakersfield. I know what you're thinking: "How on earth could anyone get tired of living in Bakersfield?" One day after my on-air shift, I was reading through a radio industry magazine. I ran across a job listing for a creative director at a very popular rock radio station in Santa Barbara, California. I thought to myself, what a dream it would be to live at the beach doing what I loved. I sent off my resume and a tape of my commercial work and forgot all about it.

Several weeks later the sales director from the station in Santa Barbara called me about my tape and resume. He told me I was a finalist for the creative director job and they wanted me to come to Santa Barbara for an interview. A creative director is responsible for writing copy and producing commercials in radio and television.

I decided to come clean with my current boss, telling him I was up for a job in Santa Barbara and I needed a few days off. Fortunately, we were on good terms and he had started to sense that I was getting restless. He was kind enough to allow me to take the time off. We remain good friends to this day.

My Santa Barbara interview was scheduled for a late Wednesday afternoon the following week. So I called ahead and booked a room for that night, not wanting to make the round-trip in the same day. I left Bakersfield early that following Wednesday morning in my beat-up '78 BMW heading south on Highway 99. I caught Interstate 5 south of town and headed over the southern mountains known as the "Grapevine." I-5 connects with Highway 126 West just north of Los Angeles and 126 dumps you out to the Pacific Ocean just south of Ventura, California.

As long as I live I will never forget making the merger from Highway 126 to Highway 101 that runs north and south along the Pacific Ocean. Immediately as I made the merger on to the 101 the Pacific opened up and I can distinctly remember thinking to myself: "I have to get this job." The view was breathtaking. The ocean seemed endless. The sun was bright and the water glistened with its light. The sky was so blue it almost hurt your eyes to look up. I opened all the BMW's windows and took in the ocean air. The smell was addicting. The salt, mixed with the cool ocean air, was like an aphrodisiac to my senses. It was heaven on earth: a vast beautiful ocean to my left, and spectacular coastal mountains on my right. The stretch of highway along Highway 101 between Ventura and Santa Barbara is, in my opinion, one of the most beautiful, scenic drives on the planet. As I drove I started to prepare mentally for my afternoon interview, determined to somehow make station management want to offer me that creative director job.

I arrived for my interview right on time, in suit and tie—the typical attire I wore working in radio. Even though it appeared to me that the general manager didn't like me, I got the job. The sales manager loved my resume tape—clips of some of my award-winning commercial work in Bakersfield. He and I also connected immediately, both complimenting each other on our taste in clothes. It was my dream job because I was going to have the opportunity to write and produce commercials, work with high-quality equipment and I wasn't going to be live on-air. As much as loved being a disc jockey I had grown tired of the long hours alone in the studio.

I was about to live and work near the ocean. I couldn't ask for anything more. I loaded up my old BMW, sold everything I didn't want to take with me and moved to Santa Barbara.

Santa Barbara is, quite simply, one of the most beautiful places on earth. It is a relatively small community nestled against the mountains of the Angeles National Forest facing the Pacific Ocean and the Channel Islands. The vegetation is beautiful, the trees lush and the air constantly brims with the ocean's aroma. There is the constant sound of seagulls in the air, the distant low roar of a ships' horns and waves breaking onto the shore. The beaches along famous Cabrillo Boulevard are filled with tourists, volleyball players and on the weekends, artisans lining the walkway selling their trinkets and artwork. The tree-covered mountains to the east always seem lightly shrouded in a damp gray coastal fog giving off such a surreal feel you want to drive up there just to see what's going on. The people who live in houses along those hills and mountains, known as the Riviera, have the most breathtaking view of the harbor, the ocean, and on a clear day, the Channel Islands. The feeling as in the Neil Diamond song is "lay back" and everything seems to move at a slower, more casual pace. One gets the sense that everyone is in no hurry, always in a good mood and eager to help you out even if it takes a bit longer than you'd like.

After settling into my first apartment in the University of California at Santa Barbara college community in Goleta, just north of bordering Santa Barbara, I would venture out on weekend excursions of discovery in my newly loved hometown.

Weekend nights I would park my Beemer in one of the parking structures downtown and wander up and down famous State Street. State Street runs west from the beach going east, right through the heart of downtown Santa Barbara. The street is narrow, lined with quaint shops, antique stores and taverns. Dozens of taverns. On Friday and Saturday nights the streets are lined with college kids, and young professionals doing the "club crawl": wandering from tavern to dance club in search of a soul mate. Or at least, a long-term overnight relationship. As I was already in my mid-thirties, I took an observer's approach and just took in all of the sights, and smells, content to watch inebriated young adults put pathetic moves on members of the opposite sex in hopes their night didn't end with that long, dejected, lonely ride home or to their dorm rooms.

On one of my first ventures out, I found a road that headed toward the beach and I happened onto a state beach: Arroyo Burro State Beach. I would later learn that it was better known as Hendries Beach or simply, "the dog beach." When you first pull into Arroyo Burro State Beach Park, you see a restaurant and grassy park area on the right and the vast Pacific, dead ahead. The restaurant, Pelican's Wharf, would close in the summer of 2007 due to economic hard times. But in 1989 it was always packed with patrons, either inside the quaint restaurant with bay windows facing the ocean, or the outdoor patio area depending on the weather. And when it came to the weather there and anywhere else along the California coast, there was no in between. It was either clear or foggy. In either case it was beautiful. On sunny days the sunshine glistened off the water and the hair of the people walking along the beach. On foggy days you often couldn't see more than a few hundred yards up the beach or out to sea. The cold, coastal fog has a way of cutting right through to your bones. But it was still beautiful, albeit damp and cold.

On one of my first weekend nights in town, I decided to hit one of the movie theaters on State Street and catch a new movie starring Mickey Rourke. I got downtown early and after purchasing my ticket for the 9:00 showing, I walked down to a local coffee shop, bought a cup and sat outside to do a little people-watching. Within seconds of sitting down, there walking up the sidewalk toward me was Mickey Rourke himself. He was arm in arm with one of the most beautiful women I'd ever seen. I must have had a pretty interesting look on my face. As he passed by he gave me a little wink and a smile as if to say, "Yeah, it's me."

I did really well at the radio station in Santa Barbara. Everyone seemed to like me. The sales department, in particular, loved me because they could take me on sales calls because I always dressed in a suit. I didn't wear cut-offs and flip-flops, the standard attire for most disc jockeys. I was in hog heaven. I was working with the most up-to-date, cutting-edge equipment and technology I had ever worked with. I had never worked with equipment like that before but I was eager to learn how to use every piece of equipment at my disposal. Eventually I was given a state-of-the-art, eight-channel mixing board and some high-end harmonizers so I could create any sound or even change the pitch of my voice. I wrote and produced all of the on-air commercials, promotions, and sweepers —the pre-recorded sound effects and messages you hear between songs. And I won several local awards for my commercial work. I worked twelve, sixteen, even eighteen hour days and I loved every minute of it. The job became my life. I had no social life and didn't care. I'd walk to work before the sun came up and wouldn't return home until after dark. I had a car I could barely drive because the transmission was going out. By the time I sold it there was neither second gear nor reverse. I'd have to push the car if I wanted to go backwards. But the beach, the job and I were a match made in heaven.

After I'd been working at the station for only a few months, the male-female morning show team decided to up and leave for another job—a common occurrence in the radio business. The station put ads in the industry paper but they still needed someone to fill-in during the interim. Knowing my background in morning radio, they turned to me.

It was a great time of my life. I got to do morning radio again knowing it would only be temporary and there was really no pressure on me to perform. I was just the fill-in guy. The station has, to this day, a very high reputation in the industry and would routinely get some pretty high-level musicians to stop by. They used this opportunity to bring in "guest" disc jockeys in the form of well-known rock musicians. Two of the most memorable for me were Jimmy Messina (of Loggins and Messina fame) and Kevin Cronin of REO Speedwagon. Jimmy was a very engaging, intelligent man and he told the viewers and me the story of producing

Buffalo Springfield's self-titled first album. The group, which included Steven Stills and Neil Young, was having trouble recording one of their final tracks for the album: "On the Way Home." Take after take went by with mixed results. They worked into the night and they couldn't get a single take down on tape that they liked. Finally, as Jimmy told the story, he told them he could "fix one" and sent everyone home for the night. He ended up editing portions of several takes together and the song became one of the group's biggest hits.

Kevin Cronin of REO Speedwagon was just a super nice guy. He had a quick wit and was a joy to be around. Not once did I get the sense that his celebrity had ever gotten the better of him.

I also had the opportunity during my morning fill-in stint to interview Kenny Loggins who, like Jimmy Messina, was a resident of Santa Barbara. Let's just say that I must have caught Kenny on an "off day." We'll leave it at that.

After filling in for a few months, the station finally hired a new morning DJ and I was sent back to my full-time job of station creative director.

Unfortunately, my dream job at that station only lasted a little over a year. In the spring of 1991 the economy, both nationally and locally, had taken a dump. Advertising revenue went into the toilet and lay-offs were implemented. I was one of the first people let go. The station could no longer afford to keep a full-time production director on the payroll. Many small or medium market stations require an on-air personality to double as production or creative director.

Losing my job in Santa Barbara was another turning point in my life. I had no money and no job so I moved to Seattle to live with my cousin, Ray. I looked for a job in Seattle but was unsuccessful. My self-esteem was at an all-time low. I was collecting unemployment, living with my cousin in a city I had never lived in before and it rained more days during the year than the number of days the sun shines in California. Or so it seemed. Seattle is a beautiful city but it can be so depressing with all the rain, dark skies and gloom. I was severely depressed.

My luck soon changed. After forty-five depression-filled days in Seattle, I received a call from out of nowhere from a guy who ran a Top-40 radio station and an AM news station in Santa Barbara. He knew of my work and had taken a great deal of effort to track me down. He offered me a job working for him. I politely told him I didn't think he could afford me. When he asked how much money I needed I told him at least $2,500 a month. Up to that point I had never made $2,500 a month in my entire broadcasting career. However, I needed to get back on my feet and needed to pay off some increasing credit card debt. He told me we had a deal. In a single phone conversation I went from collecting $800 a month in unemployment to making $2,500 a month. The best news was that I was going to return to Santa Barbara to do a job I knew and loved.

I had no money to purchase a plane ticket to get back to Santa Barbara so an old friend of mine—my former radio boss in Bakersfield, the same guy who gave me time off to interview in Santa Barbara—loaned me the money for a plane ticket. I flew back to Santa Barbara having no place to live and no transportation. I'd left my old BMW at a buddy's house in exchange for money I owed him. The station I was going to work for advanced me $1,000, allowing me to buy, sight unseen, a Honda 750 motorcycle. The sales manager who worked at my new station let me live with his family for a while. The motorcycle turned out to be my only transportation for over a year. I'd ride it to and from work in the cold, rain and fog. Eventually I met a guy who told me he had an extra room in the house he was renting in La Conchita, a tiny ocean-side community twenty-five miles south of town. We ended up being roommates for well over two years.

I commuted on my motorcycle to work each day back and forth on Highway 101. It was a twenty-five minute ride from La Conchita to my new job in Santa Barbara. I would shower at home, strap a travel bag to my backseat and then style my hair when I got to work. One morning my travel bag fell off in the middle of the highway and was run over and destroyed by an eighteen-wheeler. That morning I had to stop at a drug store before going into work to buy all new things.

Although my new job included an on-air shift, I really liked my bosses and my co-workers. As the station creative director, I had complete control over commercial content, production and creativity and station management really respected my work. My on-air shift was noon to 3 p.m. Monday through Friday. The production studio was directly across the hall from the on-air studio so I could run back and forth, multi-tasking throughout the afternoon. The station's music format was Top-40 and I enjoyed hearing the new songs and artists. In short, I loved my new job and I really enjoyed living back on the California coast. Unfortunately, I had a boatload of debt hanging over my head from my days of unemployment in Seattle. I'd even picked up a DJ job weekend nights at a local nightclub but I was still drowning in debt.

I was in such financial debt, having charged up so many credit cards I had to go into debt reorganization. The debt reorganization company didn't decrease any of the credit card debt I owed. They simply worked out payment plans with all of my creditors. I repaid $800 a month for two years. By the summer of 1993 I had repaid my entire debt, however, my credit score was so bad I was only able to apply for and get approval for secured credit cards.

By the fall of 1993, I'd been promoted to the position of program director at the radio station. I had been back in Santa Barbara for over two years and I had done quite well for myself. I was responsible for everything that went out over our airwaves. It was a great job that carried a huge responsibility but I was really beginning to get tired of working in radio. As if on cue, I received a call from a guy I used to work with in radio before I moved to Seattle. He still worked at my previous Santa Barbara radio station and was simultaneously employed as a reporter at Santa Barbara's only local TV station. He knew I had worked as the weekend weather guy in Bakersfield and he suggested I take some of my old tapes to show to his news director. The ABC affiliate in Santa Barbara didn't have a weekend weather person at the time. I reminded him that I hadn't been on television doing weather in several years. He told me I had nothing to lose. So I made an appointment with the news director at the local ABC affiliate. His name was King Harris. He agreed to meet with me the following week.

I arrived for my appointment the following Friday and was introduced to King Harris. He took me on a short tour of the station and then we

LIVE radio broadcast from Disneyland circa 1993

sat and talked for a while in his office. Halfway through our conversation, he asked for my tape. He popped it into his VCR and watched intently with little expression. I began to worry. After about five minutes he stopped the tape and sat silent for the longest time. I thought I was so awful that I left him speechless. Finally, he turned to me and told me he didn't know what caused me to stop working in television. He told me I'd made the wrong career choice when I left television in 1988. He also told me that I needed to be doing television

because I had "it." He said he didn't know what exactly "it" was but I had it and I should've never stopped doing television. He told me he didn't have a budget to pay me but wanted me to work as an unpaid intern doing the weekend weather.

King Harris was an interesting soul and I liked him immediately. I agreed to take the job because I wanted to be back on television for the experience and to work with a guy I respected. At that time I didn't need the money. I was making enough money working at the radio station and the nightclub.

That was in the early 1990s and as much as I hate to admit it, I still had a 1980s bouffant hairdo. Okay, I still do. You know the type: *Pretty in Pink*, male movie actor hair; a bit tall, sticking way out over the forehead. When I walked inside the television station for my first weather-cast someone announced over the intercom, "Elvis has entered the building."

At the end of my first weekend working at the television station King called me in to his office. He had a still picture on the television screen of me on the air standing sideways and he asked me, "What is that?"

I proudly replied, "That's my hair."

He told me to get it cut before going back on the air. I did.

I was back in television and couldn't be happier. And I was engaged and about to be married to the woman of my dreams. I was wrong.

Bluff where Jordan was born, Santa Barbara.

CHAPTER 2

Jordan Rescues Me

Shortly after coming back to Santa Barbara in the summer of 1991, I had met a young woman and fallen head over heels in love. She was in college at UCSB and sixteen years my junior. She was way too young for me but I didn't care. I was smitten. I met her while she was working part-time at the radio station where I had just been hired. We eventually got engaged and were together for over two years. It was a match destined for failure but I loved her with all of my heart. She eventually left me for a guy her own age, which, in retrospect, makes perfect sense. But I was heartbroken and severely depressed. On the weekends, with nothing else to do, I'd drive for hours at a time, not even knowing where I was going or where I had been. And while driving up and down the streets of Santa Barbara can be great fun, putting 130 miles on the odometer, having no recollection of where I'd been, was pretty dangerous. Somehow I managed to function at work. For some reason throughout my entire professional life, during times of personal adversity I've always been able to focus all of my energies on my work duties. I guess it's just a way of my mind forcing me to take a break from my emotional issues.

When I think back on it, the entire event seems rather childish. I'm not the type to need a significant other in my life to be happy. And yet when I fall, I fall hard. Worse still, I don't handle break ups well. In short, I was miserable. I once heard that life is all about having something to look forward to. It was the early spring 1994 and I didn't think I had much to live for. I was wrong.

I became friends with a female co-worker at the radio station and on many occasions I would talk to her about the break up with my fiancée and how devastated I was. I know this person befriended me because she had a crush on me. And even though she was smart, witty and extremely attractive I just couldn't disengage from my feelings for my ex-fiancée. What I didn't know at the time was that this wonderful woman, was about to change my life dramatically for the better, and for good.

On the morning of April 5, 1994, my radio station friend suggested we take a drive together. I agreed and within a few miles from the station it became clear to me that she was driving with a purpose and a specific destination. We headed to an area of Santa Barbara referred to as the Mesa, a beautiful residential portion of the city situated on a bluff that overlooked the ocean. I kept nagging my driving companion about where we were going as I was getting impatient. I had a bunch of work waiting back at the station. My friend kept blowing me off. Each time I'd inquire as to our destination she'd either ignore me or just tell me to be quiet.

Several minutes later we pulled into the driveway of an old ranch-style home. It sat on the edge of a cliff directly above the Pacific Ocean and Arroyo Burro State Beach—the dog beach.

I don't know why, but I can remember clearly what the house looked like. The driveway was one of those semi-circular jobs and at the top of the drive was the front of the house. It looked like your typical seventies rambler, quite common in California, a single story, shake or shingle roof, low ceilings and plenty of big windows on the front, side, and back. To the side of the house was a driveway with a big double gate. My friend got out of her car and told me to follow her.

I could hear commotion coming from the right side of the house behind where the gate was. My friend motioned toward the double gates. When we turned the corner I saw a fenced-off area with an adult yellow Labrador retriever that I later learned was named Happy. She was with what remained of her litter: nine-and-one-half-week-old puppies. My eyes were immediately drawn to one of the pups sitting off to one side in the corner of the pen. Our eyes met just for a split second and I knew I had to have him, right there and then. I had no idea why. I wasn't even looking for a dog. In fact, up until that instant, caring for a dog was probably the furthest thing from my mind. I was having a hard time caring for myself. How could I care for a dog?

I've often thought back on that day and why that particular puppy captivated me. It wasn't because he looked significantly different from his siblings. He wasn't the runt or the biggest of his remaining littermates. In fact, they all looked very much alike at first glance. What was different about this puppy was his attitude and demeanor. What drew me to him? He seemed content to be off to one side of the pen away from the other pups. He actually seemed disinterested in the proceedings, as if to say, "Look, I don't mind having to share this space with the rest of you, I just want to be left alone over here by myself." After our initial eye contact, when he looked in my direction he never actually made direct eye contact. Instead, it was as though he was looking through me with a definite level of disinterest and ambivalence. I was looking at a four-legged version of myself.

You have to understand something about my genetic make-up: my father Joe, when leaving my mother, was heard to say, "I don't like no clinging vines." My sister Joanne used to put it a bit differently: "There's something on my back and it's not my shirt. Get off." That describes me to a tee. I need my space. And that was what I saw that April day in 1994. I looked into the eyes of my future best friend looking back at me and he let me know: "I may grow to like you some day. But I don't really need you. I may want you in the same room with me, just don't expect me to climb up in your lap or fawn all over you."

I told my friend which puppy I wanted and she called the owner on her cell phone to give him the good news. He never asked to speak to me. He had no idea if I would be a fit parent. I would later learn how irresponsible his behavior was. Regardless, we ended up taking two puppies back to work with us that day: the puppy I picked out and one of his siblings for a different co-worker who had been looking for a retriever. Sadly, that sibling had to be put down due to serious genetic issues—confirmation that this breeder's practices were well below standard.

Sub-standard breeders often don't check to make sure they're not drawing the parents from the same gene pool, resulting in inbreeding and all of the genetic defects that result from such improper practices. This is why we have laws in this country that restrict how close within our own gene pool we can marry and procreate. All of the puppies, including the puppy I took, would suffer from some sort of genetic-related medical issue. Most had to be put to sleep at very young ages. At the age of seven months, my puppy was diagnosed with mild to moderate hip dysplasia. I wasn't savvy in the ways of purebred AKC dogs. And had I been looking for a dog in the first place I would've gone to the pound. All the dogs my family had in the past came from the pound. And I just assumed that all dogs were like pound puppies, happy, healthy, and just thrilled to be rescued.

In the years to come I would learn how puppies were supposed to be raised and properly weaned. Puppies need to have constant human interaction from the time they are born until the time they're adopted by their human parent. Daily interaction with humans ensures that the pup will bond properly with his or her two-legged parent. Early human bonding often prevents emotional problems as the dog grows older. This is why I have come to despise the practice of pet stores selling puppies. Those poor animals spend days and weeks on end stuck in tiny cages with little human interaction. Pet store puppies are also notorious for having genetic-related health problems. Quite often they're purchased from disreputable puppy mills that run rampant in the south. For the past several years, after learning the proper way to adopt from a breeder, I've always advised people who are dead set on getting a purebred dog from a breeder to get to know the breeder personally and to make sure they have all the proper credentials and references. I believe that having different breeds of dogs is important. And I respect the wonderful work of the American Kennel Club. However, I've also learned that we euthanize more than 3 million animals each year in the United States. That's why I have the highest regard for those people who rescue their pets from shelters and rescue organizations.

Picking a name for my new puppy turned out to be easy. Because he was nine-and one-half weeks old I briefly thought of naming him "Mickey," after Mickey Rourke who had starred in the recent *9 ½ Weeks* film. Just as quickly as that thought entered my mind it made way for another one: this puppy's name was going to be Jordan—the name that my ex and I had picked out for our future child, girl or boy. It was my way of thumbing my nose to the girl who broke my heart. I was subconsciously telling her my dog would be named after the child she denied me. How pathetic, immature and idiotic was that?

While it is true that Jordan and his siblings were the product of a backyard breeder, one who was more interested in making money than properly breeding purebred animals, he was an AKC registered yellow Labrador retriever and I had an obligation to register his name with the AKC. Jordan's registered name turned out to be Frederick McDuff of Jordan. Frederick was for my mom's brother, Fred. McDuff was for my childhood boxer, Duffy. Duffy and I shared the exact same date of birth and even though he really belonged to my aunt and uncle, we became inseparable. Duffy's registered name was Sir Windy McDuff of Creston— Windy because he could clear a room when he broke wind. Duffy and I stayed best friends for all of his eight years. I loved Duffy dearly and wanted his legacy to live on as part of Jordan's name.

Jordan was a huge hit at the radio station. I sat on the floor and played with him and everyone in the station came by to fawn over him. Fortunately, station management had no problems with dogs being in the building. Radio people can be weird and quirky at times. But for the most part they're good people.

Jordan wasn't such a big hit with my roommate. When I took him home that first afternoon, my roommate was irate. He yelled at me for not discussing my decision to get a dog, before I brought him home. I told him that I didn't have a choice in the matter. I explained that as soon as I saw the look on Jordan's face, I knew I had to have him. My roommate simply didn't get it.

That was a real cause of contention in our relationship. My roommate told me that I should just take the dog back where I got him or there would be problems with our friendship. Getting rid of Jordan wasn't an option. That new life in my depressing existence had suddenly given my life purpose. I no longer had just me to think about. I had a pet and I was responsible for his health and welfare. No matter how little I might have cared about my life I knew I had taken on a huge responsibility. For the first time in many months I felt as though I finally had something to look forward to.

Fortunately for Jordan, a few months earlier I'd decided to get rid of my motorcycle. Although it had served me well I was tired of riding in the elements. I sold my Honda 750 and bought a 1970 Volkswagen Fastback Sedan.

The following morning Jordan and I drove through the dense fog to a Starbucks in Montecito. On the way, we stopped at a gourmet pet boutique and I bought Jordan a special treat—a pig's ear—on the recommendation of the person working behind the counter. Those nasty things immediately became his favorite special treat and, in the years that followed, we'd never go more than a month without him having one.

We left the pet store and headed to the Starbucks on Coast Village Road. Coast Village Road is the main drag that runs through downtown Montecito. Montecito is the unincorporated area on the south edge of Santa Barbara—home of the rich and famous. Think Oprah Winfrey. Coast Village Road is a narrow, two-lane street, lined with huge trees, shops and restaurants. Tourists and celebrities alike wander up and down the sidewalks, window-shopping, eating at expensive eateries and browsing through high-end boutique shops. On many occasions after work I'd drive down to one of the nicer lounges on Coast Village Road to listen to comedian Jonathan Winters. He was a Coast Village regular and liked to impress the patrons, telling tale after tale of his younger days in the entertainment business. I ordered pizza at the same place as Michael McDonald of the Doobie Brothers, as well as the Grammy award-winning Christopher Cross. I'll never forget walking right past the actress Sela Ward one afternoon thinking the television and film screen did not do her justice. She is stunningly beautiful. Later, when I started doing the weather, actors sometimes approached me at the local Vons to ask me about the forecast for the upcoming weekend. I'll never forget taking Jordan to the Starbucks there some months later, only to have Rob Lowe ask me if I had matches so he could light his cigar. I had no matches to give him but he struck me as a pretty regular guy.

Our first day. Starbucks, Montecito, CA, April 6, 1994

I put Jordan on the leash and found a place outside the coffee shop where he could relax and I could people watch. I gave him his first pig's ear treat and got him settled on a small blanket I'd bought for him the previous afternoon. I looped his leash around a table leg and asked a couple at the next table if they'd keep an eye on him while I went inside to get my coffee.

It was a foggy Saturday morning in Santa Barbara and I was hanging at Starbucks with my new little buddy. That morning I learned the true meaning of animal magnetism. I didn't have a moment's peace. My coffee got cold while I fielded questions from interested strangers and watched in amazement as men and women, mostly women, fawned over my dog. Had I known just what "chick magnets" puppies were, I would've had one throughout my entire adult life. However, I should caution you that animal magnetism does not transfer from dog to owner. Trust me on this one. Never once did I get a single phone number or date with a girl who was fawning all over Jordan. Why do I admit these things? But puppies are great conversation starters and I loved that added benefit of being a new pet owner.

Day One, Starbucks in Montecito, CA

I took Jordan with me everywhere I went because I didn't know what else to do with him. When I deejayed at the local night club Friday and Saturday nights, I took Jordan along and he slept in the back room where they kept the liquor. Don't worry. The liquor was kept in a separate caged area. I'd set him up with his bed and toys, and he seemed to be content. At the end of my shift, as Jordan and I walked to my car all the club-goers would stop and comment on him. The girls, usually inebriated, would tell me they wanted to "take my puppy home" with them. The guys, usually even more inebriated, would ask if they could "borrow" my dog to impress some girl who had apparently blown them off earlier that evening.

My mother had a favorite expression: Ignorance is bliss. That certainly applied to me in the days and weeks that followed. I had stepped up to the edge of the dog-owner-responsibility-abyss and I didn't even know it. I had no clue about proper diet, potty or obedience training, veterinary care, vaccinations and socialization. Everything I learned in the days and months to follow would be the hard way, trial and plenty of errors.

CHAPTER 3

Jordan the Terrible

My roommate and I shared a house in La Conchita, a small coastal community located right along Highway 101, adjacent to the Pacific Ocean, about twenty-five miles south of Santa Barbara. La Conchita, Spanish for "The Little Shell" is famous for a couple of reasons: it is the community that had several homes destroyed in a mudslide there in 1994, and again in 2005. And it sits directly across from Rincon Beach, made famous in the Beach Boys' "Surfin' USA." Rincon Beach is a favorite for surfers because the waves break not only to the shore but also along the shoreline as it is a "south facing" beach. The adjacent land juts out for several hundred yards into the Pacific Ocean, leaving shoreline to the north and to the east. Be sure and look for it if you're ever traveling along Highway 101 between Ventura and Santa Barbara.

In our rented La Conchita house I lived downstairs and my roommate lived upstairs. We shared a common living room that was located upstairs. Each day we recorded the soap opera *All My Children* and watched it over dinner that evening. Male bonding at its best: two grown men laughing and crying over a soap opera. It was really one of the few things we had in common and our evening soap opera get-togethers were some of the best times we shared. Truth be told, I was an *All My Children* fan from 1970 through the mid-nineties. How can you not love Erica Kane, A.K.A. Susan Lucci?

When I brought Jordan home, my roommate gave me explicit instructions that he would not be allowed anywhere upstairs. But, with my crazy work schedule and a brand new puppy, it was easy for me to fall asleep without realizing it. One day while I was upstairs in the living room, I fell asleep on the couch. I must have left my bedroom door open and Jordan, who I later learned was an escape artist, managed to get out of my bedroom. He went upstairs into my roommate's bedroom and pooped in three different piles all around my roommate's bed. Knowing my roommate didn't want him there, Jordan was sending him a message: "I'll show you, buddy boy!" And he didn't stop there. With me sound asleep on the couch, Jordan went to the end of the couch and ripped the fabric off the arm.

When my roommate returned home he woke me up and ordered me into his feces-covered bedroom. If he weren't so pissed I would've cracked up. Not because I condoned Jordan's behavior. I didn't. I was laughing inside because I knew that Jordan had made a statement. And secretly I was a just a little proud of my boy. My roommate was not a pet person and Jordan sensed it.

I cleaned my roommate's bedroom and promised to pay to have his couch repaired. I apologized profusely, all the while explaining that Jordan was just a puppy, and he didn't know any better. My roommate didn't want to hear any of it. Tensions in the house continued to mount. I knew it was only a matter of time before the situation reached the boiling point and I would have to make a decision.

Jordan wasn't able to stay at the radio station every day because I would become busy with my job and I couldn't always keep my eye on him. I couldn't leave him at home because I worried that he would get out of my room and destroy the house, so I had to find a place for him to stay during the day. They didn't have all the pet services available back then like they do today. I couldn't just look in the yellow pages and find a petsitter. Not only that, the idea of hiring a sitter never even crossed my mind. Moreover, I knew nothing about kennel training; the most humane way to keep pets safe when you can't keep a constant eye on them.

One of my pet-loving co-workers was kind enough to let Jordan stay at her house during the day. She rented a beautiful home with a great yard and she had a Doberman, named Rory. I was thankful Jordan finally had four-legged playmate.

I don't ever remember Jordan being a biter, but he sure was a chewer and a digger. He destroyed everything in his path. He was like a bulldozer, ploughing his way through countless yards, bushes, flowerbeds, grass and even sprinklers.

I would drop Jordan off at my friend's house in the morning and then pick him up on my way home from work. This arrangement only lasted about two months because he destroyed practically everything in and outside her house.

Baby Sitters Bed Pre Eviction June 1994
4 mo old. Photo by Mo Gettings

Each day after I dropped Jordan off at my co-worker's house, he was left alone to wreak havoc. He tore through all kinds of stuff. One problem was that the house wasn't puppy-proof. My friend's dog Rory was older and had already gone through his puppy stage. My friend finally had enough when she came home and found that Jordan dove into a twenty-pound bag of powdered diet drink mix that was on the laundry room floor. Powder was all over the house. It was everything I could do to keep from busting a gut laughing. But to my friend and co-worker, that was the final straw. When I picked Jordan up at the end of that day my friend gave me the bad news: She loved him, but Jordan couldn't come back until he grew out of his puppy stage.

Thankfully, I knew another co-worker who was renting a house with some friends and he agreed to allow Jordan to stay in the backyard while we were at the station. Because the weather in Santa Barbara was mild all year long, I didn't mind Jordan being outside during the day. The yard was nice and well landscaped. At least it was until Jordan got there. He ripped up the entire sprinkler system. He didn't just rip the sprinkler system out of the ground, he chewed through the PVC pipes too. Jordan also managed to rip through my co-worker's bowling bag which was kept on a porch upstairs. The bowling ball bounced down the stairs where it crashed into a beautiful flower bed. While my co-worker and his roommates tolerated Jordan a lot longer than I expected, he was eventually evicted from their backyard. The property management company decided they didn't want a pet on the property shortly after the bowling ball incident.

It was now the summer of 1994 and Jordan was four months old and growing fast. And though he had proven to be a real handful, I loved him to pieces and we had a blast just driving around Santa Barbara. He'd ride either on the passenger side floorboard or when he got old enough, he'd sit in the front passenger seat next to me. I had no idea how dangerous that arrangement was. Had I ever needed to slam on the brakes, Jordan may have flown right through the windshield. Years later I learned about properly transporting pets; in kennels, in enclosed areas in the back of an SUV, or properly secured by a safety harness. I got lucky. Jordan was never injured while riding in the front of our car. He'd just sit next to me on the passenger seat looking forward like he was my co-pilot. People would pull up next to us, do a double-take and then laugh. I'd laugh right along with them. Jordan was better therapy than any shrink. Some of you may have been around long enough to remember when you had to use lettered tickets, "A" through "E" for rides at Disneyland; "E" being the ticket that would get you on the best rides. I used to tell people Jordan provided me with hours of free entertainment like an "E" ticket at Disneyland. Only better.

CHAPTER 4

Our New Home

The longer I had Jordan the more the tension grew between my roommate and me. One day my roommate received a call from the owners of our rented house. They wanted to put the home up for sale. The owners called my roommate to confirm there were no pets living in the house. California disclosure laws require that house sellers must notify potential buyers of any pets in the home. My roommate told the owners that we did in fact have a dog in the house. They informed him the dog "had to go." That day.

That afternoon when I got home from work my roommate explained the situation to me. He let me know I had to get rid of Jordan. I told him I wouldn't give up my dog. He could not believe I was choosing my dog over our friendship and my home. I really wasn't choosing between the two but it probably seemed like that at the time. My roommate even tried to convince me that getting rid of Jordan wasn't a big deal because I'd only had him for a few months. My roommate simply didn't understand that Jordan was a member of my family. And I wasn't going to discard a member of my family. I was given an ultimatum: either give up the dog or move out.

I grabbed my sleeping bag and some toiletries, loaded up my duffle bag and threw them in the car. Jordan jumped in and we drove away. It was the middle of the week and I had nowhere to go. I couldn't afford a room at the only local pet-friendly hotel, Fess Parker's Red Lion Inn. We drove to my office at the radio station, and Jordan and I slept on the floor.

Fortunately, once I moved out and tensions eased, there was never any lasting animosity between my roommate and me. We soon reconciled and he even became my boss for a time at the night club where I deejayed on weekend nights. I still consider him a dear friend. Furthermore, I will never forget that he befriended me and gave me a home when I moved back to Santa Barbara from Washington in 1991.

Jordan and I spent the next two weeks living on the floor of the radio station. At night, I'd crawl into my sleeping bag and Jordan would curl up on the floor next to me. He developed a cute habit of letting me know when he had to go to the bathroom. I would wake up in the middle of the night and could sense Jordan's presence. He'd be standing right over the top of me, his face inches from mine. I'd ask him if he had to go potty and he'd trot over to my office door.

The nights are cool in Santa Barbara and when it's foggy, as it usually is during the summer months, it gets chilly outside, with temperatures sometimes dropping into the forties. I'd take Jordan outside so he could do his thing and we'd race back inside. I'd crawl back into my sleeping bag and Jordan would plop back down beside me until it was time to start another workday. To make sure no one took issue with us being there, I always went back outside after the sun came up to clean up Jordan's mess from earlier that morning. Fortunately, I had understanding owners. They were seasoned broadcasters and knew that people in our profession were not paid the best and often were in need of a helping hand.

Although the radio station had restrooms it didn't have shower facilities. Each morning I would drive down to Cabrillo Boulevard, located along the beach in Santa Barbara and I would take my daily shower in the public showers. On several occasions I found a homeless person asleep in the shower room. I couldn't complain. I was homeless as well.

The water in the beach showers was so cold. I would hurry up and take my shower and leave with my hair wet. Then I'd head back to the station where I'd blow-dry my hair and finish getting ready before I'd start work on another day.

While living at the radio station, I searched though the classifieds each day looking for a home that was located close to work, affordable and would allow big dogs. By now Jordan weighed close to fifty pounds.

One day I found an ad for a room for rent on an avocado ranch that happened to be atop a mountain directly above where our radio station was situated in the southeast end of Santa Barbara. Jordan and I went to look at it.

The owner of the ranch was a retired fighter pilot, having served in the Iranian Air Force. He was a friendly man and spoke broken English. He had clearly done very well for himself and bought the ranch in the late 1970s before the market had become completely cost-prohibitive for most. He owned a beautiful, horseshoe-shaped home at the top of the mountain in an area of Montecito known as The Rivera: a very expensive and exclusive part of Santa Barbara. The deck at the back of the house overlooked the entire Santa Barbara harbor and all the Channel Islands. An avocado orchard surrounded the house and the property had horse stables. The owner of the house had two horses, some dogs, and a few other tenants who lived in other parts of the property, either in other rooms of the house or in a few small travel trailers on the ranch.

Jordan was welcome but the property had no fence around it. I had three choices if I rented the room: I could keep Jordan locked inside my room all day; keep him tied up outside or leave him outside unsupervised and hope he didn't run away. The rent was $600 a month for one bedroom and one bathroom with no kitchen. I was told I would not be allowed in the main house. The room had its own private deck with the best view of the city. I rented the room, got my stuff that was being stored by my old roommate in La Conchita and we moved in the following Saturday morning in late August 1994.

My room had a sliding glass door that led to a private deck and when I sat up in bed I had a beautiful view of the Santa Barbara harbor. Because I didn't have a kitchen, I purchased a microwave, and a little portable refrigerator. That was all I needed because I didn't cook. I was so happy to have a home for myself, and Jordan. In the course of a single day, we'd left the doghouse, for the penthouse.

John & Jordan at our Santa Barbara home circa Spring 1996.
Photo courtesy of Robert Johnson

I chose to let Jordan have free rein of the property. I just couldn't keep him locked in one room for hours at a time. I didn't want to tether him to an outside post either. Having the knowledge I have now I wouldn't make the same choice. At the time I did what I thought was best for Jordan.

During the day I left my sliding glass door open for Jordan to come and go as he pleased. While he was still welcome at work, he was a real handful and I couldn't trust him not to chew through carpet or destroy something at the radio station, unless he was by my side at all times. That was not always possible. When I would leave the house Jordan followed me down to the end of the driveway and somehow he instinctively knew to stop there and head back to the house. I took that as a good sign. Somehow he seemed to know he wasn't supposed to venture off the property.

On our Santa Barbara Ranch Deck SB Harbor in distance circa Spring 1996.
Photo courtesy of Robert Johnson

Many days I came home from work and found Jordan had left me a present right inside our sliding glass door. He would leave the gifts there as opposed to any other place in my room, to make sure they were the first thing I saw when I got home. Some days I'd find a dead rat. Other days he'd bring me a dead bird. Sometimes it would just be a dead bug. He never killed any of these animals as it was clear that rigor mortis had long set in. He'd find them dead around the property when he was out on his adventures during the day. I like presents but not the ones Jordan left for me; however, I knew Jordan was just trying to impress dad and his gift-giving only served to further endear me to my sweet young boy.

Jordan loved his new home. He had free rein on the avocado ranch. He ate the avocados that fell to the ground causing him to put on some extra weight. Every morning Jordan ran down to the stables to chase the horses and then they'd turn around and chase him. Jordan also loved to play with the ranch owner's dogs. That turned out to be a bad thing.

My greatest fear came true on an early fall day in 1994. While I was at work, Jordan left the property. He took off with a terrier mix that had just been adopted by my landlord. Terriers are known to be roamers. Early that afternoon, I received a message on my pager from a woman who found Jordan and the other dog and brought them to her home. By the time I called her back both dogs had escaped from her yard.

I was horrified to learn that the woman lived at least ten miles away from the ranch, in vineyard country. To get to her house the dogs had to cross major streets, roads, hills and rugged terrain. It took me nearly thirty minutes in my car to get to where she lived. She told me she didn't think the dogs could have gone far since they left her yard. I got back in my car and drove up and down the vineyards searching for them. All of a sudden I spotted Jordan and the terrier.

I was so relieved. I sat and watched the dogs for minute and noticed how unbelievably free and happy they both looked. They were romping around in the vineyard, caked with mud and dirt, having the time of their lives. When I called Jordan's name he got excited, ran right over to me and jumped into the car and the other dog followed. Once Jordan was safe in my car I cried like a baby. I was so angry at him and at the same time so happy that he hadn't been killed. By this time I knew better than to scold him after he'd come to me. He had no idea what he had done was wrong. I'll never know how those two dogs traveled so far without being hit by a car.

When we got back to the house, I explained to the landlord what happened and that I could not afford for it to happen again. I was thrilled that Jordan had a new friend but there was too great a chance that they'd take off again together.

My landlord liked Jordan and me so much he immediately adopted the terrier back out and went back to the shelter and got an older, calmer dog that seemed content just to stay close to the property. My landlord liked to have dogs on the property to scare off varmints and anyone else not welcome. The ranch was located at the dead-end of a winding road. Anyone who ended up there was either a resident or lost.

Jordan did leave the property one other time during our stay at the house. However, he had only gotten a few blocks down the hill when a nice man picked him up and called my pager number that was on Jordan's dog tag.

CHAPTER 5

Our Life at the Beach

Some of my fondest memories of life with Jordan happened during our daily trips to the beach. The weather was beautiful almost all year round and the ocean was just a short drive from home, and work. For Jordan the beach was a giant pool and sand box. For me it was a place to clear my head and prepare for another day. Jordan could romp up and down the beach with other dogs—his new canine companions—and I could get some exercise, unwind and find joy in watching my new best friend.

I've always heard and read that being near the ocean has a cleansing quality. I'm sure it's true. I seemed to gain a renewed sense of hope and happiness while I walked the beach and Jordan romped in the sand or water. Two great musical examples of the cleansing effects of the ocean are Jackson Browne's "Rock Me on the Water," and the Grand Funk Railroad song "I Can Feel Him in the Morning." I'm sure you can find them online.

The first time I took Jordan to the dog beach in Santa Barbara it turned out to be an educational experience. The sand was like one big litter box to Jordan and he would poop almost as soon as we stepped foot on the beach. That first day I started to cover Jordan's poop with sand when a guy came up to me and told me not to do that. He pulled out a plastic bag, picked up Jordan's poop, then looked at me and said, "That's how you do it." I told him it was all new to me and thanked him for his help. That was the one and only time I would fail to clean up after him.

When I first started taking Jordan to the beach he wouldn't go into the water. If I threw a stick into the water he wouldn't retrieve it. I figured I could lure him into the water if I went in first. One day I put my swimming trunks on and went into the ocean. It was summertime, 1994, and the water was warm enough for an afternoon swim. I was shoulder deep and called for Jordan to come join me. At first, he wouldn't come in. He just ran back and forth on the beach in front of me whining. Eventually, he couldn't stand it any more and slowly walked into the water. Then he swam over to me. Thinking I might be drowning, he started trying to grab on to me with his paws. It took me a while to convince him I was fine and loving the water.

Once Jordan got in the water he found out he loved it. Following his first swim, anytime I ran into the ocean or threw a ball or stick in the water he would jump right in. I made a promise to him that if we ever had to move away from the beach one day I would buy a house with a pool in the backyard for him.

One morning after we had just gotten down to the beach, another yellow Lab came running up to us and seemed to take a special interest in Jordan—and Jordan in her. A young woman I didn't recognize came over to get her Lab and I asked her what her dog's name was. She explained that she was just dog-sitting for the owner and the dog's name was Happy. I could hardly believe it. I was so excited. I told her that Happy was Jordan's mom. The coolest part about the meeting was that the two dogs seemed to recognize each other. It turned out to be the last time Jordan saw his mom. However, it made me feel good to know that Happy got to see her growing son at least one more time.

Jordan made many doggy friends at the beach, but one of the friends he seemed to like most was a pot-bellied pig. I never saw the owner of the pig—it just ambled down the beach like he or she owned it. How do you tell a pig's sex? Jordan just loved following that pig around and would do so each time he saw it on the beach. The pig seemed oblivious to dogs, in general and Jordan in particular. But the pig didn't seem to mind the attention, so Jordan continued to hang out with it until it stopped coming to the beach altogether and we never saw him or her again. I never had occasion to speak to the owner so I surmised that the pig might have gotten too old for walks on the beach.

Shortly after the first year of our beach visits, Jordan stopped using the sand as his litter box. When he had to take a dump, he'd walk out into the water about knee deep, squat and unload. Then a wave would come up and wash it away. I had no idea why he started doing this but I was grateful that I didn't have to pick up his poop anymore. I wasn't too worried about it either because crap is biodegradable, right? And no one from the Park Service ever took issue with the new arrangement.

One day when Jordan was taking his morning ocean dump, a guy walked by and said: "That's disgusting."

I replied to him, "It's a good thing the fish don't crap in the ocean."

He just walked away.

Because I didn't know much about raising a puppy, I took advice from anyone who was willing to help. Pet owners at my workplace told me not feed Jordan human food. They told me once a dog has a taste of people food, begging would become a serious problem. So I made a vow that Jordan would never eat people food. Years later I would find out through our vet that human food is also not healthy for pets with all the calories, carbohydrates and preservatives. Maybe we should be eating dog food.

When Jordan was about six months old, he and I met a friend at Pelican's Wharf restaurant at the beach we went to each day. I picked a table next to the fence that separated the restaurant from the sand, and tied Jordan to it. He was on the beach side of the fence, right next to our table.

It was a beautiful summer day in 1994. The fog had cleared earlier in the morning and the air was so clear you could see the Channel Islands way off in the distance. The beach was packed with partiers, swimmers, dogs and their owners, and many others just content to walk along the shore. My friend and I ordered our food while the people at the table directly behind us were talking to and about Jordan. The man asked me if he could give Jordan a piece of bread. I thanked him for the gesture but told him Jordan was not allowed to eat people food. I turned back around and continued my conversation.

A moment later I heard something behind me so I turned around again and the guy was feeding Jordan a big piece of French bread. I looked at the guy and asked what he was doing. He said it was no big deal for him to give the dog a piece of bread. I told him that I couldn't believe he disrespected what I told him, and went against my wishes. We got up, paid our bill and left immediately without finishing our meal. In my business, you can't afford any notoriety for restaurant confrontations and the like and I had learned to just walk away when faced with such a situation.

From that moment on, if Jordan got a whiff of human food he would do anything in his power to steal it. If I ever left something on the counter or coffee table and turned my back for a split second, it was history.

Many years later I did a live broadcast with the Las Vegas arena football team. We went into the locker room to interview the quarterback. The quarterback had just arrived and had a breakfast sandwich in a bag that he hadn't had time to eat. While I was interviewing him, Jordan caught whiff of something and went slinking into the other room.

When Jordan came out of the room the quarterback said: "Oh my God, he's got my breakfast." We were live on the air and I looked over and there was Jordan with the entire breakfast sandwich in his mouth. It was one of those magical, on-air moments that you just can't script and everyone busted up laughing. How can you get mad at a dog for stealing your food if it's within his reach?

That probably would never have happened if that guy at the beach hadn't given Jordan a piece of bread. Or maybe it would. I'll never know.

Like most dogs, Jordan had a keen sense of smell. When we drove to the beach, he could smell the ocean air a mile away and would get so excited because he knew where we were headed. Once we crossed the Mesa and were on the ocean side of the hill he'd start pacing in back of the SUV, his nose sniffing the ocean air, his tail wagging and smiling like only a dog can smile.

Jordan also loved the smell of anything rank. And the higher the stink factor the more it attracted him. He didn't care if it was a dead fish, a dead seal or seagull. When Jordan found something stinky in the sand he would rub his body in it like it was expensive perfume. It was all but impossible to stop him. By the time I got to him he'd already rolled around in whatever was the foul fare of the day and he reeked to high heaven.

Fortunately, right next to the parking lot was an outdoor shower. I was usually able to get most of the smell off Jordan before he jumped into my SUV. However, even with my best efforts to get Jordan clean, my SUV stunk and I was embarrassed to let anyone else ride with me.

Years later I was auctioned off as a date during a benefit for the Arthritis Foundation. One of the women I met there gave me her number and we went out shortly after the event. The look on the woman's face when I opened the passenger door was priceless. Not only did she make that oh-my-god-what-stinks-so-bad look on her face, she physically recoiled for a moment before getting inside. She never actually said anything to me about it but I did overhear her complaining to a valet guy later that evening. That was our first and last date.

Another one of Jordan's favorite pastimes was chasing horses that people were riding on the beach—not for the exercise, for the horse poop. Man, did he love those road apples. And not as a perfume. He'd gobble them up like caviar and I couldn't stop him until I caught up to him, often several hundred yards down the beach. Maybe it was a good thing he didn't give kisses.

Like most retrievers, Jordan loved to fetch. Each morning at the beach I would throw a stick into the water and he would fetch it. It didn't matter how far I threw the stick into the water. Jordan would always retrieve it.

One of my fondest beach memories occurred when Jordan was in the ocean fetching a stick. On his way out to the stick something more interesting caught his eye. Whatever it was had him swimming farther and farther out from the shoreline. I wasn't quite sure what he saw until a dark figure popped its head out of the water and then went back under again. I couldn't believe it. Jordan was playing with a seal! Each time the seal's head popped up Jordan stopped swimming. Then the seal would go back under the water and Jordan would start swimming toward it again. The seal was playing a game of hide and go seek with my dog.

The game continued for quite some time. The next thing I knew a crowd of onlookers formed on the beach, watching this amazing sight. Everyone was laughing and clapping. Looking back, it never occurred to me at the time that Jordan might have been in danger. At the time it was obvious to me the seal was playing with Jordan. By the time the seal finally disappeared altogether, there were over one hundred people watching the fun.

Like most everything else that had to do with puppies, I had no idea how to train Jordan. For a long time I could not get Jordan to come to me when I called him. I would get so frustrated with him. Most of the basic commands he learned were taught to him by my pet-loving co-workers. Because Labs are bright and love to learn, Jordan knew the sit, stay and down commands in no time. Best of all, I got an education in obedience training.

As Jordan got older, it became impractical to take him with me to my weekend club DJ job. He was getting too big for the storage area and the owners of the club were growing impatient with the situation. I found a quick remedy. My radio station was on the way, so each Friday and Saturday night I'd drop Jordan off there on my way to the club, leaving him in the care of the disc jockey working the night shift. That was when he learned one of his best tricks.

Jordan took a real liking to the evening disc jockey working for me at the time, and would do just about anything the guy wanted him to. Somehow he taught Jordan to bark whenever he said, "Tell me you love me." I didn't see it, so I didn't know how he got Jordan to bark on that command. But I loved it all the same, and it became one of the few tricks that I would have Jordan perform over the years. A few other tricks I taught Jordan included smiling and yawning on command. I'm not making this up. Years later, when we'd visit school kids together, I'd look over at Jordan and say, "Am I boring you?" Right on cue, Jordan would yawn and the kids would burst out laughing.

The one command I couldn't get into Jordan's head when he was young was "come." If I said: "Jordan, come" he would either ignore me or go the other way.

When Jordan and I arrived at the beach each day we'd see a man playing with his German shepherd. The shepherd was the most obedient dog I'd ever seen. The guy must have noticed my growing frustration with Jordan. He came up to me one morning, telling me about a book I needed to read: *How to Be Your Dog's Best Friend*, written by the monks of New Skete. They're a religious group that live on a farm in upstate New York. To make ends meet, they train guide dogs and they wrote a book about dog training.

I bought the book and read it in one night. I learned that I was doing everything wrong. Not just in training Jordan, but with raising him as well. After reading the book, I realized I wasn't giving Jordan positive reinforcement. I was giving him negative reinforcement. When I called him and he finally came running to me, I was so frustrated I'd scold him. That book taught me I should have rewarded Jordan for obeying me.

I also learned how to properly correct his undesired behavior. A minor rule infraction was met with a "bad dog." More severe infractions would result in me rolling Jordan over in the submissive position. Then, while straddling him, I'd get right in his face and say: "You're being a very bad dog." And when he did something that was completely unacceptable I would make him sit in front of me. I'd get right in his face and with an open hand I'd gently tap him under the chin, simultaneously telling him he was a "bad dog." This did three things: it reinforced me as the alpha dog in Jordan's mind; the tap under his chin got his attention without him ever seeing any part of my body as a physical threat, and it let him know his behavior was unacceptable. I learned to refer to him as a dog when he was bad and a boy when he was good. Furthermore, I learned how important it was to praise Jordan when he did something I expected of him. Employers, are you reading this?

How to Be Your Dog's Best Friend also gave me the idea to take Jordan to obedience school. So when he was about seven months old, I signed us both up for a local obedience class. One of the prerequisites for the class was that all dogs had to be neutered prior to attending.

That obedience class plan got put on hold because up to that point, getting Jordan neutered wasn't an option. I wanted to breed him. After all, I loved him to death and I wanted a few little Jordan's running around. I was completely ignorant to our pet overpopulation problem. I was also unaware that Jordan's health might impact his ability to produce offspring.

CHAPTER 6
Jordan's Hips

In early fall of 1994, even though Jordan was still very young, I noticed he had trouble standing up after periods of inactivity. Knowing several of his littermates were put to sleep because of genetic defects because of poor breeding practices, I became very concerned. I made an appointment with his veterinarian.

Jordan was diagnosed with mild to moderate hip dysplasia. The vet gave me two options: he could perform surgery on Jordan's hips or let it go and let him live with the condition. The vet told me if I elected to have the surgery on Jordan's hips it would be best to have it done while he was still young. Young dogs recover from surgery easier and faster than older dogs, just like people. The surgery involved breaking Jordan's hip socket, rotating it back over the ball of the hip joint and then fusing the bone back together.

Not knowing what was in Jordan's best interest, I asked the vet what he would do. He said he wouldn't put Jordan through the surgery. He told me that Jordan might need the surgery later in life but he might also be just fine with a couple of aspirins each day. He also explained that any surgery, simple or complicated, carried risk.

I chose not to put Jordan through surgery. He continued to be a little slow getting up in the morning but I felt I'd made the right decision. I could live with giving him a few aspirin as he got older. Unfortunately, as Jordan got older he would need much more than a few aspirin. But I have no regrets.

Even though I wanted to breed Jordan, it was no longer an option. I couldn't allow a genetically defective bloodline to continue. Jordan was seven months old and it was time to have him neutered. Veterinarians disagree on the best age to have a dog spayed or neutered, but most will agree the critical growing months for puppies are from four to six months. According to vets I've spoken with, before the age of six months, spaying or neutering can result in growth problems

I took Jordan down to a local animal shelter where they provided spay/neuter services for just thirty-five dollars. I dropped him off on my way to work one morning and I cried as I drove away because I felt so bad that I would never have any of his offspring. I'd grown to love him very much and I wanted to continue his bloodline. However, that would've been irresponsible and I knew I was doing the right thing. Even so I was crushed.

Having Jordan neutered was one of the best things I did for him. It really calmed him down and he never wandered away from home again. It's also generally accepted that spayed or neutered pets experience fewer health problems as they get older. Sadly, I can't say I had Jordan neutered because I was a responsible pet owner. I knew nothing about being a responsible pet owner, nor about the terrible pet overpopulation problem we have here in the United States. It wasn't until I got involved with animal adoption and rescue that I learned we euthanize over 3 million dogs and cats each year in this country.

After Jordan was neutered, I enrolled him in an obedience training class conducted by a local group in Santa Barbara. The group met once a week and had ten to fifteen dogs in each class. The dogs ranged from completely out of control to moderately obedient. Jordan and I attended two classes, then quit. By that time Jordan had learned everything the class instructors taught. Jordan knew all the basic commands and heeled without being on a leash. He walked right next to me, stopped when I stopped and sat and stayed on command.

Jordan got to be so well-behaved I'd leave him unleashed sitting outside of stores for extended periods of time while I shopped. When I'd come out he'd always be waiting patiently for me. He listened only to me so if anyone tried to get him to go with them, he wouldn't move. He just sat and waited for me. As Jordan got older and I learned how stupid that was of me, I never left him alone outside a store again.

While Jordan got better with his commands, he was still a Lab and a puppy and boy, did he love to chew. Anything that smelled like me, whether it was a piece of clothing, a shoe, or a pair of sunglasses, Jordan destroyed it. I eventually learned chewing things that smelled like me was just Jordan's way of letting me know he missed me. Jordan chewed everything to bits. Still ignorant of many obedience-training methods, it never occurred to me to put anything I really cared about out of his reach. I was actually encouraging him to misbehave without even knowing it. I've never claimed to be the sharpest knife in the drawer.

Even though Jordan could drive me absolutely bat-crap-crazy, I loved him dearly. That is not to say he didn't test my patience. He did. And on more than one occasion I know now I went too far in scolding him after he did something unacceptable.

One weekend evening I came home after my weekend club DJ gig to find that Jordan had torn apart some of the plastic blinds that covered our sliding glass door. I'd brought a girl home to meet him and she was mortified when she saw me lose my temper and start yelling at Jordan. She left right then and there, having brought her own car. Her presence probably kept me from doing anything that I would've really regretted later on. I wish I could say that I never did anything to Jordan that I would later regret, but that was not the case and it would be a lie to suggest otherwise.

CHAPTER 7

Television Weather

Early on in my internship at the ABC affiliate in Santa Barbara, I learned that pets were welcome in the building as long as they behaved. As soon as I got Jordan, I took him to work with me each weekend. Since he was just a puppy I really had to keep an eye on him. When each newscast started I'd lock him in the weather office and head out to the studio. I'd been doing weekend weather there for several months and had settled nicely into my job. I got along well with my co-workers and it was long before they looked forward to seeing Jordan each weekend. As he got older and more trustworthy, I'd let him have the run of the station, even during the newscasts.

One Saturday afternoon before we headed off to work at the TV station, Jordan must have eaten something that didn't agree with him. He had been potty trained for a while and didn't have accidents so I wasn't concerned that he'd do something inappropriate inside the station. However, while I was live on-air doing the Sunday evening weather, Jordan was wandering around the television station trying to find a way out because he had to go to the bathroom.

The newsroom was on the bottom floor of the building, and the technical equipment and news control room was upstairs. By the time he made his way upstairs, Jordan lost control of his bowels. The poor guy had a huge accident just inside the door to the master control where the employees were producing and directing the newscast. They were a captive audience and sat there gagging and puking until the newscast ended.

After the newscast, one of the employees brought Jordan downstairs to me in the weather office and told me Jordan had taken a dump all over the floor in the news control room. I went upstairs to survey the damage. I did my best to clean the diarrhea off the carpet but it was still a mess.

I left work after my shift that Sunday evening knowing I was probably in big trouble with station management. The next morning, just after 8:00 a.m., while I was at the radio station doing some of my consulting work, the office manager at the television station called me and started screaming at me about how dare I bring my dog to the station and let him ruin the carpet there. She really went off on me. I thought for sure I was going to get fired. Management at the television station had to call in a carpet cleaning service to get the crap stains out. They billed me for the cost of the cleaning service. They couldn't take it out of my paycheck because I was an unpaid intern—at forty-plus years of age. As a former personnel director in industry, I knew wage and compensation laws were being violated, but I didn't care. I was on television.

The next weekend I went into work and popped my head into King's office. He looked at me and cursed, then started laughing. He told me he didn't know what was funnier—Jordan crapping all over the master control room floor or listening to the office manager rant and rave about it.

In the fall of 1995, after I had been interning for over two years, the television station went through some major changes. A new general manager was hired and he wanted to add a morning newscast to complement the noon and evening newscast. They thought King, with his quick wit and his ability to ad lib and banter would be perfect for the mornings, as morning newscasts tend to include more light features and personality-driven segments. King would not only anchor the new morning show, but he would also be required to assume the anchor duties of the noon newscast as well. Something had to give.

To prevent King from having to split his time between his roll as news director and being a full-time anchor, the station hired a new news director to lighten his load. The woman they hired as his replacement liked me, thank God, and made me an offer. They needed a full-time weather person for the new morning show and King recommended me. After seeing some of my weekend work, the new news director agreed that I was a good style and fit for the new show and offered me the full-time job. I was about to receive my first television paycheck since 1988.

The new morning show had no real direction or format and it ended up being a rip-off of the morning formats you see on network television. The show had a single anchor to report the news from the main anchor desk. King and I sat in big-cushioned chairs in the interview area of the news set. I did the weather and King and I did light-feature reporting. Because we had no real direction we were left to our own devices. Some of our ideas turned out okay. Many others fell flat as a board.

One problem was the timing of the show. We either were constantly dropping stories because we were too heavy with news or we were ad-libbing for minutes on end because we didn't have enough stories to fill the newscast. Once, at the end of my weather-cast, just having finished the extended forecast, the floor director gave me a five-minute cue. They wanted me to fill five minutes on live television with no script. I'm not making this up. They didn't want me to walk back over and sit and chat with King and fill the time, which would've been a cakewalk. King was the ad-lib king. They wanted me to fill five minutes on my own. Thinking back on it and knowing his twisted sense of humor, it was probably King's idea to throw me to the viewing audience wolves.

Somehow I actually managed to fill a full five minutes and to this day I have no recollection of what I talked about. The studio floor crew said I was hilarious. Apparently I broke into an impromptu stand-up comedy routine and had the crew and many viewers in stitches. I realized that day that I had the ability to speak extemporaneously for as long as I wanted to and it would serve me well, not only in front of the camera but also for personal speaking engagements in the years that followed.

Now that I had a full-time job in television, I felt it was time to get out of the radio business for good. I used to tell friends that I "didn't want to be a forty-year-old disc jockey." Not that there was anything wrong with that. I just didn't want to be playing records into my middle years.

I told my boss at the radio station I'd been offered a full-time job at the television station and needed to resign my radio position. He said he still needed my help and asked if I could stay on as a paid consultant. When he offered me $1,000 a month I knew I couldn't turn him down. All he needed was for me to monitor the station's song list, recommend new songs and artists, and train my future replacement in the art of being a radio station program director. The program director for any radio station is in charge of on-air talent, promotions, play lists, song rotation and frequency of airplay. The most popular songs are played with the greatest frequency and oldies or "gold" songs are played with the least frequently. It's a tried and true formula that works. It's also the reason songs get played over and over again until you get sick of them.

Back to television. I read a quote once that went something like this: "Television is the only industry that eats its young." After twenty-plus years I can honestly say I understand the meaning of that quote. I've seen a lot more young anchors, reporters, and producers wash out, get fired or frustrated, and just all together quit the business within their very first year on or off of the air. Part of this is because many seasoned veterans, having to learn the business on their own the hard way, expect and believe that newcomers have to pay their dues as well. These veterans don't offer a hand up and probably take a perverse amount of pleasure when a rookie fails. I don't understand or buy in to this way of thinking, as I believe people deserve help when they're new to the business. And I'm proud to say I've helped and trained many young forecasters over the years.

Television can be a very cutthroat business and the people who've been in it for awhile know no one's job is safe. There is always someone younger, smarter and better looking than you who'll work for half your salary to take your job. If you're not at the absolute top of your game, no matter what market you're working in, you're going to lose your job to someone else. I've seen it happen time after time. I've known too many forecasters, and broadcasters in general, who've relied on their experience and familiarity within the market to lose their jobs because they got lazy, arrogant or both.

In my business, the smartest thing you can do is to adopt the attitude that each broadcast might very well be your last. So you must be determined to make each broadcast your absolute best. That's why I was determined to earn my meteorology "Seal of Approval." I wanted the viewers to know that I knew what I was talking about. I have a history of being a jokester and a pretty fun-loving guy on the air, and that can hurt your credibility. I had a news director once tell me I had "no credibility." I had another news director tell me, "I can either fight you or take credit for you. I choose the latter."

King Harris and I had a great relationship. We worked very well together on the air and the viewing audience could tell. We would also joke and pal around off-air and pretty much drove people nuts. We quickly became known as the station outsiders or "rebels" because we'd say and do whatever was on our minds, on or off-air. On-air we'd intentionally try to make the other slip up by making faces off camera at each other, unless of course we were in the middle of a serious story.

My two funniest King stories: Shortly after starting the new morning show, the two of us would sit in the newsroom after the morning newscast ended and joke around about the events of the day. I think King was kind of relieved to no longer have an obligation as a manager to wave the corporate flag or be a management cheerleader.

One morning, the new news director was giving a potential new reporter the tour of the facility and as they walked by us, King yelled out, "Don't do it!" He was telling the prospective employee she shouldn't take the job at our station because it was a bad place to work. The funniest thing about the incident was neither the recruit or the news director seemed to realize who King was talking to, and we just sat there and laughed until we cried. The other station employees thought we were complete idiots.

My second favorite King story happened just before the end of my employment at the Santa Barbara station. We were doing "cut-ins;" brief news updates during the network show *Good Morning America*. These updates had two segments, news and weather, separated by a brief commercial break. Moments before going to air, King was told that a fatal car accident had just occurred on Highway 46, which runs east from Paso Robles and ends at Highway 99 in central California; the same highway that took the life of James Dean during a fatal, head-on collision on September 30, 1955.

The only information King had before he went on-air was that one person had been ejected from his car and died at the scene. In these situations there is no script or teleprompter, so the anchor or reporter just takes his or her notes and ad-libs the story. King was the best ad-libber I'd ever worked with and he was usually seamless when he had to do breaking news. However, in this instance he couldn't think of the word "ejected" and he stammered and stumbled and was really struggling when finally, out of sheer frustration he said, "And on impact (imagine his hands motioning forward) the man was set free."

I was standing at the chroma key wall, which I'll explain in detail later in this chapter, and did a full on spit-take with my coffee. We immediately went to break and King and I lost it. We were laughing so hard I had trouble composing myself before the break ended and I came back on the air for my weather update. Understand that we were laughing about King's on-air faux pas and not the actual incident. After the update was over, the station went back to network programming, and we went into the newsroom. The phone lines were flooded with people calling to complain about King's insensitive comment.

When the news director came in, she read King the riot act and I thought they were going to fire him right there on the spot. Fortunately, they didn't. Privately we laughed about the incident for years to follow, as we stayed in touch for some time after I'd moved away. By the way, King did eventually leave that station and has been teaching college and doing other broadcasting work ever since. He truly is one in a million. I feel fortunate to have worked alongside such a seasoned, knowledgeable and professional broadcaster. I can't count the number of anchors and reporters who've been forced to learn their craft from someone who has no business even being in broadcasting.

Let me explain a little of the history of weather technology: The first television weather-casters had to draw graphics on a pane of glass that was placed between them and the camera. Because the on-screen images are reversed by the time you see them at home, early weather forecasters had to learn to draw in reverse. These are the first forecasters I remember as a kid. Quite an art but pretty antiquated.

In the seventies and eighties, station graphic artists created the weather forecast graphics which were then superimposed on a chroma key wall behind the weather caster. The weather-caster would compile the forecast and provide the data to the graphics person with a list of the order he or she wanted them to appear on the screen. This was a real advancement but there was one major problem: the weather-caster had no control over what appeared on the screen. If a graphic appeared out of order or there was a technical glitch, the forecaster would be stuck out there on live television with no option but to toss back to the anchors at the desk or wait until the problem was solved. This, as they say, is what separated the men from the boys.

Forecasters who aren't good at ad-libbing can look like a fool on the air. Those who are quick on their feet can turn uncomfortable situations into some of the funniest and most memorable moments for the viewer. This is why so many weather people get their start in radio. Disc jockeys have to be good ad-libbers. Unlike news anchors, weather anchors or meteorologists don't work from a prepared script. I actually worked with a guy who would type out his entire weather-cast, memorize it word for word and proceed to recite it back on-air. All was fine until the wrong graphic popped up and then he was reduced to a babbling idiot. He ended up refusing to learn the new computer software technology and subsequently lost his job.

In front of chroma key wall during appearance by Chef Gustav Mauler September 27, 2001. Photo courtesy of Mary Vail, Publicist.

Current weather software is much more sophisticated. I use a weather software computer system that gives me full control over all of the graphics I use on-air. And it's fun to use. The graphics are so lifelike and sophisticated it's almost like playing video games. But one has to be pretty darn good working with computers. Fortunately I seem to have a knack for it and I enjoy building compelling graphics that help me tell my weather "story" each day to the viewers. I build all of the graphics viewers see on-air on my computer and I place them in the order I want during the weather-cast. Weather graphics or scenes are advanced with the use of a hand-held "clicker" that looks and operates much like a garage door opener. So if there is a glitch, I have no one to blame but myself, which really keeps me on my toes. While the occasional screw up is okay, constant on-screen mistakes don't sit well with one's employer. Many weather forecasters and meteorologists have seen their careers end abruptly with the advent of weather computers as they simply refuse to learn the new technology.

Television weather people work in front of a chroma key wall, better known as a "green screen." This is the same technology used by movie producers to create most special effects and action sequences: An actor appears to be fighting a monster when in fact he's alone in front of a green wall, and the special effects are added in post production. So when you see me standing in front of a map or graphic, there's nothing behind me but a big wall painted a pastel green; hence the name, "green screen."

To be honest, I've never really understood exactly how this works, but it's something like this: a computer program, the "chroma" part of "chroma key" tells the system to "key" on green, the "key" part. Computer generated graphics are "looking" for a particular shade of green and they "attach" themselves to the green wall behind me. The only thing not keyed on is me, making it look as though I'm standing in front of the graphics. If I wear clothing the color of the wall behind me the only thing you'll see is the exposed parts of my body. Confused? So am I.

When standing in front of the green screen I don't see the graphics like you do at home. What do I see? I'm actually looking at three different television monitors: one on either side of me, outside camera view, and one in front of me which is actually part of the camera. Because I'm not reading off of the teleprompter like the anchors, the camera on me can be switched to a television screen mode. This way, when I'm looking at the camera, I see the graphics behind me even though there is really nothing there. I can then look at the monitor on the left, right, or in front of me and use the image of myself as a guide to point at graphics or places on a map.

The real trick to working in front of the chroma key wall is to make the viewer think that I'm actually looking at what I'm pointing to. In the business we call this "chroma cheating." Here's the way chroma cheating works: while I'm looking at the monitor in front of me, I point at something I want to reference, hold my finger on that spot, turn and look briefly at my finger and then look back at the camera. This creates the visual illusion that I'm actually looking at what I'm pointing to. Conversely, if I were to point to Miami while looking at the monitor to my left, it would appear as though I'm looking off into space. To you at home, Miami appears behind me to my lower right. However, the monitor to my right is at eye level. If

I'm looking at the monitor and pointing to Miami, it's obvious to you that I'm not looking where I'm pointing. The next time you're watching your hometown weather forecaster, see how well he or she has mastered the art of chroma cheating.

The chroma key wall can be a load of fun, especially during Halloween. One year I painted a glove green and to the viewer at home it looked like my hand was missing. Another year I wrapped a green blanket around my body and my head appeared to be floating in space. You're probably getting a sense of why one of my former news directors had issues with my credibility. But he was devoid of any semblance of a sense of humor. He also once told me, "I didn't hire a comedian."

I said: "No, your predecessor did !"

In 1996, after we'd been doing the new morning show in Santa Barbara for about eight months, the Olympic torch was being transported around

the country on a special train. At nine one morning the torch was scheduled to stop in Santa Barbara. The reporter who was supposed to cover the story couldn't be found.

This was a pretty significant historical event for Santa Barbara and the station had no one to cover it so they sent me. I had never done live field

LIVE broadcast DT Santa Barbara with Spencer Christian of GMA Spring 1996

reporting before and I ended up being live on the air that morning for two straight hours. King and I went back and forth between my live shots and his coverage in the studio.

When I got back to the station, I was treated like Moses after he parted the Red Sea. The news director told me my coverage of the event was some of the best work she'd ever seen. She went to the general manager that day and told him the station needed to get me under a written contract. She tried to explain to him that I would not stay in a market like Santa Barbara unless I was under contract because some other news station was going to hire me. The general manager blew it off because he didn't like me. Two months later, I was offered a job in Las Vegas, Nevada.

When I broke the news that I was leaving Santa Barbara for Las Vegas, the news director told me what she had said to the general manager and how he had blown it off. When the general manager heard the news about my leaving, he walked into the weather center and said, "You know what there is in Las Vegas, don't you? Nothing." With that, he turned and walked out, never speaking to me again.

I have no idea what it is about me that rubs some managers the wrong way. Yes, I like to cut-up and joke around on TV. But if it helps ratings isn't that a good thing? For many years I'd do or say anything that came to mind, no matter how politically incorrect it was. The old adage about broadcasting is, "Do first and then beg for forgiveness afterward." Until I got older, that described me to a tee. Anyway, I had virtually no contact with the general manager in Santa Barbara, but it was pretty obvious by his behavior he didn't have much use for me. During my entire tenure at that station, whenever I passed this guy in the hall or the newsroom, he simply ignored me.

Speaking of tees, I got in trouble for saying, on-air, "I'd like to take a five iron to Ted Kaczynski" right after his arrest. My news director at the time ripped me a new one and I learned a valuable lesson about making editorial comments with regard to news content. There are three things in the broadcasting business that will get you fired: first, you never, ever comment about a commercial sponsor. You piss off a sponsor and they'll pull their advertising. And you've just lost a job. Second, you never use profanity on-air. Okay, this sounds like a no-brainer. But what if you don't know the camera or the microphone is on? I saw it happen to a guy doing a live field report during a storm in Los Angeles. The anchors had tossed to him in the field but he didn't know it. So he stood there on live television, tapped his earpiece and said, I can't hear a f**king thing!" That was the last time I saw him on-air on that or any other station. Third, never editorialize a news story. Your job is to report the news. Just because you think a suspect is probably guilty, and a dirt bag, you keep those comments to yourself. Period. Sure, there are some other sure-fire ways to get fired, like lying to your boss or theft of company property. Those things will get you canned anywhere.

It was now late spring of 1996, and I was about to get an agent, a new job and a life in a new city. But first, my boy Jordan was about to become a TV star.

CHAPTER 8
Jordan's Television Debut

One day after work I brought Jordan home because I had to run some errands and I was going to be gone too long to keep him in my car. I ran my errands and when I returned home I couldn't find him anywhere. That was so unusual for him. He always greeted me in the driveway when I got home. After searching for what felt like hours, I finally found him hiding underneath my bed.

I called his name and asked him if he was okay. At first he just ignored me and lay there licking one of his back legs. He was hesitant to move, and I didn't understand what was going on. Finally, he crawled to me from under the bed and stood by my side. Something just wasn't right. It suddenly occurred to me there might be something wrong with Jordan.

I reached around to the back of the leg he'd been licking and felt a large wet spot. When I turned him around, there was a hole the size of a silver dollar in the back of his leg and I could see tendons and muscles. Fortunately, Jordan's instinctual survival mode had kicked in and the wound was wet and clean from his constant licking.

I panicked. I never had to deal with something like that before. I remembered there was an animal emergency hospital nearby, so I put Jordan in the back of the SUV and raced him to the hospital. When we got to the emergency hospital, the staff took Jordan in immediately and a few minutes later the vet came out to talk to me. I was crying because I thought Jordan might be seriously hurt and I was somehow responsible.

The vet was fairly certain coyotes had attacked Jordan. He told me Jordan was very fortunate to have gotten away, and that he would be okay. He said the wound was not life threatening. Jordan just needed stitches and he could go home.

I have no idea if it really was coyotes that hurt Jordan that day. However, it makes sense as they are very common around the hills and mountainous areas that surround the California coastal areas, including where we lived in Santa Barbara. The hill we lived on was uninhabited just to the east and I had no doubt there were all kinds of critters and varmints roaming around within a few hundred feet of our home.

However, coyotes don't normally attack another animal unless they're running with a pack, and I couldn't imagine Jordan getting away from two or more attacking coyotes. Many years later I would find out just how tough my boy could be when meeting up with another aggressive dog. He made the other dogs back down in the two fights he was involved in. When it came to confrontation, my boy had no fear. Maybe that's how it went that day up on the mountain. Jordan was romping around enjoying an afternoon of discovery when he encountered a mad group of coyotes. His first thought would've been that they were dogs and they wanted to play. Maybe he even initiated the contact, going over to them to play. Only then would he have learned of their deadly intentions when he was quickly surrounded by raised hackles and bared fangs. I would like to think that my brave boy, in this potentially deadly encounter, engaged these would-be assassins in the fight of his life, escaping with only a wound to the back of his leg. I've often wondered what the other guys looked like after my valiant boy finished with them.

I've also thought there was a pretty good chance that Jordan simply got his leg caught on some barbed wire or a piece of glass or metal. But I like the coyote story, so we'll just go with that.

Jordan had to wear one of those big plastic cones around his head so he couldn't reach his head back and chew on the stitches. When we left the vet's office it took Jordan four tries to get out the door. Bam! The cone hit the doorway. Another try and bam! Then a third attempt. Bam! Jordan was so frustrated. When he finally made it outside of the emergency hospital, I was laughing hysterically, knowing my boy was going to be okay and from watching him trying to negotiate the open door. Jordan didn't like the cone and he kept trying to chew it off on the drive home.

After a few days the cone became Jordan's badge of honor. He seemed to get depressed whenever I needed to take it off to bathe him or to get him into our SUV. The minute I started to put the cone back on him, he would get excited and he'd strut around like, "Man look at me! I am sooo cool. I have a cone!" Jordan ended up loving his cone so much I saved it.

A few of my co-workers at the television station signed Jordan's cone as if it was a cast. His Santa Barbara TV debut came one morning when the cameraman showed him on the air wearing his cone. He then panned the camera up to me standing next to Jordan, wearing a matching sympathy

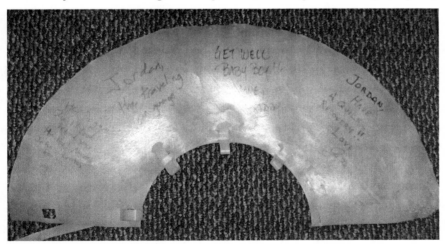

Jordans Cone Spring 1996

cone the floor director had made for me. Everyone in the station laughed. The viewing audience loved it too. Immediately following the newscast, the station started receiving phone calls from viewers.

Years later, I was asked to be the keynote speaker at an insurance conference. Jordan attended the conference with me. Being the fun-loving guy I am, I thought it would be funny to walk into the conference with a neck brace on, and with Jordan wearing his cone. The conference was about five years after the coyote attack. When I found his signed cone in the garage the day before the conference and showed it to him, Jordan got so excited and looked at me like, "Oooh my cone! Look at me! I get to wear my cone again!"

If a room full of insurance agents didn't find that funny, I didn't know who would. When Jordan and I walked into the insurance conference, the audience went crazy, laughing and clapping. To this very day that old plastic cone hangs on the wall in our garage, and I smile each time I look at it with fond memories of Jordan and his beloved cone.

After Jordan's initial television debut, he appeared on television more often, most of the time by accident. Somehow Jordan learned almost immediately that when I went on-air live to give my weather report, he could get up and walk around the station because I couldn't do anything about it. He would walk around and say hi to the employees or greet a guest who was in the studio. Sometimes he would walk right in front of me and his tail or ears would end up on television. The production staff and floor crew loved the spontaneity of it all and engineered brief, Jordan on-camera moments whenever they could.

Because Jordan was in the studio with us each day, and the crew and management seemed to be cool with him being on camera, we tried to make sure he got some on-air time at least once each morning. Viewers would call up when they saw Jordan on television and want to know why we had a dog on television and who was his owner. Soon, when one of our news crews was in the field, the viewers would stop them to ask about Jordan. They didn't seem to care about the news or me, they just wanted to know how their new favorite Labrador retriever was doing, and would we be showing more of him during our newscasts. We had created a new Santa Barbara TV celebrity. I had no idea at the time what events we had set in motion or what impact my boy would have on future viewing audiences.

Not everyone was thrilled about Jordan being in the television station. The station's chief meteorologist apparently hated animals. He posted a sign on the door of the weather office that read, "No Food or Animals in The Weather Office, Ever!" Luckily, shortly thereafter he left our station for a new position in upstate New York.

After our animal-hating meteorologist left for his job in New York, the station replaced him with a brilliant young man from Colorado Springs. His name was Steve Stewart, and he had a degree in meteorology, unlike me who stumbled into my first weather reporting job by having the gifts of gab and ad-lib due to my radio experience. Steve was truly one of the smartest young men I had ever met. He showed me things on the weather computer I couldn't even fathom. And he did all of his own weather research and forecasting; something that, up to that point, I was incapable of doing. My business has three types of forecasters: 1) those who do all of their own forecasting based on their education and experience, 2) those who rely solely on the information provided by someone else, in most cases the National Weather Service, and 3) those who do a little of both. There is nothing wrong with any of the three. The only exception I take with forecasters who fall into category 2 or 3 is that I believe they have a duty to credit their sources for the information they provide. If you use someone else's data, give them credit.

With Steve's help, I am now able to put myself in the first category. I do all of my own forecasting. The information I give my viewers is based on my research, education and experience. If I'm right, I don't want anyone else taking the credit. If I'm wrong, I don't want anyone else taking the blame. The only thing I am not qualified to do is issue weather-related advisories, watches and warnings. That is the National Weather Service's responsibility. My duty is to pass these advisories and warnings on to my viewers, whether I agree with their issuance or not.

Meteorology is not an exact science. No matter how good I am at forecasting the weather, at the end of the day my forecast is an educated guess. Thankfully, technology has gotten better to the point that I'm usually pretty confident in my forecasts up to seven days in the future. There was a time that even a one-to-three-day forecast was, at best, a crapshoot. But still, if I say it's gonna be 100 degrees on a certain day, there is absolutely no formula or broadcast research tool available that can guarantee I will be right. But I'm pretty accurate, primarily because I hate being wrong and it pains me when people come up to me and say, "You said it would rain today and it didn't!" Pat Sajak, of *Wheel of Fortune* fame, was a weatherman in another life. It is said that he was once quoted as saying, "Weather is the only job you can be wrong three days out of five." That might have been true when he was doing it, but I don't think I'd last very long with that track record today.

Forecasting is a process whereby you look at several layers of our atmosphere, from the surface, up to 30,000 feet or higher, near the jet stream, and by doing so, you get a sense of such things as temperature, wind, sky condition, rain, snow, or thunderstorm probability. What I use to do this is called "computer model data." The forecast "models" are graphs and graphics that, when you understand how to interpret their meaning, can give you a very good idea of what is going to happen in a given area for a given time, up to ten days or even longer. The model data is less reliable the further out you go in time, however, once you learn how to read and interpret the data, the models can be pretty darned accurate.

What I really considered myself strong in is forecasting wind and the probability of thunderstorms. Our thunderstorm season in Las Vegas, known as the monsoon, lasts typically from the first week of July through the first week of September. And yes, we do get severe weather here. Not like what you'd expect in Tornado Alley or the Midwest or Gulf states, because we don't have the atmospheric dynamics—warm, moist, unstable air off of the Gulf clashing with cold unstable air aloft—but we do get our fair share of flash flooding and severe thunderstorms.

I also have a great interest in forecasting winds for a couple of reasons: 1) I grew up in Southern California where you encounter the Santa Ana winds—very strong winds that accelerate and descend down and through mountain canyons and passes. As these winds descend and compress, the air becomes warmer because when you compress air, it warms. Think about using a manual tire pump. The more you pump, the hotter the metal on the outside of the pump becomes. 2) In all my years of doing weather, the number one complaint I get from viewers is about wind. People, by and large, don't like wind. Wind, in most cases, is merely the product of the difference in pressure at the surface of the earth. The primary exception is winds produced by violent downdrafts during thunderstorms.

I am proud to say I earned my Broadcast Meteorologist "Seal of Approval" from the National Weather Association in the fall of 2003. This is not to say I didn't know what I was doing before that. The seal simply gives viewers an indication that I have the experience and the educational goods to back up my forecasting. And the only reason I didn't try to earn the seal prior to that time was because I was afraid of failing. Like the Bar and the CPA exam, the meteorology seal of approval process is a difficult one, testing not just your knowledge of your craft, but how you present yourself and your information to the viewer. I've heard that many forecasters fail this process on several occasions before passing. I've also heard that some never pass. Some weather people never bother to go through the process because they don't know anything about forecasting.

I got lucky and passed on the first try, thank God. Luck aside, I had studied for several weeks after work each day and I'm sure that had something to do with me passing the exam.

Despite being young enough to be my son, my new 1995 colleague, Steve Stewart, became my mentor and to this day I still use some of the tools and knowledge he passed along to me in my daily forecasts. He remains one of my dearest friends.

In August of 2003, we had a severe weather event in northwest Las Vegas, and I was the only weather person who accurately predicted it. With rain and hail pounding my home office window, the phone rang and on the other end of the line was the young man who became my mentor. Before I could say anything, Steve screamed into the phone, "Please tell me you called this." I held the phone up to the window so he could hear the rain pounding on the pane and I told him, "I sure did!" His response? "Thank God I taught you something!"

Steve has since gone on to be a weather software trainer and graphics developer for many NBC stations across the country. He also continues to do on-air weather forecasting in the southeast.

CHAPTER 9
Las Vegas Bound?

Less than two weeks after I covered the Olympic torch story, a TV agent contacted me. King had just signed on with him and, unbeknownst to me, had given him a tape of some of my on-air work. Apparently the agent liked what he saw. He'd recently gone into business for himself as an agent after years in network television management, and King and I were two of his first talent sign-ups.

An agent can be a great thing. They can get you interviews when you can't seem to get a foot in the door on your own. They negotiate your contract with your new employer. This is probably their greatest asset as they act as a buffer between you and station management. If there any hard feelings after tense negotiations, your agent usually takes the heat, not you. The downside? You usually have to pay them between 7 and 10 percent of your contract, for the life of the contract. Plus, that person stays your agent and you're on the hook to him or her for as long as you stay at the station where the original contract was negotiated. Even if you negotiate all subsequent contracts, you are still obligated to pay that agent for the life of your current employment.

Worse yet, breaking one of these contracts is very hard, as I would learn less than two years after signing on with my first and only agent. I had to prove breach of contract with the governing body, AFTRA. The deciding factor for them letting me out of my contract was the fact that my agent did not get me one single interview or audition during the two years he worked for me. Not one. And this was after he pretty much promised me I'd "be in Vegas for two years and then on to a major market." Well I'm still in Vegas. With no complaints. And, no agent. And I've personally negotiated all subsequent contracts after the first one that he did for me. AFTRA agreed there was a breach but I still had to pay him through the first two years.

Back to May of 1996. The agent and I met for lunch one afternoon and I signed up with him for the standard eight percent of any contract that he might negotiate for me. At the time I was elated. Here was an industry veteran who believed in me. He was convinced he could sign me to another station, in a bigger television market that would garner a higher salary. Within a month I had an interview at the NBC affiliate in Las Vegas, Nevada. If hired, I would be working the same morning and noon hours that I currently worked in Santa Barbara.

In early June of 1996, I took two days off from work in Santa Barbara and flew to Las Vegas for my interview. I left Jordan home at the ranch and our landlord agreed to take care of him. I booked a room at Bally's, the former MGM Grand, spent part of that evening walking the Strip and checking the sites, and settled in for a very restless night, knowing I was facing my biggest job interview in my professional career.

The following morning, I showered, shaved, put on my best suit and headed down to the valet to hail a taxicab. I'd gotten directions to the station the previous afternoon when I'd checked into my room, and the cab ride to the station took less than ten minutes. Bally's is right in the heart of the Strip at Las Vegas Boulevard and Flamingo Avenue, and the station was located just off of the Boulevard, north of downtown.

The cabbie dropped me off in front of the station and I immediately noticed how large the building was and that there was an actual news helicopter sitting on a helipad on the station roof, emblazed with the station's logo. I was impressed. I went through the front door and introduced myself to the receptionist who was aware of my interview. She called the news director as I waited in the reception area.

I met with the news director and the general manager. The general manager asked me where I thought I would be in five years. I told him I hoped to be working for him and have my Meteorology Seal of Approval. They had me do a mock weather-cast. I was introduced to the current morning team and the guy I would replace. He was being promoted to the evening shift as the current evening weather guy was about to retire—hence, the reason for the opening and my golden opportunity. I could sense that the news anchor liked me immediately, which made me feel more comfortable. I shook off the jitters and did my mock weather-cast, starting first at the news desk and then walking to the chroma key wall. That was where I really started to settle down. At one point, while I was in front of the chroma key wall, I glanced over and saw the news director looking at the anchor. The news director's facial expression was obvious: "What do you think?" I looked over to see the anchor giving me a nod of approval.

Despite the anchor's stamp of approval, I didn't have a good feeling about the interview. When I left, I thought of all the things I should have said. I felt my attempts at humor were lame and fell flat. The best thing I could come up with was that I was afraid they would "pay me in casino chips." Not my best work.

A month went by before I heard from my agent that I had gotten the job. He told me I wasn't the news director's first choice. However, my agent and the news director were good friends so he asked the news director to hire me as a favor. My agent had only been in business for a couple of months and hadn't placed anyone in a job so he really wanted me to get the position. I found out later the news director decided to hire me because of my sense of humor. Apparently, he didn't care if I knew anything about forecasting the weather. It's Vegas, right?

I was elated. I was going to be moving out of state for the first time in my life to start a new job in an incredibly exciting city—a city that I had loved for over twenty years. It was a dream come true. However, I was concerned that my present employer would learn of the job offer and do something to sabotage the impending deal. So I decided to tell no one until the contract was actually signed. My agent sent me the contract within a few days and I immediately signed and returned it. Only then did I feel it was safe for me to give notice to my current employers.

When I found out I got the job in Las Vegas, I told the manager of my Santa Barbara radio station I was moving to Las Vegas. He told me they loved the job I did and asked if I would continue to consult for them from my new home. I worked for them, via the Internet for my first two years in Las Vegas. The extra thousand dollars a month really made a big difference. Unfortunately, I had accumulated some debt and I really wasn't making that much more in Las Vegas than in Santa Barbara. Eventually I'd have to get financial help from high interest check cashing services during my first few years in Las Vegas.

I will never forget the Santa Barbara TV station news director's reaction when I went in the following morning and gave her the news. She looked at me and said, "Damn it! I told our GM we needed to get you under a contract or we were going to lose you!" Then she composed herself and told me how happy she was for me. This was the same news director who once chose to "take credit for me" and I know she was proud of me. The employees I worked with in Santa Barbara had a nice little party for me following my last weather cast, and presented me with a beautiful watercolor print of the Santa Barbara coastline. I cried like a baby right in front of my boss and my co-workers. I had no idea how much they had come to like me and respect my work during my brief, full-time on-air tenure. To this day, that beautiful framed print hangs on the wall just inside the hallway that leads to our garage as a daily reminder of where I've been, and where I've come.

When I first arrived in Las Vegas for my new job, I asked around the station about local dog parks. Station management station got a big kick out of that. Of all the questions I might have asked, I wanted to know about dog parks for Jordan. To me it was no different than asking about local schools. I should've been asking as to the availability of dog-friendly apartment complexes. And to this day I don't know why I didn't ask the question that should've been at the top of my list: can Jordan come to work with me? At that time, Jordan's television career had been short and limited and I still really didn't have the mindset that we were a team. That's not the way my agent sold me to my new station. And I didn't think that far ahead. I was just happy to have a new job.

I was excited to move to Las Vegas. It had been my annual birthday destination location for many of my adult years. The only other place I ever found as magical as Las Vegas was Disneyland. Of course you usually leave Disneyland with money in your pocket, having had a great time. You always leave Vegas broke, having had a great time.

I felt like I had finally made it to the big leagues. After being on television full-time for less than one year, I had a two-year contract at the top-rated TV station in Las Vegas, Nevada. However, there was a provision in my contract that could be exercised by either party: the contract could be voluntarily terminated after one year. Thankfully, it wasn't a six-month provision, as I would have exercised my option and left Las Vegas. It's one thing to visit Las Vegas on vacation, but something entirely different to live there.

I was very lonely the first several months I lived in Las Vegas. And I struggled financially. There were times I called my agent and begged him to find me another job. Each time he'd tell me to "hang in there" and things would get better. He was right. Within a year, I began to feel comfortable in my new job, and surroundings. And, I had a new Las Vegas two-legged buddy: my co-anchor, John Overall. More on him, coming up.

On a late June Friday afternoon, the week before I was to start my new job, I drove to Las Vegas to find a place for Jordan and me to live. Once again, I left Jordan back in Santa Barbara with my landlord. When I arrived, I checked into the Luxor Hotel. I've since learned that the Luxor is home to two modern marvels: the world's largest atrium, and the world's brightest light. Nightly, the beam shoots directly from the top of the atrium into the sky, and it is said to be one of only two man-made objects that can be seen from space. The other is the Great Wall of China.

When I learned I got the job in Las Vegas, I called my new news director and asked him where I should look for an apartment. He told me the "west was best." I quickly learned that would be the extent of any help I'd get finding local housing.

After spending a quiet night in my room at the Luxor I got an early start in my hunt for a new home. I left the Strip and drove to the western part of the Las Vegas valley: Summerlin.

Summerlin is an extended name of the Summa Corporation, which is owned by the Howard Hughes Corporation. Summerlin is the biggest single-family home community development in the world and Howard's brainchild. As you might remember, Howard Hughes spent his final years in seclusion in the penthouse suite at the top of the Desert Inn, which he eventually bought. The story goes that Hughes, facing eviction from the current Inn owners, simply ordered his accountant to buy the property so he could stay. He also bought most of the undeveloped land in the west and northwestern part of the Las Vegas Valley. Howard may have had his phobias but he was no dummy.

I drove from apartment to apartment in and around the Summerlin area. At each location I was told the same thing: "We only take dogs under twenty pounds." By this time Jordan weighed ninety.

One apartment manager went one step further. She told me to give my dog away. She suggested that I run an ad in the newspaper and get rid of him. I was horrified. I couldn't believe what this woman was saying to me. I asked her if she'd give up her kids. She said no, but that it wasn't the same. I told her it most certainly was the same. Jordan was my son.

I turned around and walked out. I figured there was no point in arguing with her because she obviously didn't get it. Only a certain kind of person gets it—that special bond we have with our pets. It is a bond that God has blessed us with. However, millions of people view pets in a much different way—like property. These people will never understand what our pets mean to us: pets are full-fledged members of our family and deserve to be treated as such.

I searched all day Saturday but didn't find an apartment. It was late June and the temperature was well above 100 degrees. Each time I stepped out of my air-conditioned car, the hot Las Vegas air slapped me in the face. It was like stepping from the freezer to the oven. I dreaded having to search for an apartment all over again on Sunday in the desert heat.

Sunday morning I loaded up my car and checked out of the hotel. Once again I drove west, away from the Strip in search of an apartment complex that allowed big dogs. I had to leave Las Vegas by noon. I needed to get back to Santa Barbara in time to get enough rest for work the following Monday morning.

By 11:00 a.m. the desert sun was blazing and I was still looking for a suitable apartment. I was running out of time. I stopped at one final complex and threw myself at the mercy of the property manager. Fortunately, she took pity on me. She recommended I check out the Angel Park Apartments. I could've kissed her. Maybe I did. She gave me directions and off I went.

The Angel Park Apartments were located just east of the Angel Park Golf Club, thus the name. They're on the west side of the Las Vegas Valley, near Summerlin and very close to U.S. 95, the route I would take to get to work each day. They had single and two-story apartments and it was a very clean complex with a beautiful pool area, workout room and beach volleyball courts. I told the apartment manager that I needed a one-bedroom apartment and that I had a dog that weighed ninety pounds. She told me she had an apartment unit but it wouldn't be available until July 13, 1996. I started my new job on July 8 but I knew I could find a place to stay my first week in Las Vegas. I filled out an application, put down a deposit on the apartment and felt relieved.

She took me on a tour of the complex and showed me an apartment with the same floor plan as the one I'd applied for. It was a single-bedroom job with a large front room, fireplace, built-in washer and dryer and a huge bedroom. I was thrilled. It was one of the nicer apartments I'd seen. I couldn't thank the apartment manager enough. I got in my car and drove back to Santa Barbara, fairly confident that my application would be approved.

As I drove south on I-15 through the resort corridor, I was awestruck. This was going to be our new home. To this day, I don't get tired of driving along I-15 near the Strip, marveling at all the hotels and casinos. Las Vegas is a very magical place to me. Thank God I'm not much of a gambler. My dad, Joe, was hooked on the ponies, but apparently the bug didn't get passed down to me.

When I pulled into the driveway at the ranch back in Santa Barbara late that Sunday afternoon, Jordan raced down to greet me. He was so happy I was back. Jordan wasn't overly affectionate and he didn't like to sleep in bed with me, but anytime I was gone for more than a few days he'd sleep in the bed my first night back.

For years I tried to get Jordan to show some sign of outward affection toward me but he wouldn't. I loved him to death and couldn't understand why he wasn't affectionate toward me. I later learned that Jordan's lack of affection was a direct result of how he was weaned. He failed to get the human contact he needed during the first several weeks of his life. Human contact and interaction early in a puppy's life is vital to the bonding process that should take place with their new, two-legged family members. That's why I don't believe pet stores should be in the business of selling pets. Pet store pets receive little human contact.

Jordan would let me hug him from time to time, but only for a few seconds. It wasn't until many years later that I realized how wrong I was about how Jordan felt about me.

CHAPTER 10

Vegas Bound!

My apartment in Las Vegas wasn't ready until a week after I arrived so I left Jordan back in Santa Barbara, at the ranch. It was the longest time we were ever apart. I was upset and nervous about leaving him, but I didn't have a choice. Deep down I knew our landlord loved Jordan and would take care of him. I left Santa Barbara and arrived in Las Vegas on a Sunday, the day before I started my new job on July 8, 1996. All I brought with me was a week's worth of clothes and toiletries.

I drove to the Palace Station, hoping to find a room. The Palace Station Hotel and Casino is located just west of I-15 and the Strip on one of the major east-west arteries in town, Sahara Avenue. And it was only about a ten-minute drive from the television station. A few years earlier I had spent a weekend at that property and found the rooms to be clean and reasonably priced. I also knew that they had a food court in the casino so I wouldn't have to go far for dinner each day. I've always been a fast-food type and can live on McDonald's, Taco Bell or Del Taco. I explained to the Palace Station front desk clerk that I was on a limited budget and needed a room for five nights. She told me the cheapest room they had was $20 a night, but it was located next to the loading dock and it could be really loud. I told her I didn't care; I just needed a place to stay.

That first Sunday night in Las Vegas, I was all alone and I already missed my home in Santa Barbara and Jordan. I hardly slept because I was so excited about my new job and delivery trucks roaring around near my room woke me up whenever I did fall asleep. I woke up early the following Monday morning and arrived at the TV station for my first day of work at four in the morning. I was so early I actually got there before the morning weather person I was replacing and who was responsible for training me.

I trained for the first couple of days and then went live on the air on Wednesday. The station introduced me with a rather inventive pre-taped segment: They showed me from the back walking into the station. I had on a vest, chinos, and fedora and carried a whip. I looked just like Harrison Ford from the back. The broadcast then cut to me live walking on air. The weather guy I was taking over for introduced me and tossed over the "baton," the weather graphics clicker.

I met some great people at my new job. A few of us spent a lot of time hanging out outside of the television station. John Overall, the guy I had auditioned with, immediately became my Las Vegas best friend. I later learned that he lobbied pretty hard on my behalf because he liked me immediately, as I did him.

The viewing audience's initial reaction to me was decidedly mixed. I replaced a very popular weather guy who'd built up a tremendous amount of goodwill in town over the years, and television viewers can be quite fickle in their likes and dislikes of on-air talent. Plus, my unconventional shoot-from-the-hip on-air style rubbed a lot of viewers the wrong way for the first few years in Las Vegas. My news director, having looked over research done on me early in my tenure, said I had a very "polarizing" effect on our viewers: they either loved or hated me, nothing between. But he liked what I did on the air and believed that the viewers in the "hate me" category would eventually come around. Fortunately, he was right.

The Friday after my first week in Las Vegas, I left my car at the television station and John Overall dropped me off at a U-haul rental business. I rented a large truck and drove it back to Santa Barbara. I left Las Vegas on that early July Friday afternoon, right after my shift ended at 1:00 p.m. and pulled into the driveway at the ranch in Santa Barbara close to sunset. Once again Jordan was ecstatic to see me, greeting me in the driveway. After being gone for five days we were both thrilled to see one another. He was all over me. He jumped up in my bed and we rolled around and played for over an hour.

I had most of my stuff already packed. My Santa Barbara meteorologist buddy, Steve Stewart, helped me load up the U-haul early Saturday morning. We made a nice comfy spot between the two seats for Jordan. Around 9:00 a.m., Steve, Jordan and I hit the road. Steve followed in his car for the return trip to Santa Barbara the following Sunday morning.

By the time we got to Baker, California it was time for a potty break. When we left Santa Barbara it was about 65 degrees. In Baker, home of the "World's Largest Thermometer," I looked up and that big thermometer read 115 degrees. The three of us got out of the truck and were kissed by the scorching heat. None of us were happy. Jordan jumped out of the truck, quickly peed and pooped and then looked at me like, "Uh, this is not happening." I put him right back in the U-haul, cranked up the air conditioning and we were back on I-15 north to Las Vegas.

We arrived in Las Vegas around 5:00 p.m. on Saturday, July 13, 1996. We drove straight to my apartment complex. It was blazing hot, still over 100 degrees. I didn't turn off the truck because I knew the heat would be dangerous for Jordan. I walked to the security office and told the guard on-duty I was there to pick up my key. The manager had promised she'd leave the key there for me. The guard told me he didn't have the key and that I should come back on Monday because the office was closed for the weekend.

I told the security officer that I was moving into my apartment that night with my dog, so I really needed him get a hold of someone. Finally the guy realized I wasn't going anywhere and contacted the manager. While we were waiting for the manager to arrive with the keys, I let Jordan out of the U-Haul. He looked at me like "What the hell were you thinking?" and immediately jumped back into the truck.

The manager arrived about an hour later and was very apologetic. I had left the engine running with the AC on the entire time so Jordan wouldn't get hot.

Our New High School Soccer Field July 1996

I later learned some very valuable lessons about pets and temperature extremes. One of the saddest things I learned was that local enforcement codes regarding animal neglect and abuse are so vaguely written nothing can be done if someone leaves their pets outside, year-round. As long as a pet has access to water, food, and shade the owner is not breaking the law.

When the National Weather Service reports an outside temperature of 115 degrees, the temperature is actually taken in the shade. That's to prevent the direct sunlight from hitting the thermometer, thereby giving a false reading. Obviously it's even hotter under direct sunlight. Every week during the summer someone e-mails me with another horror story about a neighbor's pet stuck outside all day during the heat of the day.

By this point Steve and I were exhausted. All I wanted to do was get Jordan in the apartment where I could feed him and get him some cold water. My friend and I decided we were not going to unload the U-haul that night because it was too hot, so we each took a shower. I made sure Jordan was secure and then we headed to the Las Vegas Strip; exhausted but excited to be in Las Vegas, my new home.

We went to several of the casinos. Not having much money between us, we were content to wander the casino floors and marvel at the sights, sounds and people. There is a constant, consistent sound in casinos: a mixture of electronic sounds from slot machines, the roar of people when an occasional jackpot or correct roll of the dice is hit, and music from some lounge or club in the distance. The décor is loud to keep you wide awake and filled with hope and excitement. But there are no clocks. Time is on the casino operator's side; the

longer the tourist or local gambles, the higher the odds reach in the casinos' favor. Eventually someone loses, and in most cases it's not the casino.

We went back to the apartment, fell asleep and then got up early Sunday morning to unload the U-haul. Steve had to get back to Santa Barbara so he left as soon as the U-haul was unpacked. We said our goodbyes and I headed back to my new home and to Jordan.

Temperatures across the valley were approaching 90 degrees by mid-morning, so I took Jordan for a brief walk around the complex,

High School Soccer Field
Las Vegas Fall 1996

then loaded him up in the SUV to investigate our new surroundings. After driving around aimlessly for about an hour, we happened on a high school soccer field, which looked like a perfect place for Jordan to exercise each weekend and for me to practice my golf short game. This particular high school would become a place that we would grow quite fond of and would visit for many years to come. Besides Jordan and music, golf is my passion and I felt lucky that I was going to be able to play at many wonderful golf courses in our area. And in the summertime, you can play cheaply as long as you can take the heat.

CHAPTER 11
Old Las Vegas

I've always been fascinated by Las Vegas. I'd been visiting the city since I turned twenty-one back in the 1970s. Even back then, despite the lack of mega-resorts and hotels and casinos in general, I thought Las Vegas was a magical place filled with fun and possibility. I thought the old Desert Inn was the grandest resort of all. It became the birthday destination each June for me and my best buddy, John Tutora, for many years during the 1980s and even into the early 1990s. I never left Las Vegas with a dime in my pocket because, at the end of the night, the house always wins. Sadly, the Desert Inn Resort was imploded in 2000 to make way for the new Wynn Resort.

Las Vegas, Spanish for "the meadows" is by far the most populous city in the state of Nevada and is an internationally renowned major resort city for gaming, industry shopping and gambling. Las Vegas, billed as the "Entertainment Capital of the World," is famous for the number of large casino resorts and their associated entertainment. The city's tolerance for adult entertainment has given Vegas the

The famous Welcome to Las Vegas sign South LV Blvd Spring 2001

nickname Sin City, and this image has made Las Vegas a popular setting for films and television shows. Outdoor lighting displays are everywhere on the Las Vegas Strip and can be seen elsewhere in the city as well. As seen from space, Las Vegas is the brightest city on earth.

Established in 1905, Las Vegas officially became a city in 1911. With the growth that followed, at the close of the century, Las Vegas was the most populous American city founded in the twentieth century. The population of the Las Vegas metropolitan area now exceeds 2 million residents.

Old Vegas, run by the mob, was a place where people were always treated with respect, regardless of whether the individual was a high roller or not. But as rumors go, if you got out of line, you were quickly escorted from the casino or hotel. And if you tried to rob a casino, you'd end up in the trunk of a car on your way to the desert and your final resting place. That's the rumor anyway. Back then, visitors dressed in suits and evening gowns when they went to dinner or shows. I always had fun people-watching inside the casinos. I was even propositioned by a couple of "ladies of the night" as my friend John and I were leaving a casino. I turned them down, of course.

Today, while the city still has all the magic, flash, and razzmatazz, you are more likely to encounter guests in shorts and flip-flops at shows, restaurants, and buffets than you are to see someone dressed to the nines as in the old days, which actually makes it more fun to people watch. You're more likely to see an "I'm With Stupid" T-shirt than a shirt and tie. I've grown to love this town over the years. If there is a show you want to see or a concert you want to go to, more than likely it's here or it's coming. This truly is the "Entertainment Capital of the World."

That being said, this town is not for everyone, especially those prone to addictions, compulsions and vices. You can find anything here, anytime, any day. And I do mean anything: drugs, alcohol, hookers, Asian massage parlors with their patented "Happy Endings," at your door escorts and twenty-four-hour stores. My biggest vice is being hooked on my local twenty-four-hour Wal-Mart.

There is also an under-belly and seedy side of Las Vegas. If you are looking for that type of lifestyle, you don't have to look far. The stories and news headlines are constant of people coming to town looking for a quick buck, a big payday, a place to hide from the law, topless clubs and fame and fortune. There is also a very high crime rate, including burglary, theft, domestic violence and murder. The stories rarely have a happy ending. And don't believe the "What Happens in Vegas, Stays in Vegas" slogan. Many tourists have left Las Vegas with a notice to appear or with a communicable disease. And even though gambling drives our economy and many local residents work in casinos, locals rarely venture out to the Strip or casinos if they don't have to. Why intentionally put yourself in the middle of the Strip traffic nightmare unless you have to? About the only time locals head to the Strip and the Strip casinos is when company comes to town and they're forced to act as tour guides and chauffeurs. Locals would rather stay away from the resorts and enjoy what residents enjoy in any other large or small town. Yes, there is life away from the Strip. There is a long-running joke about residents being bussed in from out of town trailer parks to work at the casinos each day and night. Las Vegas residents really do live in Las Vegas.

When you get away from the Strip and the resorts, Las Vegas is very much like any other city. We have wonderful communities, both new and old, beautiful parks and public pools, some great dog parks, and tons of culture, including history and art museums. And yes, there actually is a Las Vegas Philharmonic. We have hundreds of churches of all denominations and a very large Mormon population, as Las Vegas was founded by Mormons. You can even visit the Old Mormon Fort on Las Vegas Boulevard, just north of downtown.

Las Vegas is surrounded by mountains, and the desert sunrises are simply breathtaking. Hikers and bikers head en masse to the loop at the

Red Rock National Recreation Center, west of the valley less than twenty minutes from the Strip. People even ski during the winter, within forty-five minutes of the city, at Mount Charleston. The Lake Mead National Recreation Area attracts hundreds of thousands of boaters, jet-skiers and divers each year and Hoover Dam is only about thirty minutes from the Strip. The area has many other great sites, literally minutes outside of the Valley and there is no shortage of recreational activity for locals and tourists alike. And no, I don't work for the Chamber of Commerce or the Convention and Visitors Authority. I just love this city .

CHAPTER 12

Heavy Hand

After moving to Vegas in July of 1996, Jordan and I quickly settled into our apartment. I didn't have a lot of furniture. All we had when we moved into our new apartment was a dresser, bed, a nineteen-inch television—which I received as payment for some commercials I produced back in California—and my stereo equipment. I had to stack up some milk crates to set my television and stereo on.

Once settled in to our Angel Park apartment, the weekend after my first week at my new job, I returned to work the following Monday leaving Jordan alone in our apartment. I didn't feel comfortable taking him to work with me because I didn't know the station's policy on having pets in the workplace. Had I asked I would've been able to avoid some of the very dark days for Jordan and me that were to follow.

Jordan was potty trained so I could leave him for several hours and not worry about him having an accident in the apartment. I would leave for work around 3:00 a.m., then would return home just after 9:00 a.m. to let him out to pee and poop. I played with him for as long as I could, then went back to work from 11:00 a.m. until the noon newscast ended, and I was done for the day at 1:00 p.m.

Within three months of our arrival to Las Vegas, Jordan began experiencing separation anxiety. I had restricted his living area from an avocado ranch to a single-bedroom apartment. And though he was now two and one half years of age, Jordan still hadn't outgrown his puppy behavior. He became destructive. Anything I left out was fair game. I never knew what I was going to come home to each day.

Three out of five days I would get home from work and Jordan had destroyed something. Somehow he figured out how to open the door to the pantry, where I kept the trash. One day I came home and trash was everywhere. The next day he got up on the kitchen counter, grabbed something and tore it to shreds. This destructive behavior went on for several weeks before I hit my breaking point.

I will never forgive myself for some of the things I did to Jordan when I got home from work and found yet another thing he destroyed. When I think back on it, I can honestly say this was one of my darkest periods.

One day I got home and Jordan had taken something off the kitchen counter and destroyed it. I grabbed him and lifted his front legs onto the counter. I put what he had destroyed up to his face and I hit him underneath the chin. I hit him hard.

Even though I hit Jordan with my open hand and he never saw my hand as a weapon, I knew I had hit him too hard. On top of hitting him, I screamed at him and he had this look of fear in his eyes that I had never seen before. Thankfully, his look stopped me in my tracks before I actually caused him physical pain. I knew at that moment I'd let him down. I cried and tried to hug him and to apologize to him but he didn't want anything to do with me. Jordan didn't yelp or give me any indication that I had physically hurt him, but I knew I had abused him and would never do it again. What I had done was wrong and something had to give. Jordan retreated to the bedroom to hide under my bed, and I went over and sat down on my newly purchased couch. I started crying over my feelings of guilt and the realization that had it not been for the look of fear in his eyes, I might have actually caused Jordan physical harm.

I called my co-worker and friend, John Overall, and told him I didn't know how much more I could take. I told him I was afraid I was going to seriously hurt Jordan if I kept leaving him home alone all day. John suggested I start bringing him into work with me. At that point I had nothing to lose, so the next day I brought Jordan to work with me. That was the last day he stayed home. And I was to soon find out that I could've taken him to work with me from day one.

I later learned that Jordan's destructive behavior was not his fault at all. He was simply acting out because he was unhappy, bored, wasn't getting enough exercise—and he missed me.

Jordan spent his first few days at work in the dog run in the backyard of the station. That lasted for about a week. Then I started bringing him in the studio with me. He would just sprawl out on the floor or greet my co-workers or station guests when they walked into the television studio.

Taking Jordan to work was the one and only thing that saved my relationship with him. It also enhanced my overall well-being at work. My attitude improved and I was no longer constantly stressed over what I might find when I got home each afternoon. I was amazed at how it seemed to solve so many issues for me, almost overnight. And though I had John Overall to thank for my renewed happiness and positive attitude, it wasn't long before I thought he might be to blame when I thought I might lose my new job.

CHAPTER 13

Was I Going to Get Fired?

I was still finding my way around my new surroundings. Because John Overall and I became friends as soon as I arrived in Las Vegas, he was helpful in giving me a lay of the land, both inside and outside of the station. Having been nice enough to befriend me, we spent a lot of time together outside of work. We played golf, played the role of tourists and hung out together on the weekends.

I quickly found out that John was a prankster. He loved to play practical jokes on people. One day I was in the station men's room, sitting on the toilet and John walked in and turned off the lights. He waited until I had my pants around my ankles and was waddling out of the stall. Then he opened the bathroom door and turned the lights back on. I turned around and got half way back to the stall when he came in again and turned off the lights. This went on for several weeks and drove me nuts. But John was hard to get mad at after each of these embarrassing occasions because he was such a likeable guy.

The first week I brought Jordan to work, John thought it would be funny to let him loose in the station. None of the managers had met Jordan, though they knew I had a dog.

I walked into the studio and Jordan was gone. My immediate reaction was panic. I raced around asking everyone I encountered if they had seen Jordan. After searching frantically for several minutes, one of co-workers told me John let him out of the studio. Someone else told me they thought

Jordan had gone upstairs. I knew I was in trouble. All the administrative offices were up stairs, including that of the station owner.

I raced upstairs and ran around frantically when all of a sudden I heard, "HEY!" I stopped, turned and walked into the general manager's office. I had only met him once before, the day I auditioned for the job. He asked if that was my dog running down the hallway and I told him: "yes." He told me Jordan went that way and pointed with his finger toward the hallway. I went searching in the direction he pointed until I heard another, "HEY!" I stopped, turned around and almost died when I saw it was the station owner. He asked me the same question and told me Jordan went that way, again pointing in the direction Jordan ran down the hall. I saw my career flash in front of my eyes.

I finally tracked Jordan down and took him downstairs. John Overall was laughing hysterically when I walked into the newsroom and thought letting Jordan loose was the funniest thing he'd ever done in the workplace. I was so angry I screamed at him and told him he probably had just cost me my job. He told me no one at the station would care because dogs were welcome. He was right. I never heard a word about the incident from any of my bosses. Station management had absolutely no issue with people bringing their pets to work. For goodness sake, the station owner even had a doggy run and doghouse built for his pets in the station's backyard. I can't believe how naïve I'd been. At that moment I knew everything was going to be okay. I could get through anything as long as Jordan was by my side. Before long, he was much more than just at my side. He was about to become a bona fide Las Vegas television celebrity. I just didn't know it or plan for it at the time.

CHAPTER 14
Our New Las Vegas Home

It was now winter of 1998. I was in my third year with the station and Jordan had become somewhat of a fixture on our morning and noon newscasts. Our viewers were beginning to think of him as part their on-air family. However, they still didn't consider us a team. That would soon change.

I had grown tired of living in an apartment because all the rooms had the same eggshell white walls and the same generic features, and I wanted a place that Jordan and I could really call home. I had just signed my second contract and felt reasonably sure that Las Vegas was now our home. I negotiated the deal myself, having dumped my agent. It wasn't the best deal in the world but it was for another three years and did include a decent increase in pay. I was ready to buy a house. I hadn't owned my own home since my divorce was final in the early '80s. My marriage had ended amicably, and I gave my ex-wife the only thing she cared about: our home. She is one of the finest people I've ever known and I'm happy that we've stayed on good terms through the years.

I called a realtor who had come highly recommended by one of my co-workers. I told her I would be staying in Vegas for several more years and I wanted a place that Jordan and I could call home. She said she'd be thrilled to be our agent. When I told her I didn't have any money for a down payment, I thought she was going to hang up on me. After a long period of silence she told me that having no money for a down payment would be a challenge, but there were programs available for individuals in my situation. She told me she'd call back when she had more information regarding my financing options. My hopes were immediately dampened and I felt like she wanted nothing more to do with me.

A funny and unbelievably coincidental thing happened later that same day. When I got home from work there was a message on my answering machine from the human resources director at the farming corporation I had worked for in the '70s and early '80s. The corporation was being sold so they were tracking down all employees who had been vested in the company's retirement plan. When I called the her back, she told me I had money in the company's retirement program and wanted to know if I wanted to roll the plan over into the new company, or cash it out. I asked her how much it was and she said around $7,500. I told her I'd take the cash. I had just acquired a down payment for a new home in Las Vegas. Lady Luck had entered the building.

As soon as I hung up the phone I called the realtor back and told her I had $7,500 to put down as a deposit on a home. I told her I wanted a home with a yard that required little or no maintenance because of my work schedule. And it had to be dog-friendly. She told me she had the perfect place in mind.

There were townhouses being built in the Summerlin area and one of the units had views of the mountains and the Las Vegas Strip. When I first saw the townhouse she had picked out for Jordan and me, I was a little apprehensive. From the outside, the development looked like a generic apartment complex. And there was no fenced yard for Jordan, just a common ground that could double as his bathroom facility.

New Townhouse January 1999

Fortunately, the inside was beautiful. The town homes were pet-friendly and included a two-car garage with direct access to the house. To top it off, the builder was offering an incentive that included window coverings and a brand new washer and dryer if I closed on the house by December 31. My realtor assured me we would close by the end of the month, which we did. In the end, the down payment and move-in costs were actually less

than the $7,500 I had received from that old retirement plan buy-out, so I had a little extra money to furnish and decorate our new home.

I spent the first few weeks of 1999 working my normal shift, and then I'd meet my buddy, Snake Rock, at the townhouse for our daily "paint party."

Painting our new Townhouse Bathroom Las Vegas January 1999

Snake is not only one of the best rock musicians I've ever known, he's also a professional painter. Snake Rock is also his legal name. Snake would end up being my best friend in Las Vegas as John Overall would leave the city in the next few months for a job in Little Rock, Arkansas.

I had started painting our new home by myself, but quickly realized that I was in way over my head. I had very little painting experience and I was getting more paint on Jordan, on me, and my new carpet than on our new walls. The breaking point came when I spilled a can of dark blue paint on my brand new, light blue carpet. I wanted to paint the master bedroom and bath, and paint and wallpaper all of the downstairs. I knew the job was too much for me so Snake came to my rescue. We finished all the work

Surveying Paint on Carpet Las Vegas January 1999

on January 14, and Jordan and I moved in to our new home on January 15, 1999. I finally had a place I could call my own. I thought the place was perfect. Jordan seemed to think it lacked a personal touch. He took care of that during our first night there.

I'd pulled our entertainment center away from the wall to hook up and wire my television and stereo equipment, and Jordan walked behind it and took a dump all over the carpet. A very wet dump. He must have done it sometime in the middle of the night while I was asleep upstairs. By the time I discovered what he'd done, the stain had set in and I couldn't get it completely out. Fortunately, the entertainment center covered what was left of the mess once I slid it into place. I couldn't get mad at Jordan because I had disrupted his routine and dramatically changed his environment, and he was just acting out. Eventually I forgot all about Jordan's house-warming gift until the day I moved out, some five and a half years later. I credited the new owners $1,000 for floor covering repair.

I have tons of fond memories of my life with Jordan in that townhouse. In some ways I wish I still lived there. However, I would endure some sad times living there, usually having to do with the memory of a former girlfriend who had spent time there. Plus, we were simply outgrowing our living space, prompting me to find a new home in the summer of 2004, right at the height of the housing boom. Had I known what was about to happen to the housing market, we'd still be in that townhouse. But I do love our new home and it gave me the opportunity to fulfill a ten-year-old promise to Jordan: a home with his own pool.

CHAPTER 15
Jordan's Popularity

It was now 1999 and I was into my second contract in Las Vegas television. Jordan had become a staple on our morning and noon newscasts and was quickly becoming a Las Vegas television celebrity. He wasn't on the air every day, but he was on more days then not. Every Friday we would put him in front of the chroma key wall— the weather "green screen"— and the crew in the control booth would superimpose images so it looked like Jordan was surfing, in the mountains or even parasailing. I think the news crew enjoyed coming up with new ideas and the viewing audience started looking forward to seeing what Jordan would be doing next. And at the end of every Friday newscast, we'd put him up in a chair and he would close the show with us at the main anchor desk. Jordan would sit next to me and it looked like he was just another one of the anchors. But he was not just another anchor: He was quickly becoming the star of the show.

When I was sent out on live broadcasts, Jordan started coming with me and would appear with me each time I was on camera. That's when Jordan really became a celebrity.

People showed up at the remote locations just to meet my boy in person. I knew Jordan became popular when people stopped asking me about the weather and starting asking me about him. I knew then that something truly magical was happening. Jordan and I were becoming an on-air team.

Jordan's popularity really skyrocketed when the news station started doing a weekly live broadcast called "Weather on Wheels." Jordan and I would be live each week from local donut shops that were owned by the television station's owner. The station owner has over 200 classic cars and we were doing the live broadcasts to help promote his new classic car museum. Each week, several of the cars were parked out in front of one of the donut shops, and car enthusiasts would come to gawk at them,

and Jordan. People from all over town came out to meet Jordan. Some people showed up with their own classic cars and others brought their dogs. Within a few weeks, hundreds of people would show up with their dogs or classic cars, and it became kind of a weekly block party, live on television. It was during these broadcasts that Jordan's Las Vegas fame was cemented in our viewer's minds. He had become my partner and no matter where I went, people expected him by my side, on- or off-air.

On location Weather on Wheels LIVE event Circa 2000

Viewers made the transition from caring about me and the weather to caring about Jordan and me. The community seemed to have officially adopted Jordan as part of their extended family.

Jordan became so popular that a special section of the station's website was created just for him. That lasted until it was discovered, more often than not, Jordan's section received more Internet traffic than most of the other news anchors. It became too much for the television station to manage. When a web designer offered to create a personal website for Jordan free of charge, I gladly accepted. Because of my relationship with Jordan, I was asked to take over the pet adoption segment the station did a couple of times each week. The Nevada SPCA, the local no-kill animal sanctuary, and the Las Vegas Valley Humane Society would come into the station with animals that were available for adoption and we'd feature a new pet each week live on the air. It gave viewers a chance to see animals that needed a good home, and many of the pets that were featured on that segment were adopted shortly thereafter.

I also began hosting a bi-monthly "Pet Vet" segment, in which local vets come on-air to discuss pet health issues. Jordan started being associated with all things pet-related, including adoption, responsible pet ownership and having pets spayed or neutered. Viewers who previously believed there was something wrong with their strong bonds with their own pets came to see the two of us as vindication that they weren't weird, goofy or just plain crazy for loving their pet like any other member of their family. People approached me on location and told me that until they started watching Jordan and me, they would hide their true feelings for their pet out of sheer embarrassment.

Unfortunately, millions of pet owners don't believe pets should be treated as family members. They believe pets are simply property and are here on earth to serve man, get served by man or for personal security. I've always told people, "If you want an alarm system, call an alarm company." That is not to say I think it's a bad idea for a dog to bark if a stranger comes to the door. However, other than the occasional early warning device, I don't believe pets were meant to be personal security. Other than service and therapy animals, I believe pets were meant to be companions. Period.

To viewers, I was more than a talking head giving the weather. I had become their voice and conduit to the animal humane community. Jordan and I received invitations to all things pet-related, including fundraisers and walk-a-thons. I became very active in the pet community. We also started getting flooded with requests to make visits to local schools, to discuss not only weather, but also responsible pet ownership. By the fall of 2001, due largely to my relationship with Jordan and my commitment to local humane causes, I was elected to serve on the board of directors for the Nevada SPCA.

On television and out in public I made it very clear that my relationship with Jordan was special. He was more than just my dog, he was my son. Viewers who got it really connected with me. I started getting hundreds of e-mails each week praising us for our work on behalf of homeless and abused animals in the Las Vegas area.

Not everyone was happy with my on-air comments about pets. Some days I received e-mails or phone calls from viewers after I made comments about pet responsibility. Most often the e-mails came from individuals who didn't believe pets were part of the family. Some people thought it was okay to keep their dogs outside in the 115-degree heat with drinking water in a metal dish in the direct sunlight. Each time I'd learn of possible animal abuse I'd contact local authorities and humane organizations. Since local laws were probably not being broken, I was not always successful in my efforts. However, I thought if I could save just one life I was helping our pet community.

Viewers could tell I loved Jordan unconditionally. Over the years, hundreds of people came up to me in public to tell me they adopted a pet because of my relationship with Jordan and it was the greatest thing they ever did. Others would tell me how much respect they had for my employers who clearly understood what pets meant to our viewers and for allowing Jordan to appear on-air with me. Knowing Jordan and I had such an impact on viewers was more satisfying to me than any award or accolade I ever won or received.

Jordan and I enjoyed a considerable amount of on-air success, respect and appreciation. The community loved Jordan and it didn't seem that our life, professionally or personally could get any better. Female companionship, or the lack thereof, aside, we had a good life.

CHAPTER 16
Meet Chewy

Once Jordan and I were settled into our townhouse I wanted to get another dog. It was now early spring of 1999, and I still had about a year and a half left on my second contract with the television station. Plus, I was pretty sure I would be offered another contract after the present one expired. I thought Jordan could use a companion and I wanted an affectionate dog, as Jordan wasn't. That is not to say that Jordan shunned affection. He would let me give him "huggies" from time to time, but he was content just being in the same room with me, not necessarily right by my side.

Let me explain our "huggies": I would sit on the floor of the house or station weather center, and I would say to Jordan, "Come over here and give Daddy some huggies." He would reluctantly walk over to me and I would have him sit facing me and then wrap my legs around him and pull him to me in a bear hug. He would put up with it for a few seconds each time and then just pull away and go back and lay down where he'd been before I disrupted him.

I told the president of the Nevada SPCA, Jennifer Palombi, that I was looking for another dog and asked her to keep an eye out for a golden retriever. I had done some research and learned that golden retrievers have the same general disposition as Labrador retrievers, but were usually more affectionate by nature. The following Monday I was at the Nevada SPCA broadcasting live for our adoption segment and Jennifer told me a golden

Portrait Day at Petsmart March 1999

retriever had just been turned in. The owner was stationed at Nellis Air Force Base and was being moved to another base and couldn't take the dog with the rest of his family.

The owner had purchased the dog for his son, who lost interest in the dog almost immediately. Apparently no one else had time for the poor thing. The dog spent most of his life out in the backyard alone. His name was Simba and he was a beautiful eighteen-month-old golden retriever. But he had received absolutely no obedience training. He didn't know basic commands, nor was he potty trained.

Jordan was with me for the live broadcast so I introduced the two of them. The two dogs weren't aggressive but Jordan didn't show much interest in Simba. Simba took to Jordan immediately, so I thought the match could work. I would soon learn nothing could be further from the truth. I told the president of the Nevada SPCA I wanted to adopt Simba and would pick him up the next day.

The following morning, on my break, we drove back to the Nevada SPCA and I loaded Simba into the back of my SUV with Jordan. Simba just loved Jordan. He licked and rubbed against him. Jordan just ignored Simba and looked up at me with an expression on his face like, "What are you doing to me? Who is this stranger?"

I changed Simba's name to Chewy because he reminded me of Chewbacca from Star Wars. Changing a dog's name is not an issue. They are highly adaptable and will accept a new name almost immediately as I learned with my experience with Chewy.

When we got home, Jordan and Chewy followed me into our house. Chewy walked over to pick up one of Jordan's rawhide bones and Jordan growled and showed his teeth. That was the first time I had seen Jordan become aggressive with another dog. I thought Jordan was going to tear him apart. I separated them immediately. Jordan was letting Chewy know he was on his turf. After that incident, Jordan never looked at Chewy again.

I bought a kennel for Chewy because I knew I was going to have to kennel train him. It was rough on Chewy. He didn't understand why he was locked up. The poor guy got stressed out and immediately crapped inside his kennel, then lay down right in it. Fortunately, Chewy got used to and even grew to think of his kennel as "home." Over a period of three months, I got him potty and kennel trained, taught him some basic commands and showed him how to walk on a leash. I had learned my lesson on obedience training with Jordan so Chewy was much easier to work with. And all retrievers are quick to learn as they are bred to serve their human companions.

Chewy quickly grew comfortable with his kennel and each day on break I'd teach him basic obedience commands. What was so funny was that anything I asked Chewy to do, Jordan would respond to as well. I would say: "Chewy, come!" and they both would come to me. I'd say: "Chewy, sit!" and both of them would sit in front of me on command. Jordan, while having had no interest in our new family member, turned out to be quite a good influence on him.

Chewy was turning out to be a very good dog. He wasn't the smartest dog in the world. But he was a good boy. I still hoped Jordan would come around. And Chewy was exactly what I thought I wanted: a very affectionate dog. As it turned out, I really didn't want a lap dog after all. I adored the sweet young boy but he always wanted to be either right next to me or on top of me. It drove me crazy and made me realize I was just like my father, who once told my mom, "I don't like clinging vines." I'm with you, Dad.

Once Chewy was trained, I decided it was time to introduce him to our viewing audience.

I was doing a pet segment at my vet's office and Chewy was at my feet. I told the viewing audience I wanted to introduce them to the newest member of my household. Just as I said that, the camera operator panned the camera down to Chewy. As if on cue, he began licking his privates. The camera operator immediately panned the camera back to me, and I said the first thing that popped into mind. Very dangerous on live television: "You know why he is doing that don't you? Because he can!" How I got away with that comment I'll never know. I thought I was going to get fired or at least suspended, but no one ever said a word to me about it. That was Chewy's one and only TV appearance.

Years later, the producers of an NBC bloopers show called me about an incident with Jordan that happened on-air. I told them I had an even better on-air blooper for them to use, and described the incident with Chewy. The guy cracked up but said it would never make it past the network censors. I'll explain Jordan's national on-air blooper in a later chapter.

Every Saturday morning I took Jordan and Chewy to that high school soccer field I'd found when we first moved to town in 1996 to let them get their morning exercise. One morning while at the high school, a lady came up to me and said she really loved my golden retriever. She told me how her parents had just lost their golden and were looking for another dog. They were retired and living on a large ranch in Prescott, Arizona. I told her that I might be interested in giving Chewy up for adoption. I loved him dearly but he just didn't fit into our household.

I came to realize that Jordan didn't want a companion. He already had one. I also realized that I really didn't want to split my affections between Jordan and another dog. I was perfectly happy being with Jordan.

The lady took some pictures of Chewy and sent them to her parents. A few days later she called me and said her parents wanted to adopt him. I had her send me pictures of the ranch they lived on and, after hearing all about her parents and their ranch, I just knew giving Chewy to them was the right thing to do.

It wasn't easy to give Chewy up. I had grown to love him a great deal. As I put Chewy in the lady's car the following Saturday morning, I cried. I was actually surprised by how emotionally attached I had gotten to this sweet, young boy. Jordan was another story. His demeanour changed immediately. He looked at me as if to say, "It's about time." I knew at that moment I made the right decision for us and I've never doubted it since.

That day, I promised Jordan I would never get another dog as long as he was alive. When he got much older, people would often ask me if I was going to get another dog to soften the blow when Jordan left me. That made absolutely no sense to me whatsoever. How could I possibly share my affections with another pet during the time of Jordan's life when he needed me most? I couldn't and wouldn't. Besides, I'd been down that road and the experiment failed.

CHAPTER 17

Back to School,
for Both of Us

I was well into my tenth year with the television station when management hired an independent research company to conduct a study on station on-air talent. The management team shared the results of the study with me. The study showed that many people said they watched our station in the morning and at noon because of my on-air relationship with Jordan.

One of the more interesting highlights of the study was that viewers didn't particularly care about the weather report. Sure they wanted to know

On Location LIVE Fall 1999

what to wear that day and they believed I was credible as a meteorologist. But they really watched because of all the work Jordan and I did in the community.

The research confirmed what I now knew: We were a team. There was no John without Jordan and no Jordan without John. When other reporters were out in the field, people routinely asked about Jordan. What was so funny was the number of times reporters would come up to me and say that someone wanted to know "what Jordan is really like." That one never failed to crack me up. How do you answer that? "Well, he's very comfortable in front of the camera but kind of shy in public."

Thanksgiving Day 2000

Jordan really made an even bigger connection with the community when we started visiting local schools. It started when teachers asked me to participate in Nevada Reading Week, which is held annually at all local schools in late February or early March.

The majority of the time the teachers told me they wanted me to bring Jordan to Reading Week. On the occasions when they didn't specifically mention him, I'd either leave him at home or in the back of my SUV, weather permitting. When the teachers found out Jordan was waiting outside they always asked that I bring him in. If I told them Jordan was at home they were always disappointed. I was often told that I was only invited because the teachers and kids really wanted to see Jordan. As time went by, I told people I was just Jordan's chauffeur. The schools didn't care as much about the weather as they did about seeing Jordan. Later in Jordan's life, I wouldn't do any type of school visit, promotional event or charity work if Jordan weren't welcome. We were a team and if Jordan wasn't welcome I figured I wasn't either.

My busiest time of year to visit schools was during Reading Week. I went to different schools and read to the kids. So many schools wanted Jordan and me to visit that it turned into Reading Month for us. My favorite book was, and still is *Cloudy with the Chance of Meatballs* by Judi Barrett. A gift to us from a local elementary school teacher, it's about a fictional town called Chewandswallow. In the town of Chewandswallow, everything people need to eat comes from the sky. When it rains, snows, or the wind blows, food and drink fall from the sky for all the townspeople to eat. All is well in the town until the weather takes a "turn for the worse."

I've read it so many times I have the story memorized. It's not only my favorite children's book, but also a favorite with elementary school kids.

After I finished reading to the kids, I talked about weather safety, including my two favorite weather sayings: "When thunder roars, go indoors," and, "Turn around, don't drown." The deserts of the southwest, including the Mojave where we live, are prone to flash flooding during our monsoon, July and August. The coarse desert sand simply can't absorb a lot of water in a short time span and floodwaters can kill. In fact, you can drown in as little as two inches of water: you can slip, fall face down and be knocked unconscious and water can quickly fill your lungs. My talk about weather safety has always been designed to educate, but not frighten school-age children. When talking of flooded areas, I'd let the kids know about not only the drowning hazards, but also that one never knows what might be carried along in that flooded water, like germs, dead rodents, snakes or even dog poop. That usually got a mixture of laughter and boos. After talking about weather safety, I'd switch gears and talk to the kids about an even more important subject: pet owner responsibility.

I'd always let kids know how important it was to ask for permission before petting a stranger's dog. Then I explained to the kids that they had

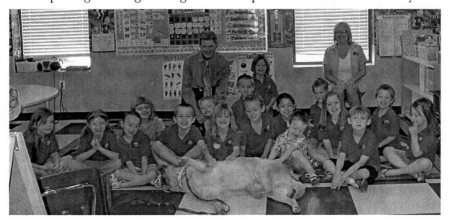

School Visit Summer 2006

to let the dog sniff them first; that way the pet would know they were friendly and had good intentions, and then they could give the dog a gentle pet and go on about their business. I explained why they couldn't tug on pets' ears or tails and why they have to treat pets like they would want to be treated. And I would always let them know that more often than not, dog bites are the result of human provocation.

Then came the best part for the kids: Jordan. They never asked me about the weather, just Jordan. The kids wanted to know everything about him. They'd ask how old was he, how much did he weigh, what tricks could

he do, why did he go to work with me every day and could he talk. I'd always tell the kids that as far as I knew Jordan couldn't talk. They'd ask if Jordan could forecast the weather and I'd say, "Sure, when his fur is wet, it's raining. When his fur is ruffled, it's windy. And when it's dry, it's sunny." Once I actually did have a viewer tell me she thought I was blind and Jordan was with me in the studio to help me see the maps. I'm not making this up.

Back of Car Spring 2001

When we were done with the questions and answer session, Jordan would stand in the middle of the room and the kids would all gather around at once and hug and kiss him. Jordan was so kind and gentle with the kids, but he never kissed them back. He would stand there while twenty or so kids practically fell down on top of him and would never bark, snap or bite. Occasionally he'd look up at me like, "What are you letting them do to me?" But I believe Jordan somehow

John and Jordan, Dog Event, Spring 2001

understood his job and role in the community and was tolerant, if not happy, to give these kids the time with him they wanted and loved.

Towards the end of Jordan's life, I was very honest with the kids. I told them that dogs don't live as long as people do and in doggie-years Jordan was approaching ninety years of age. I would never discuss the subject of death with the kids because I didn't want to traumatize them. In 2007, when I was fairly certain Jordan wouldn't make it through another hot Las Vegas summer, I told the kids that this would be Jordan's last reading week visit. I didn't want to upset them, but I wanted them to understand how special Jordan's visit was and to cherish the time they had with him.

I should point out that I have developed a theory about life expectancy in general and with pets specifically. I call it my "Mongrel Theory," in which I believe human life expectancy has increased over the years, not just because of advances in medicine, but due to the mongrelization of the societies. Up until the time of travel and societal integration, I believe that inbreeding within cultures was inevitable. This is why laws against marrying within your own bloodline exist—to prevent babies being born with inbred genetic defects. I believe this applies to all living things including domestic animals. And while I understand and support the work of the American Kennel Club, I believe that animals, in general, will live longer, healthier lives if they are the product of mixed breeding.

Jordan with Castle Made by Viewers
early summer 2001

Veterinarians I've spoken to over the years agree with me on this theory. They tell me that, with few exceptions, mixed-breed pets usually are healthier, smarter and live longer. The reason we all agree on is that the cross breeding of pets will prevent genetic disorders associated with inbreeding. I also have to admit when I've shared this theory while speaking before a group of adults, the response is decidedly mixed. It seems that not everyone is willing to buy my "Mongrel Theory" just yet. But I believe that I'm right. And while it is almost certain that Jordan was the product of bad breeding practices and inbreeding, thanks to constant care and a good, happy life, he disproved his early vet's predictions that he would most likely never live past the age of ten.

After many of my visits to local schools, teachers had the kids write thank-you letters to Jordan and me. I read all of the letters and was thankful Jordan and I could visit with the kids. Kids would always ask me what I thought was the best part of my job and I would tell them honestly that it was being able to come and visit with them.

Occasionally I'd come across a child who was afraid of dogs. I remember one little girl, a kindergartner who was absolutely petrified of Jordan. I asked if she had pets at her house and she said no because she was afraid of dogs. This little girl was cowered in the corner, shaking and crying. I didn't force her to interact with Jordan, but I felt terrible for her. She wasn't traumatized because of any experience she had with a dog, but because her parents wouldn't allow pets in her home, denying her the chance to become comfortable around pets. It was such a shame that she couldn't experience the joys of interacting with a pet. This is why I always urge parents to allow their children to grow up with pets in their home even if they themselves aren't "pet people."

I never knew my older sister, Joanne, was afraid of big dogs. Unfortunately, she passed that fear onto her son. When Joanne and her son came to visit me in Las Vegas for the first time, he was terrified of Jordan. My nephew was about nine years old. When I asked my sister about it, she would side-step the issue and just say she couldn't have pets in her home. And my sister never referred to Jordan by name. She would just ask me, when we'd speak by phone, "How's the mutt?" It was a real bone of contention with us. I guess it was her way of letting me know that to her Jordan was just a dog.

I always ended the reading sessions by asking the kids, "Who has the most important job in the whole world?" After guesses like the president, police officers, lawyers, etc., someone would finally yell out: "Teachers!" I'd tell them the only reason some people grow up to be teachers is to help others learn. They certainly don't do it for the money. Then I would have the kids give their teacher a big round of applause. I do this now because of the respect I have for our teachers and how little respect I had for them growing up. And even though my Aunt Natalie taught kindergarten for over forty years with few or no accolades, it wasn't until I got older that I realized just how special our teachers are.

Right up through high school, I was many of my teachers' worst nightmares. As early as first grade I had my desk moved next to the teacher's so she could keep an eye on me. I got kicked out of one third-grade class and assigned to another because the teacher could not control or tolerate my constant disruptions. By fifth grade, I had become so disruptive, that my playground time was spent facedown on the principal's office floor— my first taste of detention. That exile lasted an entire semester. I don't even remember the actual offense that got me in trouble. But my lack of respect for teachers didn't end until after high school when I ventured out into the real world and finally realized how valuable our teachers and education really are. Better late than never, right?

Jordan and I visited approximately 500 classrooms during our time together. We were very fortunate to interact with so many children. To be completely honest about it, I was always happy that each of our school visits lasted less than an hour. I don't think my patience would've lasted much longer and I truly admire anyone who takes on such a challenging job as teaching for a life-long career. Just before ending each one of our school classroom visits, I would always turn to the teacher and whisper: "Now we get to leave. You, on the other hand, are stuck with them for the rest of the day." And though the teachers would always laugh at my attempt at humor, I knew there was no place in the world they'd rather be than right there with their students.

Life was good for us in Las Vegas. However, life for everyone in America was about to change.

CHAPTER 18
September 11th

We were now into the year 2001 and Jordan was a well-established television personality in Las Vegas. Things were going great for us. I didn't think life could get any better and never thought anything could go wrong. I was wrong.

Jordan was about six years old and I knew he had many more years left, but I couldn't help but think he was probably getting to the halfway point in his life. It was a real eye opener for me to realize that I too had probably lived more years than I had left.

From that point on, each year I'd ask God to give me just five more years with my boy. When Jordan turned nine and started to slow down I asked for at least another three more years with him. And while I couldn't bear the certain loss of Jordan, I had already gotten accustomed to the loss of other members of my family.

In 1972, my father Joe died in his sleep at age fifty-two from heart failure. He was living and working in Los Angeles at the time of his death, but my stepmother wanted him buried at her family burial plot in a cemetery in Missouri. My father was a gas station operator by trade, but had lost every station he'd ever owned or leased. To make ends meet in his final years, he was forced to take odd jobs as a mechanic in and around the Los Angeles area. I hadn't seen my father in several years and he was dead and buried by the time my stepfather permitted my mother to tell me he had passed away. Apparently my stepfather was afraid I'd want to attend my father's funeral out of state and he didn't want to pay for my hotel and airfare. I'm not kidding. My stepfather could never understand my devotion to a man who left my mother on her own to care for me and my two older sisters. I was only four when my mom and dad got divorced. And having no formal education or work skills, my mother could only get a job as a switchboard operator for an insurance company and the pay barely covered the bills. But my love for my father was unwavering and I had enjoyed a new, positive relationship with him via letters that we'd send each other regularly up until a short time before his death.

My father and mother, Joseph and Eleanor

My mother, Eleanor, died of brain cancer four years after my father passed, in the summer of 1976. The last time I saw her she was in hospice care at my Aunt Nat's house in Canyon Country, California. Canyon Country is a small subdivision about one hour northeast of downtown Los Angeles. My older sister, Joanne, a registered nurse, was her personal care nurse at my aunt's house for the final several months of her life, when they were told that the new cancerous tumors located at the base of her brain were both inoperable and terminal. Having been given the news of her impending death, my sister and aunt wanted her final days to be in familiar surroundings. I can't imagine how hard it was on both of them.

On June 5th, 1976, my twenty-first birthday, I drove down to Canyon Country from Bakersfield, where I lived and worked at the time. Joanne told me our mother probably wouldn't live more than a few weeks and if I wanted to see her alive one more time, I needed to do so as soon as possible.

The drive from Bakersfield to Canyon Country was one of the longest two hours I'd ever spent in my life. I couldn't get there fast enough.

Fortunately, I was driving a small Toyota truck at the time, so exceeding the speed limit was not much of an issue.

I'll never forget walking into my aunt Nat's home and seeing my mom propped up in her hospital bed right in the center of my aunt's living room. My sister told her I was coming to see her that afternoon and she insisted on staying awake until I arrived. Mom had my birthday card lying by her side and when I opened it I saw that she had scrawled the words, "I love you son" on the inside. The print was barely legible as the cancer had taken over her brain and cost her the use of the entire right side of her body, including her writing hand. I looked up at her that one last time while she was alive and with tears streaming down both of our faces, she said her final words to me: "Did you ever think we'd make it this far, John?" She was actually referring to me. I was pretty wild during my youth and my mom was always worried I'd do something stupid and get myself killed. I could barely whisper my reply: "No mom, I really didn't." She died exactly two weeks from that day, on June 19, 1976 at the age of fifty-two. My sister and aunt chose not to tell my mother she was dying, thinking no good could come of it. They told her the new pain in the back of her head was the result of growing, post-surgery scar tissue and that the pain would soon subside. I think my mom always knew better. She was fond of the expression, "Ignorance is bliss." My mother may have been blissful right up to the end, but she was never ignorant. She was buried underneath a huge, beautiful oak tree on the side of a grassy knoll in Canyon Country at the Eternal Valley Cemetery.

Big Sister Joanne, Me, Big Sister Susan

My oldest sister, Susan, was a drug addict most of her adult life and died homeless and alone on the streets of downtown San Diego, California in 2000. She was a Jane Doe in the San Diego morgue for over two weeks before proper identification was made and authorities finally tracked down my sister Joanne, the middle sibling of the three of us. Susan was fifty-two at the time of her death.

Joanne, having finally broken the family "fifty-two curse," called me with the news that she had reached the age of fifty-three in January 2006. She had barely made it to the age of fifty-four years when her daughter, my niece Cassie, found her dead on her living room floor in February 2007. The coroner ruled the cause of death as inconclusive. However, we know that Joanne had been quite depressed and drinking to excess during her final weekend. Plus she had inherited my father's weak heart and had experienced some heart-attack-like symptoms during her last few years of life. However, I don't believe a weak heart is what killed her. Joanne did not spend her adult years as a happy person, never getting over the loss of our mother or her guilt over her inability to maintain a romantic relationship. Unlike me, my sister Joanne was never happy unless she was sharing her life with a boyfriend or husband. I'm more like my father, Joe. I have no problem being single as long as I have my four-legged companion.

In September 2001, my sister Joanne was my only living immediate family member. And despite the pain and suffering we went through after the loss of our father, mother, and big sister, nothing could prepare us for the events that were about to unfold thousands of miles away.

September 11, 2001 began just as any other day. Jordan and I arrived at the television station around 2:30 a.m. I went to work preparing the forecast and weather computer graphics and Jordan went out for a poop and pee and to hang out back in the station's doggy run.

The newscast started at 5:00 a.m. and the first hour was entirely uneventful; anchors reading the teleprompter and the traffic reporter and I ad libbing our traffic and weather reports. I was on the air when the first plane slammed into the World Trade Center just before 6:00 a.m., local time. During my weather forecast the newscast producer, who was in another room in the news control booth, started talking to me through my earpiece, telling me to quickly wrap my weather cast up and toss back to the anchors. Normally when a producer tells you to "wrap" it means you are to finish your current thought and then toss it back to the anchor desk. So I continued with my weather segment, as I was in the middle of talking about the seven-day forecast and wanted to finish my thought. My producer became quite agitated and started yelling at me to "wrap and toss back to the anchors." I had no idea there was breaking news. That important fact was not being communicated to me and I was becoming frustrated with the interruptions and the producer's attitude. Fortunately I didn't lose my cool and finished my thought without incident and then tossed back to the anchors. Only then did I learn what had just happened in New York.

The news anchors said a plane just hit one of the World Trade Center towers and they were going live to the *Today Show*.

Then the pictures started coming in from New York. Like everyone else, we all stood around and watched, thinking we were witnessing a terrible, tragic accident. At first, no one knew whether it was a commercial or private plane until the second plane hit. Then, on live national television, we watched, as if in slow motion, a second commercial jetliner hit the other tower.

At that moment I assume everyone had the same thought I did: "This was no accident." I didn't know why someone would do this or what the ramifications would be, but I knew then that these were intentional acts of terrorism on U.S. soil. We soon learned of another plane slamming into the Pentagon and a fourth one crash-landing in a field in Pennsylvania, killing everyone on board each of the planes and many on the ground. All of the sudden the enormity of the situation hit me like a ton of bricks. And, I lost it.

Tears started rolling down my face and I didn't want anyone to see me crying so I walked outside and into the dog run where Jordan was. I sat on a concrete slab and cried like a baby. Jordan walked over to me and licked all of the tears off my face. He never did that before and never did it again. There were many times in my life when I cried but somehow Jordan knew this time was different and I really needed him. I hugged him and cried in his fur. That was the only place in the world I wanted to be at that moment. Somehow Jordan made me feel a little bit better. In those moments immediately following those horrific acts of aggression against the United States and against innocent civilians, I knew as long as I had my boy by my side we would somehow make it through that tragic day.

Then the worst-case scenario happened: both towers collapsed.

The television station was now officially in full 9/11 mode: committed to reporting the tragedy, the rescue and recovery. Every step of the process was covered. Hope of survivors became less and less with each passing day. We discovered this was in fact a terrorist attack. The Middle Eastern terrorist group, Al Qaeda, claimed responsibility and their leader and plot mastermind, Osama Bin Laden, shot to the top of our Most Wanted list. There was little good news to report that day or for many days to follow.

These were very dark days for the news business. What was most difficult for me was the general feeling of helplessness. I had very little role in the newscasts for several days after 9/11 and I could only sit by and watch as my co-anchors delivered sad news after sad news, toss to commercial break and then cry until the break was over. Having Jordan with me certainly softened the blow but depression was inevitable.

It seemed that for some time following the tragic events of 9/11, the people of our nation had become mindful that they never really knew when their number would be up and life was truly fleeting. For a while people were nicer, more courteous and considerate. Unfortunately, that didn't last.

About a week after the attack the owner of our television station asked me how I was doing. I told him it was kind of tough going into work every day and only hearing about the events of 9/11. It wasn't that I thought the tragic events of that day didn't deserve coverage or that television viewers didn't have the right to hear the latest news updates. What I was having the most trouble with was the more I heard about 9/11, the more depressed I became. I had no doubt most everyone else in our country felt the same way. The television station owner must have agreed with me as he told me he thought it was time to get back to the business of broadcasting. He said every day we didn't move forward we allowed the terrorists to win.

We started getting back to as much of a normal broadcast as possible. As it should have been, 9/11 was the top story, but we tried to move on from the tragic day. There were days after 9/11 that I didn't appear on our newscasts at all. Reporting the weather for Las Vegas during the days immediately after the attacks didn't seem terribly important because we were living in Las Vegas and September is usually a pretty mild and boring month from a weather standpoint. That didn't mean I didn't want to be on the air contributing to the broadcast. I felt pretty much useless and invisible at times and it was tough staying motivated. Eventually the events of 9/11 faded from being the top story and I got back to my usual routine. However, I didn't "yuk it up" as I normally did for some time after that tragic day.

I intentionally did not put Jordan on the air as often for many days after 9/11 because I didn't want anyone to think I was taking the attack lightly. What I discovered when talking to people was that they were looking for any sense of solace, any act of kindness, any reason to feel better and Jordan was that source.

When Jordan and I were out in public, people would come up to me tell me that just seeing Jordan, even if only for a minute made them feel better.

TV station doggy run Fall 1998 photo by Corinna Nordin

Waiting For A Friend at the TV Station Doggy Run 2001

CHAPTER 19

One Year Later

As we neared the anniversary of the September 11 attacks, I thought it was very disrespectful that I hadn't taken time to visit our nation's capital. I decided Jordan and I would take off in our SUV one Saturday morning and would not return until we'd seen Washington, D.C. The only problem? Where were we going to get the money to fund such a venture? While we were doing an okay job of paying the bills, I knew we didn't have an extra $1,500 to $2,500, the amount I thought the trip would cost.

It was fall of 2002 and our economy was doing fine, housing prices were up and my townhouse had appreciated in value enough to get it refinanced. Fortunately, I had a friend in the mortgage business who helped me get that done. After paying off our debt, I was left with enough money to finance our upcoming cross-country trip. Jordan and I had nine days to make it to Washington, D.C. and back to Las Vegas.

Planning the route proved to be fairly easy thanks to the all of the map-making technology available now on the Internet and our handy-dandy road atlas. My idea was for Jordan and I to make a big loop around the country that included several must-see stops along the way. After looking at possible options, I decided to head south, then east, north and then back west. I knew that the farthest point east had to be Washington, D.C. After all, I had a newfound patriotic respect for our country, and where in our great land could there possibly be a place that was a bigger symbol of American patriotism than our nation's capital?

I mapped out a route that would take us south through Arizona and New Mexico, then east to Dallas and on to New Orleans. From there we would head northeast to Memphis, across Tennessee to south Virginia then north and east to D.C. The must-see stops included Bourbon Street, Graceland, Nashville's "Music Row," the National Mall in Washington D.C., the Indianapolis Motor Speedway and the Gateway Arch in St. Louis.

Getting Blood Pressure Checke Weather on Wheels March 2002

I calculated that it would take us at least eight days to cover the 6,000 plus miles, which meant I had to average close to 800 miles per day. If not, it would set us back and I wouldn't make it back to Las Vegas to return to work the following week. That didn't leave much room for a casual game of golf or seeing any of the sights. However, by this time I was firmly committed to making the journey with my best buddy, so I forged ahead with my plans.

One of my biggest concerns for the trip was my physical ability to pull off such high mileage numbers each day. I love to drive but, while I didn't inherit his weak heart, I did inherit my dad Joe's propensity for falling asleep at the wheel. His most famous story about falling asleep at the wheel was when he was in the Air Force during World War II. Late one night, while driving a military jeep, he dosed off and slammed into a telephone poll. He was lucky. The steering wheel took out all of his front teeth but he escaped serious injury.

I never hit anything or anyone while driving, thank God, but I did fall asleep at the wheel quite often during my high school and college years— once late at night on Highway 99 in central California. My car slid into the center divider and I woke up just in time to see I was headed straight for the oleander bushes in the highway median. Somehow I was able to get my Firebird under control and back up on the highway without further incident, other than pissing my pants. I also fell asleep late at night during a trip to Los Angeles in the late seventies. I was driving a Toyota pick-up and fell dead asleep right in the heart of L.A. on busy Interstate 405. When I woke up I was still in a travel lane, but my instincts took over and I slammed on the brakes in the middle of the freeway. Fortunately, no one rear-ended me and I didn't kill anyone. And if you can believe it, I actually fell asleep on a motorcycle during a trip from Bakersfield to Los Angeles, also in the late seventies. The only reason I woke up during that incident without crashing is that my helmet bounced off the front of my chest, immediately waking me up. I don't know when I was ever more scared. That time I did have to pull off the road and dry off, if you catch my drift.

It wasn't until I reached my thirties that I somehow taught myself to recognize the early warning signs of my impending drift off to la-la land and I learned to pull over and take a nap or at least get some fresh air before resuming my journey. But I had never undertaken such a huge driving task that I was planning for early fall of 2002 and the falling asleep incidents of my youth certainly were cause for concern.

Because we would be making the journey in my almost new 2002 Pathfinder, the vehicle prep required little more than an oil change and a good check of all vital functions; lights, brakes and tires. This was my third Pathfinder and I was quite confident that vehicle issues would be the least of our problems. That was one of my few assumptions that proved to come true.

Next, I needed to make sure that Jordan was medically ready for the trip. I took him to see his vet, Dr. Kristine Ziegler of the Sahara Pines Animal Hospital. She inquired as to our route and warned me of the dangers of certain problems not indigenous to Las Vegas, which included those things I was already concerned about: heartworm, fleas, ticks, rabies, mosquitoes, snakebites and whatever else there maybe waiting for us across the United States. With its dry climate, about the only real health issue for pets in Las Vegas are temperature extremes. In other areas with much higher humidity levels, all kinds of medical problems were a danger. Dr. Kristine vaccinated Jordan for whatever she felt might be an issue and loaded me up with other meds that she thought we'd need. She wished us good luck and sent us on our way. We could not have had a better veterinarian.

As a former disc jockey and all-around music lover, I knew I had to have a pretty big library of music for the long trip. For several nights before we headed out on our trip, I'd go online and download song after song, new and old. I loaded up two separate ten-disc magazines for my CD changer and was pretty sure I'd have enough tunes to make the big loop around the United States.

Because I didn't have a digital camera, I headed over to a local electronics store and purchased a 3.2-mega pixel camera that turned out to be one of the best investments I've ever made. With a rebate, the thing cost me about $150. Then I made a huge mistake. A mistake that would haunt me to this day: I only purchased one photo memory card and simply decided to delete whatever pictures I decided not to keep. Dumb, dumb, dumb.

I thought I needed some personal protection for the trip because I would be out on the open road by myself. I do not like guns, but on the advice of a good friend, I went to a gun shop in downtown Las Vegas and told the manager about my trip and asked him for suggestions. When he found out we'd be traveling through Washington, D.C., he informed me that it was a federal offense to bring a gun into the nation's capital or any federally owned area. The manager of the gun store then handed me a big aerosol can and told me it was all I needed. He said it was bear repellent. I gave him a puzzled look and asked him if bears were a big problem in D.C. I thought that one was pretty funny and started cracking up. He just looked me with a straight face and told me the bear spray would be plenty of protection. He said it would stop a grizzly bear in its tracks from thirty feet away and I could only imagine would it would do to a person. He told me he had unloaded a can of it once on a group of thugs who were getting ready to carjack him, and the last thing he saw was four guys screaming, holding their eyes and running blindly down the street. I was relieved because I wasn't comfortable having a gun with me. As I said, I don't like guns. I'm not second guessing our founding father's wisdom when they wrote the second amendment to the Constitution, ensuring our right to keep and bear arms. However, I can't help but wonder if things would've gone differently if they could've foresaw the technology that now puts Uzis, AK-47s, and other automatic weapons in our hands. Had they been able to see into the future, they may have just decided instead to arm bears. Or bare arms.

Thankfully, I never had to use the bear repellent, but years later I found out just how potent it was. I kept the can of repellent in an organizer hanging behind the front passenger seat of my SUV. I had forgotten all about it until one day when I was loading boxes into the back seat and accidentally caught the can's safety release on a box. The bear repellent sprayed across my SUV and soaked the driver's side door. Within seconds I was choking and gagging, and my eyes were watering uncontrollably. My insurance company almost totaled my vehicle before I was able to get smell and sting in my eyes completely cleaned out. It took me three weeks. Trust me, the stuff works.

The night before Jordan and I left for our big trip, I made him get up into bed with me for a heart-to-heart talk. He could still jump up onto the bed, but he preferred sleeping under it. However, I thought it was necessary to explain to him what we were about to do, even though I'd already been talking to him about it for several weeks.

I told Jordan that we were going on a really long ride in the car and we'd be seeing a lot of really cool places, but we'd be away from home from a long time and I didn't want him to think we weren't coming back to Las

Vegas. I told him I was really excited about the trip and there was no one in the whole world I'd rather have along for the ride than my best friend in the whole, wide world. My speech must have really impressed him because he made it through almost a full minute before he started snoring.

CHAPTER 20

Paws Across America I, Washington, DC

The television station webmaster thought our viewers might be interested in our trip, so the station loaned me a laptop computer. On it, I could make journal entries and upload photos and send daily summaries back to the station. He would then post both pictures and text to the television station's website so our viewers could follow along on our adventure. This later became the basis for creating Jordan's own website: www.paws-across-america.com.

As I mentioned in the previous chapter, the only thing that haunts me to this day: I deleted the photos off our camera after I uploaded them to the television station each day. I only purchased one memory card for the camera and it was full at the end of each day so I deleted whatever photos I didn't want to keep. I didn't realize at the time what precious memories I was losing. Rather than just picking up another photo memory card, I made more room by deleting all photos except the ones I considered to be the best.

Our alarm went off right at 1:00 a.m. on Saturday, September 21, 2002, and unlike the usual ritual of hitting the snooze button several times, I climbed out of bed, went downstairs and prepared Jordan's breakfast and my coffee. After Jordan ate, he went out to take care of his morning business and then I told him to get into the car. He jumped into the back of the SUV and settled in. To this day, I'm convinced the back of our SUV was his favorite place in the world.

After checking, checking again, and checking some more—I get my obsessive compulsive and neurotic streak from my mom—I finally believed we were ready for the trip of a lifetime.

After my mom and dad got divorced in 1959, we moved to Van Nuys, California to be closer to my mom's sister, my aunt Natalie and my cousins, Stephanie, Bob and Ray. Our house was a small, two-bedroom affair built in the 1950s and couldn't have been over 900 square feet. My mom and big sister Sue shared one bedroom and my sister Joanne and I slept in a bunk bed in the other bedroom; me on top and Joanne in the bottom bunk. When Sue turned eighteen and graduated high school, she moved out and Joanne took her bed in my mom's room, leaving me alone in the bunk bed. Shortly after we moved in to our house in Van Nuys, my mom began a ritual that she would continue until she got sick in the early 1970s.

Each night, after the three of us kids were in bed, my mother, assuming we were asleep, would patrol the house, going room to room checking the windows, doors, ash trays—she was a smoker—and the kitchen gas stove looking for open flames and burners that might have been left on. She'd do this several times each night, coming into our rooms to make sure we were snug in our beds, fast asleep. Only after she'd paced the floors, sometimes up to a dozen times a night, would she finally retire to her room and bed. She never knew that we knew of this late night ritual and we never said anything to her about it because we didn't want to embarrass her. After all, she was just looking out for us.

Having inherited my mom's compulsive habit, I wandered our townhouse several times that Saturday morning. I made several loops around the inside of the house, set the alarm system and locked and triple-checked the doors. I backed our SUV out of the garage and proceeded to circle our complex several times to make sure our garage door hadn't mysteriously reopened. Finally outside our gates, I looked at Jordan in the rear-view mirror and said aloud: "What the hell am I doing?" I didn't make any hotel reservations and had no idea where we would stop at the end of each day. Jordan and I drove out of our townhouse complex with a full tank of gas, a full thermos of coffee and at least one of us without a care in the world.

The goal for day one was to drive to Las Cruces, New Mexico by way of Phoenix, Arizona. The trek was about 700 miles so it would be a good test as to whether Jordan and I were up to such a long day on the road. Actually, Jordan was not the one in the SUV who had me worried.

I need to stop here and explain something that I think is pretty important: if you think you're about to read tales of encounters with interesting individuals and colorful characters during our journey, you're going to be sorely disappointed. In fact, about the only human interaction Jordan and I had during our entire trip was with convenience store employees and hotel desk clerks. This trip was strictly an opportunity for me to see our country with my best buddy. And to be completely honest, I'm not terribly gregarious outside of my job and my work in the community.

We headed south on U.S. 95 and made the crossing over Hoover Dam into Arizona within the first hour of our journey. Hoover Dam was completed in the 1935 at a cost of $49 million and over a hundred worker deaths. The dam is over 700 feet from base to top and 660 feet thick at the base. It is said that it will take over 200 years for the concrete to completely cure and that the dam was built to last 2,000 years.

We took Highway 95 south to Highway 93, which would take us to Phoenix and then south to Interstate 10 east and on to Las Cruces. The scenery though southern Arizona and much of New Mexico was much the same; desert landscape with huge cactus trees and mostly flat terrain. The journey at this point was about distance not sightseeing, so I was content driving the highway with the stereo cranked up and Jordan sound asleep in the back of our SUV. It never occurred to me that loud music in the car or home could affect a dog's sensitive hearing, but Jordan never seemed to mind no matter how loud I had the music cranked up. In fact, when we would broadcast live from the flight line at Nellis AFB during their annual demonstration, "Aviation Nation," the sound from the planes was often deafening and Jordan always seemed oblivious.

We made Phoenix just before 7:30 that morning and stopped only for gas and a few photos of Jordan looking out the SUV back window at the Phoenix skyline. During our 2002 trip, many of the pictures I took of Jordan were while he was still in the back of the SUV as I was constantly mindful of time and the ground we needed to cover each day. We'd find an interesting spot for a photo opportunity and I'd pull over, pop open the back window and snap off a few pictures of Jordan with the scenery in the background. Then I'd close the back window, hop back behind the wheel and off again we'd go.

Incorporated on February 25, 1881, Phoenix is the largest and most populous city in the state of Arizona. It is also the state capital and the largest state capital in the United States in terms of population. Phoenix is the only state capital with a population of more than a million people. It is the largest city in the Mountain Time Zone, as well as the second largest city in the western United States, after Los Angeles. The city proper is the tenth largest for land area in the United States at 517 square miles. As of 2008, the Phoenix metropolitan area was the thirteenth largest in the United States, with an estimated population of 4,579,427. Phoenix is the region's primary cultural, economic and financial center. It is also a major national transportation hub. Phoenix is located on the banks of what is now the normally dry Salt River. The city's metropolitan area is also known by its nickname, "The Valley of the Sun," or the shortened, "The Valley," because the city is surrounded by mountains on all sides. Residents are known as Phoenicians.

We caught I-10 on the southeast side of Phoenix and headed southeast, passing through Tucson and we crossed the New Mexico state line by mid-morning.

We reached Las Cruces late in the afternoon, having logged 700 miles on day one of our journey without incident. The only stops we made, as would become a central theme of the trip, was for me and Jordan to relieve ourselves, gas up the SUV and grab an occasional drink of water or snack. It was well over 100 degrees outside by the time we reached Las Cruces and, thanks to some pretty careful planning on my part, we got off the highway and into town with no hotel room reservations as I assumed Jordan and I would sleep in back of the SUV most nights. But I was simply too tired and it was too hot for us to sleep outside. I looked for a cheap, clean room for the night but what I didn't know and hadn't prepared for was the huge college football game scheduled for that night, so hotel rooms were not easy to find. After searching for an hour, I found a place that had one room left. It was a dump, but I was desperate and didn't care.

Pets were not allowed at this motel so I snuck Jordan in to the room. After getting situated, I turned on the laptop, uploaded photos and wrote my account of the day. Jordan ate and immediately climbed up onto the bed and was out like a light. He was sprawled out across the middle of the bed and I didn't have the heart to move him over to make room for me. So I grabbed a pillow and a blanket and spent the first night of our trip on the floor of a seedy motel room floor in Las Cruces, New Mexico. I fell asleep with visions of us turning back the next morning and heading home for Las Vegas. I'm glad we didn't.

Las Cruces sits just off Interstate 25 in the southeast part of New Mexico and is only about an hour northwest of El Paso and the Mexican border. By the way, borders separate countries and lines separate states— just one of those tidbits you learn when you do TV weather. The city is the second largest in population in the state of New Mexico with right around 200,000 permanent residents in the metropolitan area. Las Cruces is Spanish for "the crosses" and its vast farmland gets its irrigation water from the Rio Grande. One of its most famous inhabitants was the lawman Pat Garrett, who worked a murder case there in the late 1890s and who also shot and killed the outlaw Billy the Kid. Las Cruces is also home to New Mexico State University.

The next morning, September 22, we took off from Las Cruces just past 3:00 a.m. after Jordan had eaten, peed and taken a dump. I should've thought about my biological needs as well. We were heading almost due south on I-10 toward El Paso, Texas and I felt a rumble in my intestines. By the time we reached El Paso, I really felt the need to do a little dumping of my own, but chose to press onward and just hold off for as long as I could. However, after only getting a few miles away from the lights of El Paso, I knew I had to pull over. It was dark and we were in the middle of nowhere. I stopped on the side of the road and, without completely grossing you out, let's just say I let it all hang out over a flood wash just east of El Paso, Texas.

We made decent time and soon saw the signs for El Paso. El Paso is on the extreme western end of Texas and, according to the 2006 census estimates, the city had a population of 609,415. It is the sixth largest city in Texas and the twenty-first largest city in the United States, as well as the seventh fastest growing large city in the nation from 2000-2006. With a population of 736,310, the metro area covers all of El Paso County. El Paso is directly across the border from Ciudad Juarez, Mexico and is probably best known for the 1959 hit song by Marty Robbins of the same name.

In the years following our trips, many people have asked me what Jordan was like as a traveling companion. Simply put, he was the best. When he wasn't sleeping he would lay in the back facing me, smiling all the way. I never had to listen to, "Are we there yet?" He was just happy being on the road with his dad. Imagine a life like that. I knew when he had to go pee or poop because he would do exactly the same thing he did when we were homeless and slept on the floor of our radio station in Santa Barbara; he'd sit up and stare at me. I'd catch sight of him in the rearview mirror and would know it was time for a potty break. I always made sure we got off the highway and into an area that was safe from cars and other dangers. Jordan would jump out of the back of the SUV, do his thing, hop back in and off we'd go.

We were soon traveling east through west Texas, having merged from I-10 onto Interstate 20 which would take us due east and right through the Dallas-Ft. Worth metro area. Once on I-20, as the sun began to rise in the east, our surroundings became visible and I have to admit, no offense Texans, it was some of the ugliest landscape I'd ever seen. Flat, barren, dusty and the wind howled all the way to the west side of Dallas.

Other than my brief nature stop just east of El Paso, we made only one other pit stop until we reached Dallas. That was in central Texas at a rest stop along I-20 for me to fill up on coffee and Jordan to do his own nature thing. At that particular rest stop, I purchased a baseball cap that had "Don't Mess With Texas" embroidered on the front. I put the cap on Jordan's head and snapped off a quick picture of him before he shook it from his head. That photo, along with dozens of others, is only available online on our website in thumbnail form.

As the Dallas skyline came into view, I thought about how lucky we were that the weather, save for the wind, was cooperating thus far on the trip. Dallas is a huge city with beautiful modern skyscrapers and very sophisticated roads and highways. We had to loop around the beltway that surrounds the city, as our hotel for the night was located in North Dallas.

Dallas, Texas is the ninth largest city in the United States, and the fourth largest metropolitan area with a population of over 6 million people. The city is known for its oil and cotton industries, its location along various railroad lines and its strong financial sector.

Jordan and I quickly became seasoned travelers. I had the good sense of doing a web search the previous night and found a pet-friendly hotel in North Dallas. It wasn't the nicest of places, but the room was clean and comfortable and Jordan and I weren't picky. After checking in and getting situated in our room, I fed Jordan and took him out for a walk, as I wanted to find a fast-food joint to pick up some take-out later for dinner.

Once we were both fed and I'd had the chance to go online, upload photos and record our account of day two's travels, we both settled into bed and I read whatever novel I was reading at the time until I turned the lights off and we went to sleep, tired from a day that saw another 745 miles added to the trip odometer. Only two days into the trip and we had already logged close to 1,500 miles.

The following morning, September 23, Jordan and I left North Dallas at 4:45 a.m. The original plan was for us to drop south out of Dallas on I-45, pick up I-10 east and hit New Orleans later that Monday morning. I wanted to go to New Orleans because I had always wanted to see "The Big Easy." That plan was scrapped when I looked at the forecast data on our laptop the previous night and saw that the Gulf was bracing for Hurricane Isadore. Her remnants would catch up to us in Maryland a few days later. Instead, we took I-30 up toward Little Rock, Arkansas on our way to Memphis and Graceland. East Texas was just the opposite of west Texas—lush, green and stunningly beautiful. In fact, all across the southern states from east Texas to Virginia the landscape was so dense and beautifully green it almost hurt your eyes if you stared at your surroundings too long.

On the Road in Eastern Arkansas along I-40 PAA1
September 23, 2002

Jordan and I stopped for gas at a convenience store just east of Hope, Arkansas, home of Bill Clinton and were very impressed by how nice people were. I love a southern accent and everyone seemed to go out of his or her way to say "Hello" and "How are ya?" When I'd let Jordan out to go potty and stretch his legs, it never failed that someone would comment on what a "good-looking dog" I had. It was true, Jordan's looks, even for a lab were quite distinctive and he had the coolest expressions, always looking like he was smiling and just happy to be alive. All pet owners, even those of Chinese Crested dogs, I'm sure, feel their respective pets are distinctive and good-looking and I'm no different. But Jordan was a very regal-looking boy and I have no doubt that his celebrity status somehow added to his mystique and good looks. Thankfully, he got his looks from his mom.

Day three got us to Memphis, Tennessee with another 520 miles on the odometer. We were already behind schedule and needed to make up some ground in the days to come. Because our destination was Graceland, we never got to see downtown Memphis or the world-famous Beale Street. Dogs were not allowed on the tour of Graceland, so I took a couple of pictures of Jordan across the street with Graceland in the background, and one really good picture in front of Elvis' private plane, the "Lisa Marie." As an Elvis impersonator once said to me during a live broadcast at a Las Vegas wedding chapel: "You may not be able to afford a Priscilla, but you can Lisa Marie."

Just being near this famous landmark, Graceland, was enough to stand the hair up on my arms knowing the history and being somewhat of an

Along Elvis Presley Blvd with Graceland in background September 23, 2002

Elvis fan myself. As with John, Bobby, Martin, and even John Jr., you never forget where you were when you learned that the "King of Rock 'n' Roll" had passed away. In my case, on August 16, 1977, I was on Highway 99 just north of Bakersfield, having left work at the farming corporation I worked for in the seventies and early eighties. I was listening to my favorite local rock station, the one I would eventually work for less than two years later. That afternoon the DJ came on the airwaves at the end of a song and broke the sad news. And, as he would say, even though the station did not usually play Elvis' records, he made an exception that day and played three in a row I will never forget, "Suspicious Minds," "Kentucky Rain," and "In the Ghetto." Ironically, several years later I got into some hot water with Elvis fan clubs worldwide after some comments I made on-air regarding celebrity substance abuse issues. The anchors had just finished reading a story about some young, popular celebrity and her current abuse issues and I related it to the King's tragic death in 1977. My comments were taken out of context by a viewer, passed along to a member of a local fan club and within a few days, Elvis fan clubs around the world were calling the station demanding that I be fired. I ended up having to transcribe my exact comments for local Elvis club presidents who, realizing I was actually defending the King, finally apologized and issued statements in my defense to other clubs worldwide. Sadly, the only person who never apologized to me was the guy who, only hearing about what I said second hand, got the whole mess started. The joys of being a broadcaster.

While Memphis is almost certainly best known for Graceland and as the final resting place of the King of Rock & Roll, as of 2007 the city had an estimated population of 675,000, making it the largest city in the state and the eighteenth largest in the United States. The city sits in the southwest corner of the state, along the Mississippi and Wolf Rivers.

After we left Graceland, we headed off to our motel room to get some rest for day four of our trip. I had booked a room at a pet-friendly motel in an area of Memphis known as Germantown, a beautiful and relatively new area of the city. Hotel stays at night had become necessary, as it was still too warm and humid to sleep in the back of the SUV. After checking in to our Memphis hotel, I fed Jordan and got him settled in for the night. I then ventured out to a sports bar, ordered a cold drink and some food to go. I always tried to find a local restaurant, bar or pub each night because I knew they'd have television sets tuned to the local news so I could keep up on current events. I'd watch TV until my take-out came and then I'd head back to the room for what was becoming our evening routine: eating, taking Jordan out for a walk, turning the laptop on, going online and then e-mailing photos and our account of the day's adventures back to our TV stations' webmaster. Being a weather guy I would always check the next day's forecast on our laptop in case there was a need to detour around severe weather. Fortunately, the only time that was necessary was when we had to scrap our plan to visit New Orleans. Our Germantown motel room in Memphis turned out to be the nicest one we'd stay in for the entire trip. Plus, I had become very impressed by the courteous nature and friendly charm of the folks across the south, particularly in Memphis, Tennessee.

A resident of Memphis is referred to as a Memphian and the city sits in a region of the country known as the mid-south. By the twentieth century, Memphis had grown into the world's largest spot cotton and hardwood lumber market. It is also known for its rich cultural diversity, mid-south cuisine and some of the best blues music on the planet. The most tragic blemish Memphis must always bear is being known as the 1968 assassination location of Reverend Dr. Martin Luther King.

The following Tuesday morning, September 24, Jordan and I left Memphis a little later in the morning, around 6:00 a.m., as the strain of the long days on the road were starting to take their toll on me. I was beginning to feel the fatigue of putting several hundred miles on the odometer each day and I needed a bit more sleep that Monday morning. Once we got situated back into the SUV, we gassed up and then jumped on to Interstate 40 and headed off to Nashville toward Bristol, Virginia, home of the famous NASCAR speedway and our eventual destination for that day

Tennessee is another gorgeous state, fairly flat, with green, lush plants and trees everywhere outside the city limits. Cruising along I-40, I had the stereo and the AC cranked up and held the SUV right at or slightly above the speed limit, which was usually between sixty to seventy miles per hour across much of the south. I needed to keep the air conditioning on even during the cool morning hours as the September humidity in the south, for me, was simply stifling. I'm a dry climate person and I've never done well in humid conditions.

We could see the Nashville skyline by mid-morning and it is as pretty as Dallas' with a mixture of old and new buildings downtown. I-40 dumped us into downtown Nashville and we cruised the streets for a short while before we headed for our morning destination: Nashville's famed "Music Row."

Nashville is the capital of the state and the largest metropolitan area in Tennessee with a population of over 1.5 million residents. It is located on the Cumberland River and is a major hub for the health care, banking, and transportation industries. But the city is best known as the "Home of Country Music."

With my years spent in country radio, famed Music Row was a real treat. The street is lined with shops and nightclubs where up-and-coming country music performers hone their skills in hopes of one day hitting the big time. We stopped along the way to so I could take pictures of Jordan in front of the Nashville Coliseum, the Ryman Auditorium—home of the Grand Ole Opry—and the Country Music Hall of Fame. We stopped at a souvenir shop just off of Music Row and purchased a few hats and T-shirts. I'm not really into buying souvenirs, but I couldn't return home without getting a few gifts for friends and a few of my co-workers. We were only in Nashville for about one hour. It was going to be a long day and I was determined to make it to Bristol, Virginia by early evening. Bristol seemed to be the perfect jumping off point to head north directly into our nation's capital.

Around this point of our journey I had an epiphany of sorts: I wasn't a public figure outside of Las Vegas so I didn't have to worry about the way I looked, how I acted, or what I said as there would not be any consequences like there might be back in Las Vegas. I don't know why this struck me so profoundly, but it just seemed to make the trip a little better, knowing I didn't have to constantly worry about my appearance or behavior. Don't get me wrong. Just because it finally occurred to me that nobody would recognize me, it wasn't like I was going to strip naked and do the moonwalk in the middle of the road. I just liked being able dress down and allow my hair to start looking like I'd combed it with a firecracker.

It gets old hearing "how's the weather?" when you're standing outside under a clear sky. Sometimes I just feel like saying the first thing that comes to my mind whenever someone says that to me. But I've taught myself to just smile and laugh like it's the first time I've heard that one. There's an old saying in my profession: "Make one thousand people happy and they might tell no one. Piss one person off and they'll tell thousands." That being said, I'll never forget the time I was at a local comedy club and an audience member was heckling the comedian on stage. The comedian's way of handling the guy was with a classic line and one I have to admit I've used from time to time after a long day: "Look, I don't come into McDonald's and give you a bad time when you're working, do I?"

Once we left Nashville, Jordan and I hopped back on I-40 heading east and we drove right through Knoxville without stopping, crossing the Virginia state line that afternoon, making it to Bristol just as the sun was setting. We were getting very close to the mountain ranges in the eastern part of the country and our travels had changed from driving down a flat highway to cruising along through rolling hills and big sweeping turns along the road. It felt great to be alive, anonymous and traveling through America with my best friend and newly seasoned road warrior, Jordan. The skies were beginning to turn gray as remnants of Hurricane Isadore made their way north-northeast.

It was now the fourth day our of journey and I was getting a bit tired of the music I had downloaded prior to the trip, having listened to the same songs countless times by now. So I started listening to a lot of local radio, especially news-talk radio. The topic on a local station on this particular day was the debate over a Kentucky state lottery. And though we were driving through Tennessee, Kentucky is the state directly north and the residents of Tennessee were very interested as to whether or not their neighbors to the north would vote in a state lottery. The pros were obvious: revenue for Kentucky schools. The major con was something I'd never realized, and one to this day find quite fascinating. The vast majority of people who play lotteries are those who can least afford it. By and large, people who buy lottery tickets are barely scraping by and hoping against all odds for that one big jackpot that will answer all their problems and dreams. By the way, Nevada will probably never have a state lottery simply because the gaming industry is too powerful and they don't want to lose a single dollar to any other entity, public or private, that might deprive them of a single revenue dollar.

Just before the Virginia state line, we merged on to I-81, the road that would take us north directly into our destination city for the night: Bristol, Virginia. I-81 would also give us an almost a straight shot north into D.C. the following Wednesday. Bristol is the twin city of Bristol, Tennessee, just across the state line and has a population just under 20,000. State Street runs through the center of both towns across state lines with the famous Bristol Motor Speedway on the Tennessee side. Bristol, like Nashville, calls itself the "Home of Country Music."

Jordan and I stayed in a nice, clean motel room just across the road from the Bristol Speedway. In this room, Jordan had his one and only accident during the entire trip. I had got us checked in to the hotel, fed Jordan and secured him in the room. I was starving and found a sports bar in a strip mall adjacent to the motor speedway. I caught the news and events of the day on the TVs that hung all around the bar, ordered a meal and Coke to go while I waited. When I got back to the room only a short time later, I found that Jordan had an accident. Fortunately, he was on a high fiber diet so his poop was hard as a rock and left no stains. It was pretty hard to get mad at Jordan for his accident because our entire normal daily routine had been disrupted and I'd simply lost track of his schedule. So I just cleaned up the mess and made a mental note to pay better attention to Jordan's biological needs for the rest of the trip.

After a good night's rest, we left Bristol at 3:10 a.m. on Wednesday, September 25, 2002, and headed straight for Washington, D.C. We took I-81, which runs due northeast right up through the Jefferson and George Washington National Forests.

The George Washington and Jefferson National Forests combine to form one of the largest areas of public land in the eastern United States. They cover 1.8 million acres of land in the Appalachian Mountains of Virginia, West Virginia and Kentucky. The forest extends along the entire length of the Blue Ridge Mountains and the Allegheny Mountains to the North Carolina line.

This was one of two times during our trip that I wished we were driving during daylight hours because I missed a lot of beautiful scenery. By the time the sun came up, we had left I-81 and were headed east on I-66, better known as the "Front Royal." We took the last exit off of I-66 on the western side of the Potomac River and Washington, D.C. I pulled into a truck stop and filled the SUV with gas and Jordan and I both had some time to stretch our legs, take care of business and go for a little walk. We were too early to cross the Potomac to the National Mall because of the morning carpool restrictions. Unless you were traveling with at least one other occupant in your vehicle, you had to join the thousands of other people who did not qualify to drive in the faster, HOV or high-occupancy vehicle lane. The time was around 8:30 a.m. so we had thirty minutes before the carpool restrictions were lifted and we could finally reach our ultimate destination: our nation's capital. The sky was a mixture of sun and clouds, the air a bit on the sticky side due to the humidity and temperatures were already into the upper sixties. It would turn out to be a beautiful, warm and humid fall day in D.C. Perfect for sight seeing, picture taking and feeling happy to be alive and an American in the greatest country on earth. And the icing on the cake was that I would be visiting Washington D.C. with my boy by my side.

As we crossed the Potomac River on I-66, I saw the Kennedy Center on my left and the Lincoln Memorial on my right. The Washington Monument could also be seen in the distance. Seeing the Potomac River, then the top of the Washington Monument rising above the trees was amazing. I was simply overcome with emotion and patriotism. I was on the cell phone with my buddy John Tutora as we crossed the Potomac. Having spent several years living in the area while working for the FAA headquarters in Washington, D.C., John was able to help me navigate my way to one of the National Mall parking areas without incident. Traffic in and around the Mall is an absolute nightmare and without his help, we would've probably ended up in the Potomac.

After finding a parking space, I put the gear we needed and bottled water into my backpack and Jordan and I headed for photo time in front of the magnificent landmarks.

The District of Columbia, sometimes referred to by locals as simply the District, was founded on July 16, 1790. It's located on the Potomac River and bordered by Virginia on one side and Maryland on the other. And, though the resident population is right at 600,000, the work week commuters push it over the 1 million mark during the week and the Washington metropolitan area, of which D.C. is a part, has over 5 million residents, making it the eighth largest metropolitan area in the country. All three branches of the federal government are located in the District, as are many of the nation's monuments and museums.

Jordan and I headed across the park toward the Potomac like we owned the place. It never occurred to me to ask if dogs were allowed on the National Mall. The number of military personnel with their K-9 companions stationed all around the area was amazing to me. It was only one year after the September 11 attack, so security was still very high. All of the military

Jordan Lincoln Memorial, September 25, 2002

men and women were very nice and went out of their way to say "Hello" to both Jordan and me.

After some photos in front of the Potomac River, Jordan and I walked over to the Lincoln Memorial and I took some really great pictures of him on the steps in front of the statue of Abraham Lincoln. I can't count the number of times that people got a kick out of me taking pictures of my dog in front of all the famous landmarks. Jordan put smiles on a lot of people's faces during our trip.

After we were finished with photos at both the Lincoln Memorial and Washington Monument, Jordan and I headed for the Vietnam Memorial, stopping first at the Korean War Memorial. I was really impressed by the Korean Memorial, as I had no prior knowledge of its existence. And

Jordan Washington Memorial, September 25, 2002

though it doesn't seem to get much press, it is one of the most compelling memorials on the Mall.

After getting a few shots of Jordan in front of the Korean War Memorial, we made our way to the Vietnam Memorial.

No matter how much a person prepares

Entrance to Vietnam Memorial, September 25, 2002

for their visit to the Vietnam Memorial, one will never be ready for how emotional the Memorial really is. It is a beautiful piece of stone rising out of the earth like a natural part of its surroundings. Another landmark that you don't hear much about is a statue of soldiers guarding the entrance to the Vietnam Memorial. The photo I took of Jordan in front of that statue is, to this day, one of my all-time favorites. Just after taking the photo of Jordan in front of that statue, a woman came up to me and asked if I'd like her to take a picture of both us. I thanked her, but said that wouldn't be necessary because the trip was all about my dog. She just gave me a quizzical look and walked away.

Also at the entrance to the Memorial is a large book that lists alphabetically all of the 58,000-plus names etched on the Wall. When I found the name of my childhood friend, I was overcome with emotion and began crying. Seeing the name made me realize once and for all that he was really gone. Jordan and I then headed down along the Memorial to find his name—he was killed in action shortly after arriving in Vietnam in 1968.

While I was looking at the Wall, a woman vacationing from Las Vegas recognized Jordan. We were stopped along the Wall—I was checking my camera—and Jordan was enjoying the scenery. Suddenly, I heard a female voice exclaim: "I know that dog!" And as soon as I looked up at her, she said: "I know you! You're my weather man." That was the only time during that trip, or the trip we would take the following year, that we were recognized outside of Las Vegas. After exchanging pleasantries with our Las Vegas neighbor, I found the spot on the Wall where my friend's name was. I spent a few minutes crying and reflecting on childhood memories while I said a long overdue goodbye to my childhood friend. Unfortunately, the self-portrait I took of me saying "Goodbye" is only available on our website, another casualty of my faulty planning.

If it were up to me, there would be a constitutional amendment that required all U.S. citizens to visit Washington, D.C. and the magnificent sites and monuments at least once in their life. It was a day I will never forget and will always cherish, in no small part because I was with my best buddy in the whole wide world—my son, Jordan.

Jordan and I ended our very special visit to our nation's capital by late morning and headed back to our SUV and our afternoon destination, Cumberland, Maryland. We had to depart D.C. by noon as we wanted to avoid the afternoon traffic and high occupancy restrictions. Unfortunately, Jordan didn't qualify as a second vehicle passenger. So we got on the road just before noon and headed west via 66, 270, then 70, diverting on to I-68—the National Highway—which allowed us to avoid the Pennsylvania Turnpike and all the tollbooths. We arrived in Cumberland, Maryland at 2:15 p.m. We had traveled 3005.8 miles by the end of day five of our trip and the skies were mostly cloudy with the remnants of Hurricane Isadore. Up to this point of our trip, the weather had been beautiful. What I didn't know was we were just hours away from the post-hurricane wrath of Isadore.

Cumberland is located in the Ridge-and-Valley Appalachians, at the junction of the North Branch of the Potomac River. Interstate 68, the road that got us there, runs through the city in an east-west direction. Highway 220 runs north-south. Cumberland is surrounded by mountains and trees and the leaves were just beginning to turn when we arrived. I could really envision myself retiring in such a community. According to the census, Cumberland has a population of around 20,000.

I left Jordan in the SUV and checked us into a pet-friendly hotel. Even though I made it very clear to the hotel staff I was bringing a large dog inside to stay with me, they put us in a room on the eighth floor of an eight-floor hotel. Apparently they thought Jordan would just use the hotel room bathroom if he had to pee or take a dump. I was actually more concerned about how Jordan would react to riding an elevator, as he'd never been in one before. With Jordan still in the car, I got our stuff settled into the room, then went outside to walk him so he could take care of business. It started to rain and I was able to get him inside before he got too wet. Fortunately, that elevator ride and all subsequent ones with Jordan proved to be uneventful. I don't even think he knew the thing was moving, thank God, as I would've hated for him to freak out and get us thrown out in the rain. I got him fed and bedded down, then grabbed my umbrella and headed out to find something to eat. I found a nice Italian restaurant in the historic district of town and ordered a salad and pasta to go. I got back to the room, ate, e-mailed more photos and the day's journal account and hit the sack. I was just plain beat from spending an emotional day in Washington, D.C. and didn't wake up until just after 5:00 a.m. the following morning.

We left Cumberland, Maryland at 5:50 a.m. on September 26 and jumped on I-68, needing to cross into West Virginia and catch I-79 heading north into Pennsylvania, which would then take us to I-70. I-70 would then take us directly into Indianapolis, Indiana.

The rain continued from the previous afternoon. Fortunately, it was light and didn't slow us down much. After connecting with I-70 in western Pennsylvania, we crossed the Ohio state line and the rain let up long enough for me to stop, and take a picture of Jordan with his head out the back window of the SUV, looking over at a small pond surrounded by marsh land. The scenery was really beginning to change as fall was now in full swing and the vegetation and tree leaves were changing from a bright green to a beautiful mix of amber and brown.

Maryland, West Virginia, western Pennsylvania and eastern Ohio are very pretty—tons of trees and rolling hills. Western Ohio begins a more flat topography with lots of farmland. Still pretty, just different.

Fall is "pot-hole season" for much of the Midwest and anywhere in the nation where the roads take a beating by the harsh winter weather and all the salt applied to melt the snow from the roadways. During our travels throughout the Midwest, we were often slowed down due to roadwork and the interstates being reduced to one lane in each direction. I'm not a terribly patient man and if it wasn't for my stereo system and my traveling companion, I would've been very frustrated by the constant road repair delays.

Western Ohio along I70, September 26, 2002

We passed through Columbus, Ohio stopping only on the western side of the city for a brief gas break. Gas, as in fuel for the SUV. Shortly after that brief stop, the rain started up again and before long it was really pounding I-70, the top of our SUV and all the other vehicles on the interstate. My windshield wipers had trouble keeping up and I found myself staying in the slow lane, splashing along between fifty and fifty-five mph. The rain was really testing my nerves and I was relieved to cross the Ohio-Indiana state line by mid-morning knowing that I could make Indianapolis by midday.

When we finally arrived in Indianapolis, at 1:00 p.m. central time, the trip odometer showed just over 3,500 miles, meaning we'd only covered just over 700 miles from the time we left D.C. But the stops in Cumberland and Indianapolis were both natural stopping points, even if we were going to have to pick up the pace to make it home by the following Sunday, September 29. And though I felt fresh enough to get farther west than Indianapolis on that day five of the trip, the rain was really coming down and, like most people from California, I don't like to drive in the rain. Don't ask. I have no idea why. But ask anyone from the Golden State and they'll tell you the same thing.

Because we'd gotten used to the comforts of a warm hotel room, we booked another one just off the I-465 loop that circles Indianapolis, the same one David Letterman made such a fuss about getting named after him.

Indianapolis is the capital city of Indiana and with a population of just under 700,000, by far the state's largest city and the thirteenth largest city in the country. It is the county seat of Marion County, located almost directly in the center of the state. And, while it is known for being a center for health care, education, and tourism, the city is most certainly best known for being home to the Indianapolis Motor Speedway and the Indy 500 motor race each May. And, like many cities in the Midwest, Indianapolis is a sprawling, spread-out affair that seems to go for as long as the eye can see. The topography, unlike most of the cities we visited in the south and east, is very flat, giving a very wide open feel to the area.

I pulled the SUV under the carport leading to the hotel reception area, got Jordan out of the back and both of us walked right in to check in. I was still having trouble getting used to walking into a hotel lobby with my boy by my side. But I was also quickly learning that, more and more often hotel operators understand a traveler's need to have their pets with them on the road, and the hotel employees treated Jordan like any other guest.

Because it was still pretty early, I decided to venture out into the pounding rain and find a place where I could watch a little TV, grab something cold to drink and order dinner to go. I got back to the room at around 3:00 p.m. with some fast-food for dinner and found Jordan sound asleep on the bed. I fired up the laptop, e-mailed the day's photos and notes and fell asleep watching TV next to my boy.

You might have notice by this point that each time I ventured out and got something to eat for dinner for that day, I always got the food to go. I don't know where it comes from, but I don't like eating in front of people or alone in restaurants. On many occasions at work, my co-workers have marvelled at the fact that, in all the years they've worked with me they've never seen me eat anything. I do eat. Just alone. Another one of my odd quirks, no doubt. Jordan, on the other hand, would've eaten in the middle of a Super Bowl stadium. Why can't we be more like our pets?

We left our Indianapolis hotel the following morning, September

27, at 4:40 in the morning, navigating our way in a dark, driving rain to the Indianapolis Motor Speedway for a quick picture of Jordan under the famous landmark's neon sign. After explaining to a speedway security guard what we were doing, he allowed me to snap off a few pictures of

Departure from Hotel in Indianapolis AM 092702   Jordan looking out the back window of the SUV, with pouring rain and the motor speedway sign in the background. Then the guard shooed us along and within minutes of getting back on the I-465 loop next to the Motor Speedway, I made a critical navigation error.

Somehow in my attempt to reconnect with I-70 from I-465, I took a wrong turn and we ended up somewhere in rural Indiana and lost about an hour before getting directions back to the interstate. We found our way to a small rural town and stopped in a diner for directions to I-70. This place was like a scene out of *The Twilight Zone*. Remember the one where everyone turned out to be aliens at the end? When I walked in the diner a bell above the door announced my arrival and, in unison all of the patrons stopped what they were doing, turned and gave me a look like I had two heads. I quickly went to the counter, ordered a cup of coffee, got directions to Interstate 70 and got out of there before I was abducted.

A fun fact about our interstate highway system should you ever get lost like we did: All east-west interstates have even number designations, north-south are odd numbered.

After our early morning diversion into The Twilight Zone, we finally got back on I-70 west and the rain was really coming down. Big-rigs were passing us like we were up on jacks and with each passing truck, we were momentarily blinded by the spray of water. After each big-rig shower it took a few seconds for our wipers to catch up and those were some of the scariest moments during the entire trip. Each time one of those eighteen-wheelers threw water up on our windshield, it was as though someone threw a blindfold over my eyes. I really thought we were going to crash several times as we made our way to St. Louis. Thankfully the Man Upstairs was watching down on us.

We arrived in St. Louis around 10:00 a.m. and went directly to the Gateway Arch to get some pictures. The St. Louis Gateway Arch, also known as the Gateway to the West, is exactly 630 feet tall and 630 feet wide at its base. Work on it was started in 1963, completed in 1965 and it opened to the public in 1967. The outside is stainless steel and it is reinforced inside by concrete. The interior of the Arch is hollow and contains a unique transport system leading to an observation deck at the top that tourists can ride during daily tours of the structure. There are also emergency stairways with over 1,000 steps in the event of a failure with the tram system. Jordan and I did not take a tour as we were on a tight time budget and I was fairly certain dogs weren't allowed.

The city of St. Louis is located at the confluence of two of the world's most famous rivers, the Mississippi and the Missouri, and is the second largest city in the state, but the largest metropolitan area, with a population over 350,000. The city is named for King Louis the IX and is famous for its French, German and Victorian influences. It was also home to the 1904 World's Fair and Olympics. On a personal note: the city struck me as quite beautiful and much different than the two major cities we previously visited. Not only were there those big beautiful rivers alongside St. Louis,

but tall trees and lush vegetation grows everywhere around the city.

I took some great pictures of Jordan in front of the Gateway Arch and headed to the airport to pick up my best friend of forty years, John Tutora. In 2002, John was an executive with Northwest Airlines

Gateway Arch PAA1 September 27, 2002

and flew down to St. Louis from the Twin Cities on business and to see us, of course. John decided to take the afternoon off and give me a break and he took the wheel drove to Kansas City, Missouri. He flew back home later that same afternoon.

One of the most memorable pictures of the trip was one that I took of Jordan on I-70 between St. Louis and Kansas City. John was driving and

Central Missouri along I-70 092702

I was in the passenger seat of the SUV. I was holding onto the camera and happened to turn around to see Jordan laying there, facing forward with this big, sweet smile on his face. I held the camera up to my eye, framed him up and snapped off what has turned out to be another one of my all-time favorites. Fortunately, it is one that I chose not to delete from the camera memory card. What's really interesting is that you never really know how a picture is going to turn out until you've seen it later on a much bigger screen.

Anywhere west of western Indiana is mostly farm country and it stays that way until you reach the Rocky Mountains. Some people argue that the Midwest and Central Plains are boring but it's all in perspective. We live in a desert, and yet we live in some of the most beautiful country in the world.

We arrived in Kansas City, Missouri late in the afternoon of September 27, checking in to the only remaining hotel room I could find. It turned out there was a big NASCAR event in town that weekend and the city was packed with NASCAR fans. The odometer read 4,022.2, meaning we'd been on the road for just under 500 miles that Friday, September 27, 2002. And though a 500-mile day was now just a walk in the park for us, I was thankful to have been given a nice break from the driving duties between

St. Louis and Kansas City by my best two-legged buddy, John. After getting Jordan's needs taken care of and him situated for the night in our Kansas City hotel room, John and I proceeded to the hotel restaurant to catch up on our lives before he had to cab it back to the airport and his home

and family in Minneapolis, Minnesota.

Kansas City is the largest city in the state of Missouri. As of 2006, the city had an estimated population of 447,306, with a metro area of nearly 2 million. Kansas City was founded in 1838 as the "Town of Kansas," at the confluence of the Missouri and Kansas rivers, and was incorporated in its present

Back of Car PAA1 Central Missouri 92702

form in 1850. Situated opposite Kansas City, Kansas, the city was the location of several battles during the Civil War, including the Battle of Westport. The city is well known for its contributions to the musical styles of jazz and blues, as well as to cuisine: Kansas City-style barbecue.

The next morning, Saturday, September 28, we left Kansas City at 2:50 a.m. under a beautiful clear sky with outside temperatures cool but comfortable, in the upper 50s. We drove across much of Kansas in the dark, encountering dense, patchy areas of what is known as "Tule fog," that rises up from the cool, moist ground especially around marshes and farmland. Fortunately, I had learned how to navigate my way through this soupy mess during my years in the Central Valley of California. You simply ride the backside of a big-rig, letting the truck run interference; all the while praying to God he doesn't run into anyone. Big-rig drivers refer to people who do this as "Bumper Stickers."

By the time the sun came up, we were in the western half of the state. It's pretty obvious why Kansas is known as the "Wheat State." Man, is there was a lot of it.

After crossing the Kansas-Colorado state line by early afternoon, we blew right past Denver on I-70. Almost immediately east of Denver are the Rocky Mountains and the elevation changes dramatically in height with each mile you travel. It had been a long day and I decided to stop at the closest town we came across, which turned out to be Silverthorne, Colorado.

We arrived in Silverthorne, which is about twenty miles east of Vail, at 5:30 p.m. Mountain Time under a bit of light rain and snow. Total mileage traveled by that time was 4722.5 and we'd been traveling on I-70 all the way from western Pennsylvania. We had logged right at 700 miles on that Saturday and I was beat. Jordan just needed to take a dump and have his dinner.

The Rocky Mountains are simply spectacular and there was already snow in the highest elevations. Silverthorne is very convenient, right off of I-70 and just east of Vail right at 8,730 feet in elevation. The town is situated between the Gore Range to the west and the Continental Divide to the east. It's a quaint place of small boutique shops, restaurants, gas stations, and convenience stores and is home to roughly 3,500 permanent residents. The standard dress code for locals appeared to be boots, Levi's or Wrangler's and Pendleton shirts for the men and pretty much the same for the women. The town was named after Judge Silverthorne, Summit County pioneer and judge from the late 1800s, known as "Hangin' Judge Silverthorne" for his strict demeanor. It's a pretty cool place, very similar in look and feel as South Lake Tahoe.

I gassed up the car for the final leg of the trip and found a quaint diner-saloon where I could grab a meal and e-mail back the photos and account of our trip between Kansas City and the Rockies. This was the one and only night of the trip we both stayed in the back of the car. I pulled the car around back of the restaurant, covered the windows as best I could and crawled in back next to Jordan. I was so jacked up about getting back home that I only slept until just before 10:30 p.m. on that Saturday night.

We left Silverthorne at 10:30 p.m. on September 28th, Mountain Time, under light to moderate rain. The outside temperature was right at 40 degrees and by the time we'd reached the Eisenhower Tunnel, the outside temperature had dropped enough that the rain turned to snow. The tunnel is really cool and it's right at the very top of the Rockies. Once you emerge out of the west end, you pretty much drop straight down to Grand Junction, Colorado. On the other side of the tunnel, the snow quickly turned to rain and it was still coming down when we stopped for gas and a bathroom break in Grand Junction. From there, I-70 took us across the Colorado-Utah state line and it was a straight shot across to I-15, marking the final leg of the trip. Unfortunately, we missed most of Monument Valley, where they used to film all those old westerns, as we drove across Utah in the dark. I got a couple of really cool pictures of Jordan just as dawn was arriving in western Utah. It was now day nine, the final day of our trip and I was feeling the adrenaline rush of our impending arrival back home in Las Vegas.

Just after dawn and right before we got to St. George, Utah the sky opened up with severe thunderstorms and I counted three jackknifed big-rigs on the side of the road. These turned out to be the scariest moments of the trip because at times the rain was coming down sideways and the winds made it very hard to keep the vehicle on the highway. Lightning lit up the early morning sky like the Fourth of July and at times it seemed the thunder was originating from inside our SUV. Fortunately, Jordan never had a fear of loud noises and he slept like a puppy through the entire event. I had a death grip with both hands on the wheel and I came close to pulling off the road on several occasions for fear of ruining the trip with a last day accident, or worse. But I was determined to keep going as I couldn't wait to get home. We had been on the road for eight-plus days and the fatigue and exhaustion of the trip was really wearing on me.

Speaking of noise, the only noise that ever scared Jordan was that of our vacuum cleaner at home. For some reason I never figured out, a vacuum cleaner was the one and only thing that could make Jordan freak out. Any time I started to vacuum, he'd head for the safety of the area under my bed. That was fine with me. I didn't like to vacuum and Jordan gave me an excuse not to do so unless company was coming over or things were starting to grow out of the carpet.

Then, just as quickly as the skies had opened up with the wrath of God near St. George, Utah, they cleared just east of the Nevada state line. We crossed over into Nevada just before 8:00 a.m. on that final Sunday morning, stopping briefly for a photo opportunity at the Casablanca Resort/Casino in Mesquite, Nevada. The Casablanca is one of several properties in Mesquite owned by Black Gaming in Las Vegas, a company that has been very supportive of my on-air trivia contests, "Fredericks Facts" by providing weekly getaway packages for both that property and their sister property, The Oasis.

Mesquite is a favorite golf, resort/gaming and vacation destination for people from Las Vegas, Utah, and several neighboring states. It was first settled by Mormon pioneers, incorporated in 1984 and is growing in population with transplanted Las Vegans and retirees who love golf, small-town living and the generally mild and dry climate. Merv Griffin was briefly involved in the resort development of Mesquite in the eighties and nineties.

We gassed up one last time in Mesquite and headed west on I-15 for the final eighty miles it would take to get us to our garage door. We continued west, under now clear skies on I-15, catching I-215 west, the north part of the Las Vegas "Beltway" just north of Vegas, and then we dropped south on U.S. 95 and were home in just over an hour.

We arrived in Las Vegas under sunny skies at 9:17 a.m. that Sunday, September 29, 2002. We had finished a journey of 5,428.6 miles. I got

Jordan out of the car and got my next door neighbor to take a picture of us in front of the bug-stained SUV, giving each other a celebratory high-four. Another photo that is only available in thumbnail size on our website.

Of all the supplies I purchased for our trip, the one that ended up being the most valuable was a simple compass. There are times, due to spatial disorientation, that you simply don't know if you're traveling north, south, east or west. So there would be times I'd hold up the compass to get my bearings. I think the thing cost me about $2 at Wal-Mart.

I can't remember a time when I was happier to be back home. I think Jordan felt it too as he couldn't wait to get inside and crash on the living room floor. We had just logged another 700 miles on that final day of our trip, mostly in the dark, and some of it through some pretty nasty weather. I was frazzled. However, the only casualty of the trip, besides breaking my thermos in Grand Junction, Colorado, was that I noticed part of the kitchen floor tile had buckled when we arrived back home, presumably from the heat as the central air conditioning was turned off for the entire trip and daytime temperatures were still averaging in the nineties in Las Vegas—another reason I later had to credit the buyers of my townhouse $1,000 for a flooring allowance.

After checking my mail and grabbing something to eat, I fell asleep on the couch and didn't wake up until the alarm clock went off the following Monday morning when it was time to go back to work. I knew then that I should've taken one more day off to recover, but the original plan was to get us back home on Saturday morning, not Sunday. But that idea was scrapped by about the third day of the journey. We wouldn't have even made it back by Sunday if we'd stuck with the original plan that included New Orleans in our travels.

The one thing I was sure of was that I would never attempt another trip like the one we just finished. Yeah, right. I was already planning "Paws Across America II" within weeks of returning home from the first trip.

Trip Summary:
- 5428.6 total miles driven
- 259.639 total gallons of gasoline consumed
- 20.91 average miles per gallon
- 17 states, plus the District of Columbia
- Zero speeding (or other) tickets
- 1 broken thermos

One final note about our trip in 2002: Before leaving, our station webmaster asked me if I had a name for our trip. For lack of a better one, I told him to title it: "Jordan's Trip." But sitting in the hotel room on day two in North Dallas, "Paws Across America" popped into my mind and that, as they say, is the rest of the story. I had remembered the old "Hands Across America" thing that took place back in 1986.

Hands Across America was a benefit event and publicity campaign staged on Sunday, May 25, 1986 in which approximately 7 million people held hands in a human chain for fifteen minutes along a path across the continental United States. Participants paid ten dollars to reserve their place in line; the proceeds were donated to local charities to fight hunger and homelessness and help those in poverty.

"Paws Across America," like "Hands Across America" seemed to have a cool ring to it. It would eventually become the name of our website, calendars, shirts, and hats to commemorate our trips and raise money for local animal causes. We would end up doing four Jordan-themed calendars and a half-dozen different shirts, sweatshirts and hats to commemorate the trips and his life. Thousands of dollars were raised through the sale of all of these items and I'm proud to say that lives were saved thanks to my best friend, Jordan.

CHAPTER 21
Dog Attack

When Jordan was young, in addition to our weekly jaunts around a local high school soccer field, I began taking him to run around at a local dog park, appropriately named "Woofter Park." It was a great place for Jordan because it really leveled the playing field. At the dog park he was just another dog. He wasn't a celebrity to the other dogs there; he was just another dog sniffing other dog's butt and vice versa. This, by the way is simply a dog's way of shaking hands. Can you imagine?

If a dog at the dog park tried anything aggressive toward Jordan, he would just ignore him. But if the dog persisted, Jordan would let the other dog know that their behavior was unacceptable. He would turn around and growl and the dog would leave him alone. Jordan was never aggressive. To my knowledge, Jordan was in a fight with another dog only two times in his life. Once was when I brought Chewy home and once when Jordan was in the dog run at the television station.

The television station owner had two Mastiffs, one male and one female. One day the owner brought his dogs to work with him and let them play in the dog run. During one of my breaks, I took Jordan out to do his business and play in the dog run. The female Mastiff attacked the male Mastiff, then turned on Jordan. She ripped part of his ear. Jordan immediately went after her. He grabbed her by the neck and flipped her upside down into a submissive position. Mastiff dogs can easily exceed 150 pounds in size and this particular female Mastiff was close to that. And, while I don't condone dog fighting, I was proud of my boy for standing up for himself. When the station owner learned that his dog had attacked Jordan, he immediately had her removed from the premises He loved Jordan and he wouldn't tolerate anything bad happening to him.

On a Saturday morning in late August, 2003, when Jordan was nine years old, he and I went to our usual dog park: Woofter. We'd been spending less time at the dog park and more time with each other at our favorite high school soccer parks. But dogs are pack animals and Jordan was still young and spry enough to want to run with the pack on occasion. It was a hot August morning with the temperatures still in the eighties, despite it being right at sunrise. The dog park we visited was only about a five-minute drive from our house and is one of the oldest parks designated specifically for dogs in Las Vegas. The people there, in most cases, are outgoing and friendly and go as much for human social interaction as for canine interaction.

On this particular morning, only a couple of dogs were there running around playing. One dog was pretty wild, trying to pick fights with the few other dogs there. Two of the other dogs there that morning were brother and sister. The brother wanted to play with me. His sister came up to us and without warning bit my leg and drew blood. The owner of the dog, seeing the blood running down my leg turned to me and said, "Oh, she'll do that when she gets jealous." I knew at that moment there was no sense in trying to explain to her that her dog's behavior was unacceptable, so I just walked away. Some dog owners simply don't understand a very basic element of dog obedience training: Dogs only do what we allow them to do. Period.

While I was dealing with the owner of the dog that had bit me, the dog that was being aggressive with the few other dogs in the park decided to irritate a huge dog that must have weighed well over one hundred pounds. I don't think disclosing the big dog's breed is important because any dog can be aggressive, big or small. But the big ones are usually the ones that, if aggressive, do the most damage. Still, I firmly believe that a dog only behaves in a way that is accepted and condoned by its owner.

On Location LIVE with Dad 0503

By this time, the big dog and the aggressive, small dog were snarling and snapping at one another. Jordan walked over to see what was going on and before I knew it, the bigger of the two bit his back and wouldn't release his grip. Jordan let out a yelp. Fortunately, he was smart enough to go down on all fours into a submissive position. I ran over to break up the altercation and thankfully the other dog let go. I didn't know if Jordan was hurt until I saw blood running down his side. When I moved his fur I saw a big, deep puncture wound. I was livid. I screamed at the big dog's owner and told him he would be responsible for Jordan's medical expenses. The guy mouthed off that we were in a dog park and "dogs will be dogs." Then, in one of the few instances of my broadcasting life, I lost my temper and started screaming at the guy, telling him he was responsible for his dog's actions; dogs only do what we let them do and he needed to immediately give me his contact information so I could bill him for Jordan's medical expenses. The guy was at least fifty yards away from us so I was yelling all of this stuff at the top of my lungs. I interlaced my tirade with some pretty harsh language that I'm not very proud of. I was pissed. But my behavior that morning was questionable, at best. The only other lady at the park that morning was standing next to the guy I was yelling at and I could see her talking to him, trying to reason with him. It must have worked. Eventually the guy gave in and agreed to give me his contact information and to pay for Jordan's medical expenses.

Jordan Back of Car Along Hwy 101 July 2003

Let me be very clear on this issue of aggressive dogs. Any dog can be aggressive, if we let them. Yes, some dogs are more prone to aggressive behavior, but that can be corrected if we catch it at an early age. Pit bulls get a bad rap in this country. Yes, they are powerful dogs and they can be killing machines. However, by nature they're also some of the sweetest dogs in the world. Pit bulls just happen to be the flavor of the week. In the sixties and seventies the German shepherd had the reputation for being aggressive. Then came the doberman. Next up was the rottweiler. Today, the pit bull is public enemy number one. Unfortunately, too many people get pit bulls for the wrong reason: to fight. I am not a professional dog trainer, behaviorist or veterinarian. The only thing I claim to be is a responsible pet owner and I think people who allow or train their pets to maim or hurt another animal or human being should be personally charged with whatever crime their dog commits.

I raced Jordan to my vet's office, Sahara Pines Animal Hospital here in Las Vegas. Our vet, Dr. Kristine Ziegler, told me the wound was very deep and she would have to put Jordan under a general anaesthetic to do internal stitches. I trusted Dr. Kristine's judgment implicitly. I still do to this day. However, Jordan was nine years old and I was concerned that he might not wake back up after the surgery. Thankfully, he did.

On a previous visit to Dr. Kristine's office, she noticed Jordan was getting some fatty tissue build up. Fatty tissue deposits, usually located just under the skin, are very common in older dogs and vary greatly in size. They can be anywhere from the size of a breath mint to a baseball, or bigger. But unless they're malignant or start moving around they're usually not a health issue. At the time the fatty tissues were discovered, Dr. Kristine wasn't too concerned about having them removed as they weren't harming Jordan. More importantly, she had done a biopsy on one and found it to be a benign growth. Now that Jordan was going to go under anaesthesia for the internal stitches, Dr. Kristine recommended removing the fatty tissue deposits, as well. This way Jordan wouldn't have to be put under if the fatty tissues became an issue in the future.

Dr. Ziegler removed a total of six fatty tissue deposits, requiring her to shave the area around each spot on Jordan's body before she could perform each tissue removal. When I brought Jordan home later that day he looked like a patchwork quilt. Knowing that we would soon be going on another road trip and I'd be taking tons of pictures of him again in front of famous landmarks, I knew I would have to do some creative photography to keep all of the shaved areas hidden in the photos.

That was the last time I took Jordan to a dog park. While he never had any long-term effects from the puncture wound, I thought it was in his best interest to never put him in harm's way again. After all, not only was he my dog but he was a local celebrity and I knew if I ever let anything bad happen to him the public would never forgive me. Nor would I ever forgive myself.

CHAPTER 22

Paws Across America II
Mt. Rushmore

Our second Paws Across America trip was to Mt. Rushmore, located in the Black Hills of South Dakota. I wanted the final destination for our second big road trip to be somewhere in the U.S. that screamed patriotism like our first trip to Washington, D.C. the previous year. Plus, I'd wanted to see Mt. Rushmore ever since I was kid. Now I'd have my chance.

Planning this trip was much easier because Jordan and I already had one trip under our belt. I mapped out our trip so we could drive through Death Valley, Yosemite National Park, San Francisco, Seattle, then across and down to Yellowstone National Park to see Old Faithful and then east to Mt. Rushmore. Not wanting to make the mistake of having less than twenty-four hours of recovery time as with the 2002 trip, I wanted to get back to Las Vegas in seven days so Jordan and I would have a couple of days to recover before we had to go back to work.

The other thing I wanted was for us to travel around the same time as in 2002—late September. Even though we got hammered by remnants of Hurricane Isadore the previous year and September is in the middle of the Atlantic hurricane season, early fall is historically a good time for fair weather across the United States, especially the western states and we wouldn't be driving anywhere near the Atlantic Ocean. I put in my vacation request with my boss for the last week of September and the approved paperwork came back to me in just a few days. I was really jacked up about the upcoming 2003 trip in the weeks and days leading up to it as I knew it wouldn't be as long as our 2002 trip, and that it most likely would be our last long trip together. Jordan, like any other retriever, was pretty much jacked up by life in general so I knew he'd be ready and rarin' to go as soon as I loaded him in the back of the SUV.

The biggest obstacle facing us in planning for the 2003 trip was financing. Being pathetic at personal finance and budgetary issues, I'd blown through whatever money was left over from the refinance of our home in 2002, so I was going to have to do some creative financing for this trip. A friend of mine bought me a few Shell gas cards as a gift for the trip, but they'd only get me a few hundred miles. Other gas charges could be floated on the American Express extended payment option, but there was the issue of food and boarding. Fortunately, the night before we were planning on leaving Las Vegas, I served as emcee for a private event that paid a decent talent fee. They paid me with a check and I would have to search downtown San Francisco two days into the trip for a bank that would cash it. But that talent fee check would give me some breathing room on daily expenses. As for lodging, we only ended up spending two of the nights in hotel rooms—once in San Francisco and the following night in Seattle. And because I have a good relationship with our local JW Marriott, the folks I deal with at our local properties were nice enough to put in a good word for us with their sister properties in the other two cities, where we got very good room rates for each night. So, we were set. All I had to do was drive over 4,000 miles in seven days. Piece of cake, right?

We left Las Vegas at 3:00 a.m. on Friday, September 19, 2003 and headed northwest to San Francisco, by way of Death Valley and Yosemite. We traveled over 730 miles our first day.

We reached Death Valley right around dawn. Anywhere in the desert is beautiful at sunrise and Death Valley is no different. Death Valley National Park is the lowest, driest and hottest valley in the United States. At 282 feet below sea level, it also has the lowest elevation in North America. It holds the record for the highest reliably reported temperature in the Western Hemisphere, 134 degrees Fahrenheit at Furnace Creek in 1913. It is located southeast of the Sierra Nevada range in the Great Basin and the Mojave Desert, mostly in Inyo County, California.

We got through Death Valley via Highway 374, and then caught U.S. 395 which runs north and south along the eastern base of the Sierras. The conditions were perfect and the weather was simply spectacular. I remember thinking, just as we got through Death Valley, that there was "no turning back now." Thoughts of fatigue and exhaustion from the first trip had been floating around in my head for the first few hours that morning and it wasn't until we were on the western side of Death Valley that I became determined to make it through this second trip.

Once clear of Death Valley, we gassed up in Lone Pine on U.S. 395 and from there traveled through Mammoth Lakes, Mono Lake, turned on to Highway 120 and made it to the Tioga Pass entrance of Yosemite at 11:00 a.m.

When we hit Highway 120, which is about right in the middle of the eastern side of Sierra Nevada Mountains in California, we hung a left and climbed into Yosemite National Park from the backside at the east entrance, at Tioga Pass. The surroundings became more densely populated with trees as we climbed in elevation and we made it to the guard gate and Tioga Pass. Now heading west through Yosemite's high country, we soon entered the Tuolumne Meadows area and Tenaya Lake. I was in this same area on a YMCA camping trip in July 1969 during the same week Neil Armstrong first stepped foot on the moon. The other memorable and historic event that week in 1969? A bear spent part of the night sleeping on my duffel bag, which was about six inches above the sleeping bag that I was in. I didn't have any food in my duffel, so I guess the bear just thought it was a nice pillow for him to rest on for a while. The thing smelled of wet fur and he occasionally belched or farted. I stayed as still as possible, head

Yosemite Valley of Ice and Yosemite River
September 2003

tucked inside my sleeping bag. He finally heard or smelled something more inviting off in the distance and lumbered off.

Yosemite National Park is a park located in the eastern portions of Tuolumne, Mariposa, and Madera counties in east central California. The park covers an area of 761,266 acres or 1,189 square miles and reaches across the western slopes of the Sierra Nevada mountain chain. Yosemite is visited by over 3.5 million people each year, many of whom only spend time in the seven square miles of Yosemite Valley. Designated a World Heritage Site in 1984, Yosemite is internationally recognized for its spectacular granite cliffs, waterfalls, clear streams, giant sequoia groves and biological diversity. Almost 95 percent of the park is designated wilderness. Although not the first designated national park, Yosemite was a focal point in the development of the national park idea, largely owing to the work of people like John Muir and Galen Clark.

Yellostone's Old Faithful, September 2003

We continued west through Yosemite and started dropping in elevation, making a big, sweeping turn that took us to the western entrance of the park, home of the famed Valley of Ice, with El Capitan on the left, Half Dome on the right and the expansive Yosemite Valley below. I wanted to get a shot of Jordan in front of the Valley of Ice and managed to get some really cool pictures. That cheap, digital camera had become a real asset in the Fredericks' household.

By the time we left Yosemite, it was getting quite warm and late, as we'd already chewed up more than twelve hours and would end up spending seventeen hours on the road that first day.

SF Fishermans Wharf with Alcatraz in Distance
September 2003

When we got to San Francisco's Fisherman's Wharf, by way of the San Mateo Bridge, the sun was setting over the Pacific Ocean and it was nice to be back near the water. Seeing the Pacific Ocean never gets old to me. When I was a kid growing up in the San Fernando Valley in Southern California, my buddies and I would routinely take the bus down to Venice Beach each summer back in the '60s.

Although the Marriot at Fisherman's Wharf is pet-friendly, they have a policy of charging a $100 deposit for each pet per night that stays there. When I was informed of this charge while trying to check us in, I protested and asked to speak to a supervisor. He agreed to waive the deposit but warned me that I'd be responsible for the hotel charges for guests on either side of our room if Jordan was disruptive. At that, I started laughing. When he asked me what was so funny I told them there was a better chance they'd be paying our room charges. I took my key and walked Jordan right through their beautiful lobby on the way to our room. Since he had already gone potty right when we arrived at Fisherman's Wharf, I got him fed and then secured in our hotel room bed, and I headed out for a brief walk to get something to eat and get my bearings for the photo shoot that Saturday morning. The air was damp and the fog was starting to roll in.

SF Marriott Suite
September 2003

When I got back to our room, Jordan was sleeping soundly in the middle of the bed and I got out the laptop and got to work with an account of the day's events and to upload the day's photos to send back to the TV station.

The next morning was Saturday, so we had Fisherman's Wharf to ourselves, save for a few maintenance workers. The fog was lifting as the sun came up and I got some great shots of Jordan in front of a trolley car, Pier 37, a bunch of lounging seals and Alcatraz Island and prison off in the distance of the San Francisco Bay.

Golden Gate Bridge, September 2003

San Francisco is the fourth most populous city in California and the fourteenth most populous in the United States with an estimated population just under 800,000. The entire San Francisco Bay area is home to over 7 million residents. The city is located at the tip of the San Francisco Peninsula with the Pacific Ocean to the west, San Francisco Bay to the east and the Golden Gate to the north. In 1776, the Spanish settled the tip of the peninsula and built a mission there for Francis of Assisi. The gold rush in 1848 propelled the city into a period of rapid growth, transforming it into the largest city in the west at the time. After being devastated by the great San Francisco fire in 1906, the city was quickly rebuilt. San Francisco is a popular international tourist destination, famous for its landmarks, including the Golden Gate Bridge, Alcatraz Island, little cable cars that "climb halfway to the stars," Chinatown, its steep rolling hills and its eclectic mix of old and new architecture.

After getting the pictures of Jordan we wandered around the Wharf for a short while longer. We then walked back to the hotel, checked out and drove to Ghirardelli Square—home of those delicious chocolate confections—for some more photos and then we headed north to Golden Gate Park for still more. On the way to Golden Gate Park, I found a bank that was open and cashed the talent fee check I'd gotten the night before the trip began so I now had a little "walking around" money. I wasn't sure how far north we'd get that day but I knew I wanted us to make Seattle by the following morning, Sunday, September 21. So we left Golden Gate Park after less than twenty minutes and headed north to the south entrance to the Golden Gate Bridge—Vista Point—one of two great places to view the bridge and take pictures. The other viewing area is on the north side of the bridge. By now it was close to noon and Jordan was starting to get tired as we'd been up since around 3:00 a.m., watching TV and surfing the Internet. Well, he was watching TV and I was doing the surfing. I got him out of the car on both sides of the bridge, but due to the sun angle, the best shots were from the south side. As I got him ready for his close-ups, tourists started gathering around and cheering us on—for me to get the perfect shot of Jordan in front of the bridge and at Jordan for, well, just being so darned cute. With his tongue hanging out and dressed in his favorite red, white, and blue bandana he did look absolutely adorable. I snapped off several photos of him with the bridge as the backdrop, tourists cheering all the while.

I got him back in the SUV and we crossed the bridge and, after a few shots on the north side, we headed north on Highway 101 for parts and points unknown. Just on the north side of the bridge, the accelerator in the SUV stuck wide open and the car accelerated to over 100 mph. Panicked about what to do, I finally thought to turn the key off. However, that meant no power steering and I had to really fight to get the car off to the center median. Traffic was really heavy and I couldn't believe we didn't get hit by another car and killed. After a couple of tries, the car started without being stuck on full-throttle and we got back into traffic without the cruise control on. The cruise stuck once more in Montana so, after the second incident, I didn't use it for the rest of the trip. I later found out that there was a spot that the accelerator cable was catching on and it didn't have anything to do with the cruise control. The accelerator stuck once more with my buddy John Tutora behind the wheel the following year and he ended up driving right through our townhouse front gate. The car was fine but the gate was toast and it cost us $1,000 to get it fixed.

Back out on the road on day two, we quickly entered the beautiful Redwood State Park, marveling at the majestic redwood trees that tower over Highway 101, forming beautiful canopies over the highway making it hard to focus on the road ahead. Soon the trees and highway opened back up to the Pacific Ocean and seeing the water again gave me a second wind for the rest of the day's journey

It started getting late in the afternoon and the sun was getting low over the Pacific to the west as we continued north on Highway 101, and I pulled off the road to find a logical stopping point for the evening. It turned out we were about two hours south of Crescent City, California and I decided to stop there even though that meant we would've traveled only 430 miles that second day. That was fine with me because we went over 700 miles the first day, meaning it would average out.

Crescent City is named for the crescent-shaped stretch of sandy beach south of the city. As of the 2000 census, the city had a total population of 4,006, not including the 3,300 prisoners at nearby Pelican Bay State Prison. Crescent City is also the site of the headquarters of Redwood State Park.

We got off Highway 101 at the Crescent City exit and found a decent-looking motor inn with an adjacent restaurant within a few blocks from the highway. The rooms were set back from the road and because they didn't say anything about pets, I didn't ask and snuck Jordan into our room under the veil of darkness. I fed him and walked over to the restaurant for some dinner of my own. I got back to the room and when I got the laptop out to write my account of the day's events and upload photos of Jordan, I realized I must have left the cable that connects the camera to the laptop at the Marriott in San Francisco. I panicked. I thought this was a proprietary item—one that is only available through the manufacturer—and that I might have to buy new software or even a new camera. As it turned out, the cable was a very common item and I found a replacement at a Best Buy in Seattle the following Sunday morning. I also learned from the kid who was helping me at Best Buy that my camera had been set on the lowest resolution setting ever since I'd bought it the previous year. That meant all of the photos from the 2002 trip were taken at the lowest quality, and yet they turned out great. The kid at Best Buy showed me how to change the setting and I did notice a dramatic difference in quality after that.

We got an early start from Crescent City. After a great night's sleep in that quiet, comfortable motor inn room, I awoke wide awake and well rested around 1:30 a.m. that morning, Sunday, September 21, 2003, the third day of our second cross-country trip. I fed Jordan, loaded him and our belongings into our SUV, caught Highway 101 and headed north. Our goal was to make Seattle by mid-morning so I could get pictures of Jordan in front of Elliott Bay and the Space Needle, and then check into our hotel room.

Crescent City is about an hour south of the California-Oregon state line and proved to be a good jumping off point for that leg of the trip. The plan was to take 101 north, cross into southern Oregon and then connect to State Route 199 that runs through Grant's Pass and connects to Interstate 5. I-5 would be a straight shot north through Portland and then on to Seattle.

The biggest downside to getting an early start that Sunday morning was that we were forced to negotiate Grant's Pass on our way to Oregon. Grant's Pass is a beautiful mountainous area in southwest Oregon lined with towering redwoods and littered with mountain communities that seem to pop up about every five miles. The speed limits drop dramatically through each of these towns and were designed, no doubt, as speed traps to line the city coffers with money from speeding tickets. At night, Grant's

Pass is a treacherous stretch of winding, narrow mountain roads where the speed limit rarely gets above fifty-five miles per hour and constantly and quickly drops to twenty-five miles per hour as you pass through the many small towns along the way. As for the speed traps: it was during our drive through Grant's Pass that we had our one and only encounter with John Law, better known as a Josephine County Sheriff's deputy.

I was trying to make good time—whatever that means—and I wasn't paying very close attention to my speed. About half way through the Pass, we were barreling through one of the small towns, far exceeding the posted speed limit. There didn't seem to be another car on the road and then, right at that moment, headlights came at us from up ahead. As soon as the car got to us, I realized it was a black and white, and sure enough, the officer made a quick u-turn and hit us immediately with his roof lights. I pulled over, got out my license, registration, insurance card and waited for a lecture and a notice to appear. Jordan, now awake from the stopping of the car, was up toward the front of the SUV wondering what was going on. The officer turned out to be a young guy who was actually very nice and respectful. He asked for my documentation, went back to the cruiser and made sure we had no outstanding wants or warrants, and then came back to our SUV, whereupon he asked what my hurry was and I told him about our trip. He seemed to think that was pretty cool, told me he had a dog that looked like Jordan, to slow down and that this was my lucky day as he let us off with a verbal warning—no doubt because I had acted contrite and respectful. And our SUV had Nevada license plates.

This is a good point to mention something about out-of-state driving trips: people notice your license plate and where you're from because most of the people in each state have local plates. Now if you're from California and you're driving anywhere in the Pacific Northwest, those California plates are not your friend. Californians are universally despised in many other surrounding western states. And in all honesty, except for us happily taking their gambling dollars, Californians aren't too welcome in Nevada either. There's something about that Golden State plate that raises the hackles of other states' residents, most likely because people from California are known for their aggressive driving and are often thought to be just plain arrogant. I can say this because I'm from California, even though I don't consider myself either arrogant or an aggressive driver. I was, however, on the receiving end of some rude gestures and single-fingered-salutes when we first moved to Nevada in 1996, before I re-registered my car and got Nevada plates. The point to all of this is that I'm convinced that the treatment we received during our travels, in general, and with that officer specifically, would probably not have been as positive had we been sporting California plates. Just saying.

Back on the road and back to the speed limit, we finally got through Grant's Pass and made it to the I-5 northbound junction right around 5:00 a.m. We were low on gas, so I found the nearest station and pulled up to the pump. I figured Jordan needed a potty break, so I let him out to do his business as I reached for the gas nozzle. It was then I learned a rather interesting fact: Oregon and New Jersey are the only states in the country that require gas station attendants to pump your gas. As soon as I reached for the nozzle, an attendant came running out of the station office yelling at me that he had to pump my gas, explaining the law both there and in New Jersey. Lawmakers in both states apparently don't think drivers have enough sense to keep from blowing themselves up by dispensing their own fuel. I'm not making this up. Fines for pumping your own gas in these two states can be upwards of $500. The guy wouldn't even take a tip from me. So I thanked him, loaded Jordan back in the SUV, caught I-5 north and we were on our way to Seattle.

We continued north on I-5 and made it to Portland right after sunrise, never slowing down. Portland is a really cool looking city, located near the confluence of the Willamette and Columbia Rivers. There is a whole bunch of water running through the city. The population is close to 600,000 and it has been referred to as the greenest city in the United States. Portland is

Oregon's most populous city.

We arrived in downtown Seattle just before noon, after stopping first at the aforementioned Best Buy for a new camera cable. The skies were brilliant with sunshine and the sun glistened off Puget Sound and Elliott Bay. The city was buzzing with activity and a parking spot was hard to find. The Seahawks had a home game against the Rams so the whole area was jammed. I was not a Seattle virgin, having spent forty-five days living just outside of the city with my cousin Ray in 1991, while I was unemployed. During that time, I would catch the bus

Pike Place Fish Market, Seattle, September 21, 2003

downtown each day looking for work. I would walk the downtown area each afternoon, spending a lot of time around the Pike Place Fish Market area and historic Pioneer Square.

Seattle is a beautiful ocean-side city that sits atop rolling hills surrounded by water, concrete, trees, and buildings and homes, both big and small. A port city, it is located in the western part of the state between Puget Sound, an arm of the Pacific Ocean, and Lake Washington about ninety-five miles south of the Canada-United States border. A major economic, cultural, and educational center in the region, Seattle is the largest city in the state of Washington with over 3 million people living in the metropolitan area. Seattle residents are known as Seattleites. The city is the birthplace of grunge music, with bands like Pearl Jam and Nirvana, and has a reputation for heavy coffee consumption. Coffee companies founded or based in Seattle include Starbucks, Seattle's Best Coffee, and Tully's.

Our first stop was the harbor where I got some great shots of Jordan looking out over Elliott Bay. We crossed the street and climbed what seemed to be hundreds of stairs, as the harbor is actually a few hundred feet below

Space Needle, Seattle, September 21, 2003

the Pike Place market area. While climbing those stairs to Pike Place, I noticed that Jordan was really laboring, and I realized my boy was getting on in years and how happy I was to have gone through with these trips with him. It also made me a bit sad. But my mood brightened when I got him up to the Pike Place Fish Market, home of the world famous fish-throwing workers. No one seemed to mind that a dog was walking around among a ton of fish and other fresh foods. I'm sure we were violating all sorts of local health codes, but we pressed on without interruption or incident. I got the attention of one of the employees, slipped him a $5 bill and got a few pictures of him kneeling next to Jordan and holding a humongous fish.

Getting back down the steps to our SUV proved to be much easier. Because it was getting a bit late in the day and I was growing a little fatigued, I decided to head over to the Space Needle, get some pictures and then check into our hotel room and wrap up the day.

The Space Needle, dating from the Century 21 Exposition (1962), is Seattle's most recognizable landmark, having been featured in the logo of the television show *Frazier*, and in the backgrounds of the television series *Grey's Anatomy* and films such as *Sleepless in Seattle*.

Getting both Jordan and the Space Needle in the same frame proved to be a challenge and a real education, and I discovered a technique that I would use again the following year in front of the Stratosphere Tower in Las Vegas. I found a good spot in the grassy area in front of the Needle and had Jordan sit in front of me. Next I had to lay down on my back, looking straight up at Jordan in the foreground and the Needle rising skyward in the background. It never ceased to amaze me what a great photo subject he was. He was always patient, cooperative, would pose and always come up with the appropriate expression just at the right moment. We got some great photos at the Space Needle and, having put another 550 miles on the trip odometer, I decided it was time for some rest. We had already passed the 1,600 mile mark and we were only three days into a seven-day journey.

The Lake Union Residence Inn we stayed in overlooked the Elliott Bay, made famous in *Sleepless in Seattle*, as this was where the character played by Tom Hanks had his houseboat moored. This was another Marriott property, and the Marriott people I worked with in Vegas had already greased the skids, so the desk personnel and management at the property in Seattle were all ready for us with a spacious room on the third floor, overlooking the hotel's center atrium. It was a beautiful property and the staff there made us feel right at home. We got situated in our room and I decided to venture out to see if I could find a place near the bay where I could grab a cold drink and order some food to go. I had two days of journal entries and photos to upload, so I wanted to get back to the room as soon as possible.

Directly across from our hotel was a beautiful mall area right along

Elliott Bay filled with shops and restaurants. I found a Mexican restaurant, ordered some take-out and watched some football on TV. The restaurant had a beautiful view of the bay and I enjoyed relaxing and watching the boats enter and leave the harbor.

I got back to the room shortly before sunset and Jordan ate his dinner while I ate mine. I took care of the work I needed to do on the computer, checking the forecast for our trip Monday morning. Then I took Jordan for a walk so he could stretch his legs and take care of business, and day three was a history lesson.

Monday morning, September 22, the last full day of summer, we checked out of our room in Seattle and loaded up the SUV. I fed and walked Jordan and of both us got into the vehicle. I decided to head back downtown to get some early morning pictures at Pioneer Square before hopping on Interstate 90 to begin our journey east. I wanted to get some final photos of Jordan before the morning rush hour commute got going, as I didn't want to get struck in morning traffic. We had to move as it was already past 6:30 a.m.

Pioneer Square is the spot where Seattle was originally settled and is now home to art galleries, Internet companies, cafés, sports bars, nightclubs, bookstores and a unit of the Klondike Gold Rush National Historical Park. It is often described as the center of Seattle's nightlife. We wandered around Pioneer Square for a few minutes and it took me back to my days there in 1991—unemployed and broke—and I decided it was time to get going as I had no intention of starting our day in a sour mood.

It was just after 7:00 a.m. and the roads were starting to jam with the Monday morning commute. We jumped into the fray and negotiated our way from I-5 to I-90 and headed east. This was strictly a travel day to get us closer to our next photo destination spot: Yellowstone National Park in Wyoming. The goal for this Monday was to drive east through western Washington and Idaho, and stop for the night in Missoula, Montana.

Before long the sun was rising and so were we, cruising toward

Snoqualmie Pass and Summit which rises some 3,000 feet in the Cascade Range. The Pass is beautiful and I-90 is wide and divided and immaculately maintained. The Cascade Range is dense and the western slopes are covered with Douglas Fir, Western Hemlock and Red Alder trees. By the way, the most famous peaks in the Cascade Range are Mt. Rainier and Mount St. Helens. Locals in and around the Seattle have a favorite expression when consuming their hometown brew: "Round here, it's Rainier."

On the Road in Eastern Washington, September 22, 2003

Once we were on the leeward, or eastern side of the Cascade Mountains, the topography changed immediately and dramatically from tall mountain trees to rolling, grassy hills and valleys. The hills and valleys were covered with long yellow grass, dying in the fall air and waving in the morning breezes. Western Washington was still beautiful—only different—almost like it was an entirely different state.

By mid-morning we crossed the Columbia River and Gorge, which is wide, expansive and spectacular. The Columbia River is the largest river in the Pacific Northwest and named after the Columbia Rediviva, the first ship from the western world known to have traveled up the river. It stretches from the Canadian Province of British Columbia through the Washington State, forming much of the border between Washington and Oregon, before emptying into the Pacific Ocean. The river is 1,243 miles long and its drainage basin is 258,000 square miles.

Once on the eastern side of the river, I stopped at a scenic lookout so I could take a few pictures and a break. Back out on I-90, heading east, I looked in the rearview mirror and noticed Jordan right behind me looking out the front window, just as happy as he could be to be out on the open road with his daddy. I reached back and grabbed the camera, located in the a pocked organizer behind the passenger seat, turned it on, held it out in front of us and took a self-portrait of the two of us. It has since become one of my most cherished memories of that trip in 2003 and it is part of a three-photo collage that occupies a special place in our living area to this day.

Being a Monday morning—a school and workday—there were few other cars on the road, so traffic was not an issue. We drove right through Spokane, Washington without stopping, as I estimated we had enough fuel to make it to Coeur d'Alene, Idaho. Coeur d'Alene would be the next logical where we could stop for gas, a potty break and a snack at a convenience center just west of the city.

It was at this stop that I realized my American Express card was missing from my billfold and I searched the entire vehicle for it without luck. Fortunately, we were at a Shell Gas convenience center, so I used one of my Shell Gas cards to fill up, got back on I-90 heading east and immediately called the toll-free number for American Express to report a lost or stolen card and find out about a replacement. After the nice lady on the other end of the line informed me the card had been canceled and there were no new charges after the last one at the restaurant at Elliott Bay in Seattle, she let me know the closest place to get a temporary card was at a real estate office in Bozeman, Montana. I pulled off to the side of the road, which happened to be next to Lake Coeur d'Alene, and checked my road atlas to see how far out of the way Bozeman would take us. As it turned out, Bozeman was a good jumping off point to drop down into the northwest entrance to Yellowstone, the following day's destination. The American Express lady told me they partnered with businesses all over the world to issue cards and traveler's checks in case of a situation like ours. She ended the call by letting me know the office in Bozeman would be open at 8:00 a.m. the following morning and she would fax the necessary paperwork immediately to them so they could issue me a new, temporary card. I thanked her and, having ended the call, got out of the SUV and took some pictures of Jordan looking out the back window at Lake Coeur d'Alene, which is simply breathtaking.

Coeur d'Alene, with a population of just over 35,000 as of the year 2000, is located about thirty miles east of Spokane, Washington, which, combined with Coeur d'Alene and northern Idaho, has a population of about 600,000. Coeur d'Alene is also the largest city in the northern Idaho Panhandle. Coeur d'Alene is located at the northern end of Lake Coeur d'Alenea, a thirty-mile long lake. Locally, Coeur d'Alene is known as "Lake City." French Canadian fur traders allegedly named the local Indian tribe the Coeur d'Alene out of respect for their tough trading practices. Translated from French, "Coeur d'Alene" literally means "heart of the awl," which might mean "sharp-hearted" or "shrewd." Another possibility is that the name is a corruption of Coeur de Leon, or Lion Heart. Others interpret "Heart of the Awl" to translate to "Eye of the Needle," perhaps referring to the narrow passage through which the lake empties into the Spokane River on its way to the Columbia.

Knowing that we'd have a new credit card by the following morning calmed my frazzled nerves, and we got back on I-90 east and were quickly across the Montana state line. We had just about an hour drive southeast on the interstate to Missoula. It was during this final stretch of our Monday travels that I decided to risk a chance and see if I could use the cruise control without incident. No dice. The accelerator immediately stuck wide-open, and we were soon barreling down I-90 reaching speeds of over 90 miles per hour before I could, once again turn the key off and force the SUV to the side of the road. I got the car restarted without incident, told myself that was the end of the cruise control for the trip, and traveled on to Missoula without further incident.

The road was now lined with trees that had yet to turn color in the early fall and our surroundings were green, lush and beautiful. I-90 is a well maintained interstate and we cruised into Missoula, arriving at 4:16 p.m. that afternoon under a brilliant, blue Montana skyline and an 80-degree outside temperature. Logging just over another 500 miles for the trip, the trip odometer now read 2,143.2. My only goal at this point was to find a place to sleep, eat and get Jordan fed, pooped and peed and settled in for the night. We were in for a big day the following Tuesday, September 23rd, as I had delusions that I could actually make it to both Yellowstone and Mt. Rushmore in one day. I was wrong. You'll find out why in the paragraphs to come. I would also come to find out that I had taken my last shower of the trip earlier that Monday morning in Seattle. They say you're the last one to smell your own stank, and that certainly was true in my case during the rest of our trip. I never sensed I was smelling foul. And if Jordan noticed it, he held his tongue, and breath.

As of the 2000 census, the population of the Missoula metropolitan statistical area was 95,802, making it the second-largest city and metropolitan area in Montana. Missoula is the home of the University of Montana and the birthplace of Jeanette Rankin (1880–1973), the first woman elected to the U.S. Congress. Missoula is nicknamed the Garden City. It is also the place where much of the Robert Redford movie, one of my favorites, *A River Runs Through It* was filmed along the Big Blackfoot

River. That was why I wanted to stop in Missoula—to see the river and place where the movie was shot.

As it turned out, the university campus and most of the commerce was divided by the Big Blackfoot River, so I didn't have to venture far to find what I was looking for. I drove up and down the main drag of town looking for a reasonably priced, pet-friendly hotel or motor inn. Having no luck, I parked the SUV on the side of a restaurant-saloon-pool hall and Jordan and I walked down to the edge of the river to take a few photos. Then we wandered around the campus until the sun started to sink behind the hills to the east. We got back to the SUV when it was still light enough to get Jordan fed and down for the night. I grabbed my road atlas and went into the saloon to map out the next day's journey and grab a bite to drink and eat. The place was crowded with loud, boisterous college kids and, though I enjoyed their youthful enthusiasm for about three minutes, it was all I could do to muster up enough patience to wait for my food order and take it back to our quiet SUV. Having no luck finding a place to stay for the night, I ate my dinner in the driver's seat of the SUV and decided it was finally time to suck it up and crawl in back to sleep alongside my boy. Jordan had come to enjoy a space of his own and didn't seem the least bit happy to be sharing it with dear old Dad. Too bad, old boy. My lodging choices had turned out to be slim to none for that evening. And slim had just left the building. After covering the windows with makeshift drapes, I crawled into my sleeping bag and fell asleep next to Jordan almost as soon as my head hit our pillow. And despite the cramped quarters and Jordan's snoring, I had a restful seven hours of sleep and woke up wide awake at 2:00 a.m. that following Tuesday, September 23.

After our breakfast, Jordan and I both answered nature's call and we were off and running, under clear skies and a cool outside temperature of 50 degrees. We stopped off at a Denny's near town right around when fall officially arrived, at 2:47 a.m. so I could grab a cup of coffee and do the summary for day four. I also wanted to see how much ground we'd have to cover to make it to Mt. Rushmore by that Tuesday afternoon. A lot.

We jumped back on I-90 heading southeast, determined to make it to Bozeman and that travel office when they opened that morning at 8:00 a.m.

With a population of 27,509 at the 2000 census, Bozeman is the fifth largest city in the state. The city is named after John M. Bozeman, founder of the Bozeman Trail. It is home to Montana State University, Bozeman. Bozeman residents are known as Bozemanites. We made it to Bozeman just after 8:00 a.m. and—having been given the address of the place we needed to find Montana Travel—we found their office within minutes of arriving in town. The people there had already received the paperwork from American Express and immediately made me a temporary card.

We were back in business, and back out on the open Montana road. And though I was relieved to have a new card and was no longer in jeopardy of running out of money, I would find that temporary cards can't be swiped in

Gallatin River Southwestern Montana, September 23, 2003

machines or gas station pumps and I would be forced to have to go inside each location to have the clerk or attendant check my ID and take down the card number and enter it into their cash registers. It was a hassle and cost a bit of time during the remainder of the journey, but the alternative of having no card would mean we'd run out of money well before getting back to Las Vegas.

We left I-90 and headed south on I-191 to the West Yellowstone entrance, stopping only twice; once to take some pictures of Jordan alongside the rolling hills of western Montana and once more next to the Gallatin River, a tributary of the Missouri River that is approximately 120 miles in length and runs through parts of both Montana and Wyoming. Ironically, parts of *A River Runs Through It* were filmed there as well. No wonder, since it is a stunningly beautiful river, babbling along on rocks and surrounded on each side by lush vegetation and tall trees.

We arrived at the northwest entrance to Yellowstone by mid-morning, paid our annual park fee of $20 at the ranger station and headed south and east through the park toward Old Faithful. Just inside the park, I was immediately struck and saddened by all the devastation still left over from the big fires there in 1988.

Several small fires started in the park in 1988 and, once merging together, formed the largest wildfire in the recorded history of the park. The flames spread quickly out of control with increasing winds and drought, and burned for several months. The fires almost destroyed two major visitor destinations and, on September 8, 1988, the entire park was closed to all non-emergency personnel for the first time in its history. Only after the efforts of over 9,000 emergency personnel, cooler temperatures and higher humidity in the fall air were the flames finally extinguished. If you've never been to Yellowstone, prepare to see acre upon acre of burned out forest areas. It is very sad to see. However, the park is still quite beautiful and I got a kick out of how interested Jordan became after catching sight of the majestic bison and small geysers along the western park loop.

Yellowstone National Park, set aside by the U.S. Congress as a national park on March 1, 1872, is located mostly in Wyoming, though it also extends into Montana and Idaho. The park was the first of its kind, and is known for its wildlife and its many geothermal features—especially Old Faithful Geyser—one of the most popular areas in the park. Yellowstone National Park spans an area of 3,468 square miles, comprising lakes, canyons, rivers and mountain ranges. Yellowstone Lake is one of the largest high-altitude lakes in North America.

When Jordan and I arrived at the Old Faithful Center mid-morning on Tuesday, we were told we had just missed the geyser erupting by five minutes. We also learned that Old Faithful, while still older, is no longer as faithful and the near-hourly display of shooting hot geyser water was not as high as I remembered from my only other trip to Yellowstone in the summer of 1983. My best buddy John and I made the trek that year and not only saw Yellowstone, but also visited the Grand Teton National Park, home of Grand Teton, rising 13,770 feet above sea level, making it the second highest peak in the state of Wyoming.

Even though Jordan and I had missed Old Faithful's hourly show by just minutes, and we were on a tight time schedule, it was one of our two must-see places for the day and I knew we'd wait for the next scheduled show, in just under an hour, right around noon. I still thought we might be able to make it to Mt. Rushmore later that day, even if we'd have to spend the night there in order to get some good pictures the following Wednesday morning.

Because we had some time to kill, I took Jordan for a walk and stretched my own legs before putting him back in the SUV. Temperatures were only in the upper 60s, so I just cracked the windows open and left Jordan there so I could go back inside the visitor center. After wandering around the Old Faithful Visitor Center for a few minutes and getting a Coke in their cafeteria, I went outside and got Jordan back out of the SUV for our upcoming photo opportunity in front of Old Faithful. Temperatures were now in the low seventies, and the sky was a beautiful blue with not a single cloud. We strolled around the Old Faithful parking area, briefly stopping to answer questions from other tourists inquiring about Jordan: "Was he a service dog?" "A therapy dog?" Or simply, "why did you bring your dog to Yellowstone?" Rather than try to explain the nature of our trips and his celebrity status back in Las Vegas, I just told those enquiring minds that

Jordan always traveled with me, no matter where I went.

As the time drew near for the geyser to do its thing, we got our camera and, along with all the other tourists there for that particular show, headed over to the viewing area, a semi-circular set of stainless-steel grandstands. I had to get a little creative with how I was going to get shots of Jordan while the geyser was going off, so I positioned him in front of the stands just on the other side off a roped-off area that was off limits to all but park personnel. Fortunately, no park rangers were around at the time and I got Jordan in position, only about fifty yards away from the geyser hole. I sat down in front of him on the gravel area just below the grandstands and turned the camera on. We were fortunate that Old Faithful was on time that day. At the posted time, the hot waters started rising from the ground in a grand display to the sounds of applause from the crowd, camera shutters and scalding hot steam. I was snapping pictures of Jordan in front of Old Faithful as fast as I could, hoping and praying I was getting some good ones. There was too much noise for me to talk to him and try to get him to pose, so I just had to do the best I could. I could hear the laughter coming from behind us in the stands, as people were joking about the idiot taking pictures of his dog in front of Old Faithful.

Once the geyser stopped spraying, the grandstands cleared quickly and Jordan and I headed for the parking area with the rest of the tourists. One couple stopped us in the parking lot, informing me they had taken a picture of me taking pictures of Jordan and would like to e-mail me a copy. I had them follow me to my car, got Jordan loaded in the back and got out one of my business cards and gave it to them. When they saw where I worked, they both laughed and said they were on their way to the Las Vegas suburb of Henderson, Nevada to see their son. Small world, huh? They would, in fact, forward me the photo and it is included with the others I shot that day on our website.

We left the Old Faithful Visitor Center right after 1:00 p.m. that afternoon and I was still determined to make it to Mt. Rushmore sometime that night, still feeling fresh and confident. However, I made a costly error in navigation, one that would cost us over two hours of travel time and scrap all hopes of getting out of Wyoming that day.

Yellowstone contains an interior looping road that has three arteries that branch off and serve as ways to get to and from the south, north, and east exits and entrances of the park. My bearings got all screwed up and by the time I realized the error, we were well on our way to the southwest entrance to the park, going in the exact opposite direction of the way we needed to be headed. I should've consulted my hand-held handy-dandy compass. I pulled over, checked the park map and got us turned around and headed toward the east exit of the park. However, the traffic was getting heavy and there were several delays due to road construction. By the time we actually got out of east Yellowstone, I knew we wouldn't make it to Rushmore that Tuesday. I pulled over once again when it was safe to change our strategy and final destination for that day: Cody, Wyoming. We didn't actually leave Yellowstone until 3:50 p.m. that afternoon and wouldn't arrive in Cody until 4:35 p.m., having put another 500 miles on the trip odometer. We had traveled 2,638.3 miles by the time we reached Cody on the fourth day of our 2003 trip. It was September 23, 2003 and the following day would prove to be the longest road-traveling day of my life.

Cody, Wyoming sits next to Highway 14 in the northwestern part of Wyoming and is named after one of the town's creators: William Frederick Cody, better known as Buffalo Bill. Themes surrounding Cody's pioneer and cowboy and western history are common in the cultural events and activities in the area. The Buffalo Bill Historical Center is a large and modern facility located near the center of the city, contains large collections, and is a favorite stopping point for tourists passing through the town on their way to or from Yellowstone. During the summer, a re-enactment of a wild-west shoot-out takes place next to the Irma Hotel, another historical site still open for business with a hotel and restaurant. This establishment forms the nucleus of the town. And, even though it was early fall, I got to see one such re-enactment shortly after we arrived in town that day. It was really cool. The actors all looked their part and took the re-enactment seriously. The gathering crowd of about 200 seemed to enjoy the show. As with most wild-west shows, this one included the requisite meeting up of good and bad guys, the ensuing argument and shoot-out; guns blazing that were firing blanks, of course. By the time the show was over, my ears were ringing from the sounds of gunfire and the air was filled with smoke from the gunpowder. Although I knew nothing of the show until it happened and I happened on it, I had the good luck of parking our SUV right in front of the adjacent Irma Hotel as it seemed like a good place to order something other than fast food.

I attended to Jordan's needs and left him in the locked SUV. I cracked open the windows and left him a bowl of fresh water, knowing he'd be fine as temperatures had already dropped to the upper sixties as the sun began to drop out of sight to the west. I walked through the doors of the Irma Hotel and the place was packed with locals and tourists alike. It had gotten pretty easy to tell the difference by this point of our travels. Because Cody is a western town, the locals were all dressed the part and the tourists all looked pretty much the same in shorts, T-shirts and flip-flops. There were some motorcycle riders there, as that is a favorite part of the country to ride, and they were all dressed in their leathers and Harley-Davidson garb. I ordered a turkey sandwich, fries, and a drink to go and headed back to the car just as it was getting dark. I was too tired to think about a room and had already decided that I was going to be sleeping alongside my boy once again. The SUV was parked under a street lamp and I thought we'd be fine right there on Cody's main drag. Plus, I had my bear repellant. And in that part of the country, I was actually more afraid of bears than people.

Although I had no idea what was on tap for the following day's journey, I was tired and knew Wednesday would be a long one, so I bedded down next to Jordan shortly after sunset and we were soon in la-la land, him snoring and me dreaming of the open road. Jordan, like all dogs, would often dream. I only wish I knew what he was actually dreaming about. My best guess is that he usually dreamt of his next meal, chasing rabbits or sniffing butts.

We got back on the road the following Wednesday morning, September 24 at 12:57 a.m. under partly cloudy skies and a cool 45 degree outside temperature. The plan was to take Highway 14 east through the Bighorn National Forest, and then reconnect with I-90, which would take us east into South Dakota. I-90 drops straight down into Rapid City, South Dakota, and from there it's just a short drive to the Black Hills and Mt. Rushmore.

The sky was pitch-black when we started our ascent up through and over the Bighorn Forest. Highway 14 became a narrow, two-lane affair that began twisting and turning more and more with elevation. I decided I needed to really concentrate, so I turned off the stereo and gripped the wheel firmly with both hands. Jordan had once again fallen fast asleep and I assumed he trusted dad to get us through this narrow, winding and dangerous stretch of road. He should've been a bit more concerned.

Elevations in Bighorn Forest range from 5,000 feet along the foot of the mountains, to 13,189 feet on top of Cloud Peak, the highest point in the Big Horn Mountains. Cloud Peak was dead ahead of us.

Just before reaching the summit of Cloud Peak, we encountered groups of deer alongside the roadway. The problem was—even with the high beams on—I didn't spot these huge, beautiful animals until I was almost literally on top of them, because I quickly found they would wait until the very last second to dart out onto the roadway and stop dead in their tracks right in front of our vehicle with their characteristic deer-in-the-headlights stare. On several occasions this happened, and I either had to swerve or slam on my brakes, or both to miss them. I slowed to nearly a snail's pace and it seemed like it took forever to finally leave the Bighorn Forest, thankfully having avoided collision with any deer, running off the road or crashing into the mountainside. I was frazzled and just plain stressed out. And our encounters with deer were far from over.

Just outside of the Bighorn National Forest, we left Highway 14, thank God, and reconnected with I-90, which would take us south and then east through Buffalo and Gillette, Wyoming, and on to South Dakota. And, Mt. Rushmore.

Once on I-90 the speed limit and the traffic increased, mostly with big-rig trucks; eighteen-wheelers whose drivers only seemed to know one speed: flat out. They obviously knew this stretch of interstate and the perils contained therein—dead deer right in the middle of the road. I lost count of the number of times I had to swerve to miss a carcass that had been run over and killed by a big-rig. Deer would simply bounce off the bumpers of those big-rigs without incident, other than the fact that the deer were now dead. Unfortunately for Jordan and I, and the rest of the people traveling in smaller vehicles, we had to dodge these dearly, recently and suddenly, departed creatures unless we wanted to be buying a new suspension or vehicle. Seriously, these animals are huge, lying there dead in the roadway and they pose a real, constant risk to vehicles and their occupants, from minor damage to death. Hitting one of these several-hundred-pound carcasses can send a car, truck or SUV careening out of control. Fortunately, we survived the deer-death-dodge and they became less numerous on the road by the time we stopped for gas and a potty break around 5:00 a.m. in Gillette, Wyoming.

With a population of 20,000, Gillette is a small city centrally located in an area that is vital to the development of vast quantities of American coal and oil. The city calls itself the "Energy Capital of the Nation."

We stopped at a Truck Stop of America, known for catering to long-haul truckers with showers, truck wash stalls, piping hot coffee and pretty decent food. One of the downsides of road travel is that you don't always have the luxury of deciding when and where you have to take a leak, or the other. So it's always an added benefit when you find a restroom that is actually clean. Restroom facilities usually are in these big truck centers if you're ever out on the open road needing a pit stop.

I filled my thermos at the truck stop, filled the SUV with gas and we got back on I-90 heading east and soon crossed the Wyoming-South Dakota state line just as the sun was coming up, knowing that our destination, Mt. Rushmore was just a few hours away.

Now that it was getting light outside, I could see how beautiful northern Wyoming and eastern South Dakota really were, with rolling hills, mountains off in the distance and expansive vistas that seem to go on forever. I don't know if I could ever live out in the country or a small town again, having done both in the Central Valley of California while I was in high school. But I certainly thought I could retire in the part of the country we were driving through at the time, eastern South Dakota.

I-90 turns southeast just past the state line and we made it to Sturgis, South Dakota just after 7:00 a.m. that Wednesday morning. The skies were a mixture of blue and fair weather cumulous clouds, and the air was crisp and cool, with outside temperatures still in the low 50s. It was a beautiful morning and I was really jacked up to be nearing our ultimate destination of the trip. It was our sixth day on the road and I was feeling pretty confident we could get back to Vegas sometime the following day— our original goal.

We pulled off I-90 and drove around Sturgis, the home of the biggest motorcycle rally in the world, held each year the first full week in August. Over 500,000 bikers and their bikes, of all kinds, sizes and walks of life converge on the city for a week of concerts, rallies, scantily clad women, young and old, and consumption of vast quantities of alcoholic and non-alcoholic beverages. And, despite the stories of fights and rival motorcycle gangs, most of the motorcycle enthusiasts who attend the Sturgis Rally and others like it around the country each year are usually business professionals who take a week off once a year to hang loose, feel the air of the open road and just plain let it all hang out before returning to their normal, mundane lives.

Because the rally was held just over a month prior to our stop in Sturgis, there were still banners and other signs hanging everywhere. I took the opportunity to get Jordan out of the SUV and take some pictures of him in front of the few motorcycle shops and rally venues. Then it was back in the car and back on I-90, south to Rapid City and finally to the Black Hills of South Dakota and Mt. Rushmore.

Having gassed up in Gillette earlier that morning, we blew right through Rapid City, briefly encountering the morning traffic before leaving I-90 and heading south and west on Highway 16, which runs through the heart of the Black Hills and would take us to the entrance of Mt. Rushmore.

The Black Hills aren't really black, but are hills, most of which don't rise more than a few thousand feet above sea level. A small, isolated mountain range, the Black Hills rise from the Great Plains of North America in western South Dakota, extending west into Wyoming. Set off from the main body of the Rocky Mountains, the region is something of a geological anomaly, described as an "island of trees in a sea of grass." That pretty much sums up the way things looked as we ascended the range that Wednesday morning.

Just after 8:00 a.m., we rounded a curve on Highway 16 and Mt. Rushmore came into full view. I was immediately struck by two thoughts: the monument isn't nearly as tall as I always thought it would be from the pictures I had seen in books and on the Internet, and it's even stunningly more beautiful and majestic when seen for the first time in person. I nearly drove us right off the road, as it was hard to keep my eyes off the heads of the those four dead presidents. And, as quickly as the monument came into view, it was once again hidden by another hill and twist in the road. Then, we made another turn and it was right there in front of us again, and I could barely wait to get to the park entrance. We arrived at the entrance booth at 8:15 a.m. that morning, September 24. We had made it to Mt. Rushmore. And I couldn't wait to get inside and take some dramatic shots of Jordan in front of this beautiful testament to American ingenuity and patriotism. I soon found out that wasn't going to happen that morning, or any morning, for that matter.

Mount Rushmore National Memorial, near Keystone, South Dakota, is a monumental granite sculpture by Gutzon Borglum (1867–1941), located within the United States Presidential Memorial that represents the first 150 years of the history of the United States of America with sixty-foot sculptures of the heads of former Presidents George Washington, Thomas Jefferson, Theodore Roosevelt and Abraham Lincoln. The entire memorial covers 1,278.45 acres and is 5,725 feet above sea level. The memorial attracts approximately 2 million people annually.

When we pulled up to the park entrance booth, the female park ranger inside welcomed me to the park and said that an annual pass—the only type available—was $8. As I reached in the console to pull out the money to pay her, she also informed me that dogs were "not allowed within the Memorial, unless they are service dogs" and that Jordan was "welcome in the parking area." I told her he was my seeing eye dog, and before I got him, I drove with one hand on the wheel and one hand on the road. For some strange reason, she didn't buy it. I was immediately deflated. And devastated. We had just spent over five days and 3,000 miles on the road, only to find out I couldn't take pictures of Jordan at the only place that was essential to the success of the trip. I tried to explain what the trip meant to us and that Jordan was the subject of my needed photos, but she wouldn't and couldn't budge on the issue. Jordan would not be going inside the park. Period. I told her I understood, although I really didn't. I thanked her, sort of, and proceeded on to the parking structure, with Mt. Rushmore now so close and yet so far away.

I parked, grabbed my camera and got Jordan out of the SUV anyway, thinking I might be able to reason with one of the park rangers inside the memorial. I was partially right. The ranger at the entrance actually allowed me and Jordan to walk just inside the main entrance and for me to take a few pictures of him. Unfortunately, the United States Presidential

Memorial sits at the entrance to the monument and getting an unobstructed view of Jordan and Mt. Rushmore without all kinds of structures in the way was simply impossible. After snapping off several pictures, I could tell I was testing the ranger's patience, so I thanked him for his kindness and we walked back to the SUV, me being completely bummed out and Jordan just happy to be alive. Fortunately, the Man Upstairs was watching out for us that day, as I was about to find out.

I loaded Jordan into the back of the SUV and reluctantly pulled out of the parking area, heading for the western exit and the long, depressing ride home.

Just as we turned right, back onto Highway 16, I looked up and I was staring at the most beautiful, perfect and completely unobstructed view of the monument, with gorgeous trees and their fall colors in the foreground and big, white, puffy fair weather clouds in the sky above those four big, giant granite presidents. I pulled the car over in a no parking zone along Highway 16, got my camera and Jordan out of the SUV and we walked back to the perfect spot to get him posed and for me to get my picture.

I got Jordan to lay down right where I needed him and turned the camera on. I checked the viewfinder and got him framed directly below the monument. I was sitting right in front of him on dirt and gravel, simply thrilled that we would not be denied. Right as I was about to press the shutter button, I said to Jordan: "Where's the kitty cat?" At the precise moment two things happened: Jordan lifted his head and gave his most regal pose, and I heard the camera click. I took a few more pictures for good measure, but I knew in my heart and mind I'd gotten it right the first take. And I was right. That first picture I took of my boy that morning of September 24, 2003 would turn out to be the best picture I had ever taken. He looked so presidential himself, all dressed up in his favorite red, white, and blue bandana, giving me the perfect pose under absolutely perfect conditions, both in terms of location and lighting. Mt. Rushmore faces due west for good reason: so that the sun, rising in the east, can brightly light

Mt Rushmore, September 24, 2003

those four big faces each morning. I don't think I've ever felt happier or more proud of my sweet boy. But I didn't want a ticket. So, we quickly got back into the SUV and headed for home.

We made Cheyenne right around lunch, and I took one of the downtown exits in hopes of finding a decent place to eat that had televisions, so I could get caught up on the events of the day. Cheyenne is the capital of Wyoming, with a population of just better than 55,000. It is also the largest city in the state; a sprawling city that seems to go on as far as the eye can see. The weather was still cooperating for us and the traffic was generally light. The only problem was the time of day. It was too early to settle in for the night. But I was pretty tired from all the night driving and dodging big-rigs and deer, both dead and alive. At that point, I wasn't quite sure if I could sleep during the daylight hours, but I was fairly certain I was too tired to drive much farther. I found a parking spot downtown near a sports bar and restaurant. And, because the temperatures were cool enough, I left some water and Jordan in the back of the SUV, locked it and went inside the restaurant to get something to eat and to decide what we'd do for the rest of the day.

By the time I got something to eat and watched a little TV, I was really feeling fatigued, so I decided to see if we could find a spot in a nearby area where we both could take a nap. I only had to drive a few blocks before we were in a residential area and I pulled the SUV alongside a curb in front of a house and under a huge tree that provided some shade. Temperatures were now rising into the upper seventies and, though I quickly fell asleep in the back of the SUV alongside Jordan, I soon woke, wide awake and drenched in sweat. I made a decision: We were going to get back on the interstate and get as close to home as my worn-out body could take us that day.

I got us back on Interstate 25, heading south and because Cheyenne is in the extreme southeastern part of Wyoming, we crossed into Colorado within the hour stopping in nearby Ft. Collins long enough to stretch

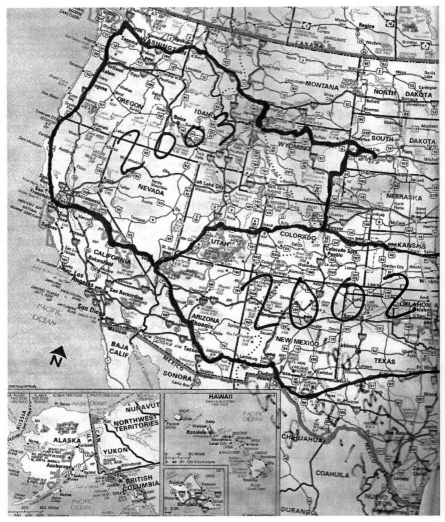

Map: © Rand McNally

our legs and gas up the SUV. Even though I had passed the twelve-hour driving mark, I caught a second wind and now that we were back in Colorado, I knew exactly where we would spend the final night of the

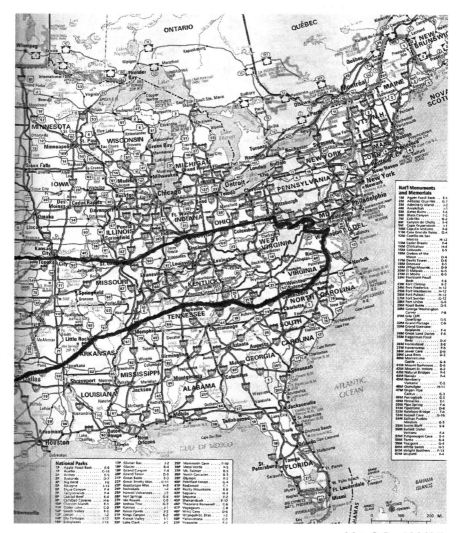

Map: © Rand McNally

trip: Silverthorne.

We blew through downtown Denver right at rush hour and left I-25, heading east on I-70 for the Rockies and Silverthorne. Having been there almost to the day the prior year, I knew that we could make it back to Las Vegas by sometime early that following Thursday morning and keep to our original plan.

We made Silverthorne just past dark and got off at the same exit as the previous year, the only exit for that small town off I-70. I drove right to the same restaurant we stopped at the previous year, fed Jordan and took the laptop inside and got right to work. Upon transferring the picture of Jordan in front of Mt. Rushmore to the laptop, I received confirmation that our second long cross-country trip had been worth the effort: The picture, as I had thought earlier that morning, was magnificent. One poster-size version of it hangs in our home hallway. The other occupies another special place that you'll read about later. I now had two days worth of journal entries to catch up on, as I hadn't sent the account of our trip to Yellowstone and Cody the previous two days back to the station webmaster. It took me almost an hour to eat and get my computer work done and I was beat. It was the longest day on the road of the two years, having driven over eighteen hours and logging more than 900 miles on the trip odometer. It was close to 9:00 p.m. on Wednesday, September 24 when I finally climbed into the back of the SUV to get some much needed rest, and spend what would turn out to be the last time I'd ever sleep with Jordan in the back of our SUV, underneath the nighttime stars. I was thrilled knowing that, barring any unforeseen disaster, we would be sleeping in our own bed the following night. It was cool outside, as the elevation was right around 8,500 feet and the temperatures had dropped into the fifties. I pulled the sleeping bag up over my head and both Jordan and I were fast asleep in minutes. If Jordan was grossed-out by my elevated level of road-weary body odor, he wasn't talking.

I woke up the following Thursday morning, September 25, cold but wide awake, right at 1:45 a.m., having slept soundly for just over five hours. I quickly got Jordan fed and outside to take care of business and we pulled away from that quaint little Silverthorne restaurant. We stopped for gas and to fill up my thermos with coffee and were quickly back on I-70 for the final leg of our trip. It was 37 degrees outside, according to my inside-outside car thermometer, which had served me so well for the second straight year. It sure felt like 37 degrees, and I blasted the car's heater and the stereo. Before we knew it, we were back in Grand Junction and then crossing into Utah to connect with I-15, which would take us all the way back to Las Vegas.

Just after we crossed the Utah state line out of Colorado, I hit the proverbial wall. I think the previous day had caught up to me and I didn't think it was safe for me to keep driving. I pulled into the nearest rest stop, locked the car and crawled into the back of the SUV and my sleeping bag next to Jordan. I had barely dozed off when my body woke me, telling me I had to use the restroom. I got out of the SUV and the cold, night air hit me like a slap in the face. And, though I'd only slept for what turned out to be a few minutes, I was suddenly wide awake and eager to get back on I-70. However, I really needed to go the bathroom, even though rest stop restrooms scare the heck out of me. There is no logical reason for this fear as far as I know. Unless you believe the urban myths about serial killers hiding out in the rest stop restroom, waiting for their next, unsuspecting victim. I didn't take any chances. I grabbed our can of bear spray, flashlight and made my way to the rest room, feeling anxious and silly at the same time.

I got back in the SUV and headed west, then south toward I-15. It was another star-drenched night and it was hard to focus on the road and not the nighttime sky or the rearview mirror. For the first few miles after leaving the rest stop, I kept checking the rearview for suspicious looking headlights. They have a very distinctive, ominous look. Important safety tip.

The rest of the trip proved entirely uneventful and we made it back to Las Vegas on that Thursday morning, September 25, 2003 just after 11:00 a.m. Our only other stop before we made it back home was to pick

Back Home, September 25, 2003

up my check at the television station, located just north of downtown Las Vegas. During that brief stop, I had one of my co-workers snap off a picture of Jordan giving me another celebratory "high four" behind our SUV. We were back home within fifteen minutes and Paws Across America II was in the can.

We arrived at our townhouse just before noon that Thursday, a warm fall day in Las Vegas, with outside temperatures still in the '90s. I got Jordan out of the car and back inside our home, shut the garage door, turned on and cranked up the AC and went straight to bed. Neither of us woke until after sunrise the following Friday morning.

Due to my odd hours, much of our driving during both cross-country trips took place during the middle of the night. That limits my descriptions of our surroundings, topography and sites. My general impression of our country, after we'd arrived back home would be as follows: the eastern half of the United States is quite beautiful. Western states west of the Mississippi, not as beautiful unless we're thinking about our western coastal states. I'm a bit biased—being from California—but for my money, the drive north or south along coastal Highway 101 is arguably the most beautiful stretch of highway on earth.

Trip Summary:

- 7 days

- 4,234.5 total miles

- 11 states including: Nevada, California, Oregon, Washington, Idaho, Montana, Wyoming, South Dakota, Colorado, Utah, and Arizona

- Close to a dozen National Parks/Recreational Areas

- 1 Lost American Express

- 2 times the cruise control malfunctioned and the accelerator stuck "wide-open"

- 0 Tickets (one warning in Grants Pass, Oregon)
- 4 near-misses with deer
- 1 wrong turn in Yellowstone (costing us over 2 hours in driving time)
- Dollars in park fees (Yosemite $20, Yellowstone $20, and Mt. Rushmore $8. Don't forget, dogs are not allowed in the Mt. Rushmore Memorial area.)

Sahara Town Center
Las Vegas Snow Day,
December 30, 2003

CHAPTER 23

Viva Las Vegas

Shortly after our trip to Mt. Rushmore in 2003, Jordan and I visited and spoke to a senior citizen group at Sun City in Summerlin—a retirement community on the west side of the Las Vegas Valley. While there, I spoke of our trips and how I thought I might use them as a basis for a book sometime in the future. One of the women in attendance suggested it might be easier if I just used the trips and photos as a calendar, proceeds of which could go to local pet charities and shelters. We had designed, printed and sold commemorative T-shirts the prior year, with the proceeds benefiting local animal causes, and I thought making a calendar to commemorate the trips and raise money for local animal groups was a brilliant idea.

It was mid-October of 2004, so I knew I had to get moving because people usually buy calendars well before the end of the year. I put together twelve photos from both of our trips, deciding which month each would be and wrote the story of each photo to be included on each page. Then I contacted a friend at the Las Vegas Art Institute and as soon as I told her what I was planning, she immediately jumped on board and told me she would have some of their students design the calendar for free as a classroom project. The kids did a beautiful job and they got to use the calendar as part of their future resume portfolios.

I contacted a local printer, ordered 1,000 copies and paid the $3,500 printing cost up front out of my own pocket. I stuck the charge on my fresh, new, permanent American Express card and prayed the calendars would sell well enough to at least cover the cost. They did. I scheduled calendar signing events all over our forecast area and the TV station management

Dealing Blackjack at Tropicana, September 2004

allowed me to promote the events on-air because proceeds would be going to animal charities. The events were a huge success, some attracting

LV Mayor Oscar Goodman Oct 2004

hundreds of viewers. People showed up to see Jordan and plop down $10 for his very first "Paws Across America" calendar, knowing it was for a good cause. I quickly covered my cost and, as promised, every other cent went to local animal shelters and charities.

Shortly into 2004, when the calendar sales leveled off, I started thinking about a theme for a "Paws Across America 2005." I had already decided our cross-country days were behind us so I had to come up with something different. It didn't take long to decide that our hometown, Las Vegas, would be the backdrop for the 2005

Caesars Marquee October 2004

calendar. Thanks again to the students at the Art Institute, the Vegas-themed calendar became the best of the four "Paws Across America" calendars Jordan and I ended up doing together. I took another week off toward the end of September 2004 and each day and night we'd venture out across the Las Vegas Valley to get photos for the upcoming 2005 calendar.

The Las Vegas-themed calendar for 2005 showed me just how significant and important Jordan had become to the Las Vegas community. Local marketing representatives and public relations people for all the local resorts and casinos opened their hearts and doors, with few exceptions, when I asked if I could take photos of Jordan in or around their properties. After all, it was great PR for them, too.

Air Force Thunderbird F16 Nellis AFB Oct 2004

I took photos of Jordan dealing poker at the Tropicana Hotel and Casino. He posed with the showgirls from the legendary Folies Bergere show there, as well. I took his picture with Mayor Oscar Goodman at City Hall. Jordan was King for a Day at the Excalibur and got his very own scene

Circus Circus Frightdome October 2004

in their Tournament of Kings show. I photographed him next to an official Thunderbirds F-16 Fighting Falcon at Nellis Air Force Base and took more pictures of him high above the Las Vegas skyline at the Voo Doo Lounge, inside the Rio Hotel. I got some great shots of him below the Stratosphere Tower, having learned the technique the previous year at the Space Needle in Seattle. We also spent a morning taking pictures out at the Red Rock National Park, on the far west side of the Las Vegas Valley. Some of the funniest shots were taken inside the Fright Dome, the Halloween-themed haunted house at the Circus Circus Resort. Despite the screams and the scary characters running around, Jordan never flinched or batted an eye. He actually seemed rather bored with the proceedings.

None of the photos for our 2005 calendar would've been possible had it not been for my good relationships with local casino and resort folks and more importantly, the goodwill that Jordan had built up in our community.

The moment of true glory during our daily photo sessions for the 2005 calendar came with help of the folks at Caesars Palace Hotel and Casino. They dedicated their marquee to Jordan for an entire day. Jordan's name and photograph, along with our Paws

Coronation Tournament of Kings Excalibur, September 2004

Folies Bergere Tropicana, September 2004

Across America 2005 logo, rotated from 10:00 a.m. until 10:00 a.m. right along the advertisements for Celine Dion's "A New Day" and Elton John's "The Red Piano." Imagine that. A dog with his own marquee on the Las Vegas Strip.

When I first saw the marquee, I was blown away. It was so incredibly moving to see my boy's face and name up in lights on the famous Las Vegas Strip. Jordan had officially won over the hearts of the city. I took a picture of him in front of his very own marquee that September day in 2004 day at Caesars Palace and it became my favorite calendar month photo of 2005.

For the 2006 calendar, the theme was Jordan's "Life so Far," and included pictures from his time as a puppy to the present. The final calendar I made with Jordan was for 2007 and it was themed "Greatest Hits," and included my favorite photos from the three previous calendars. All four calendars proved to be wildly successful and I'm proud that, thanks to the support of our viewers, we were able to raise thousands of dollars for local animal causes and charities. To this day I get calls and letters from viewers letting me know that their favorite calendar photos hang in their homes or offices, and how much those pictures will always mean to them.

Excalibur Courtyard, September 2004

Mandalay Bay 0904, September 2004

Outside Excalibur, September 2004

Monte Carlo Marquee, September 2004

Little White Wedding Chapel LV Blvd,
September 2004

Jordan Shirt Front, PAA III, Las Vegas
Proceeds to NSPCA, September 2004

Las Vegas Blvd, The Strip, September 2004

Rio Voodoo Lounge, Floor 51, October 2004

Red Rock Recreational Area, September 2004

Stratosphere Tower, September 2004

*Luxor,
September 2004*

*Fabulous Las
Vegas Sign,
September 2004*

CHAPTER 24

Our On-Air Memories

Over the years, Jordan and I shared many memorable moments during live broadcasts.

In conjunction with the *Today Show's* "Where in the World is Matt Lauer?" the television station and I worked out a segment called "Where in the West is John Fredericks?" I went out to different locations each morning and viewers would call in to guess where I was. The first viewer to guess correctly won a prize. If I went to a location that was outside or dog-friendly, Jordan always came with me.

One morning Jordan and I were at Lake Las Vegas broadcasting live from a small boat on the lake. While live on the air, I took of one of my canvas shoes and tossed it into the water. Jordan immediately jumped out of the boat and chased after it. He put the shoe in his mouth and brought it back to the boat. I pulled him back in the boat where he shook the water off him, soaking me live on-air. Later that day, I received an e-mail from a woman who said she was never going to watch our television station again because I let Jordan kill a bird on live television. After I finished laughing, I sent her a very nice reply explaining that Jordan was retrieving my shoe and not a bird.

Time for some brutal honesty here. E-mail might very well be the greatest discovery known to man. It may also be the worst. People hide behind their e-mail anonymity, sending some of the most vile, hate-filled messages to me and my on-air co-anchors that you can possibly imagine.

The vast majority of e-mails we receive are very complimentary and positive. Those you soon forget. It's the negative ones that stay with you long after they've been deleted from your in-box. My personal policy is to reply to all e-mails, snail mail and voice mail messages whether it takes me a minute, an hour or a month. I even respond to the nasty ones and I do so in a positive, professional manner, most of the time. I will admit there have been a few times when I responded in-kind to negative e-mails, either directed toward a co-worker or to me. But I learned a valuable lesson about dealing with the public many years ago.

While I was still a disc jockey in Bakersfield, the GM of the radio station I was working for had his kids call the request line to see if they could get a rise out of the DJ on-air by ridiculing him or her and calling them names. Disc jockeys who responded in- kind lost their jobs. I was lucky and it taught me a valuable lesson. The customer, or in this case, the listener-viewer is always right and must be treated with dignity and respect. My point of this subject is simply this: There are times in my life when I can't wait until I am no longer a public figure and I can be open and honest with rude, insensitive people. Personal note: Take that self-defense class you've been putting off for the past twenty years.

One of my favorite "Where in the West" broadcasts was from inside Wayne Newton, "Mr. Las Vegas's" estate. The estate, known as "Shenandoah" in honor of the place of his birth, is just east of the Strip and McCarran International Airport. But you'd never know it once inside. It's enclosed on all sides by eight-foot walls. There are hundreds of exotic birds and creatures roaming the compound, along with a huge stable area with many beautiful horses. Jordan was especially taken by the sight of Wayne's peacocks that wandered by while we were live on-air.

Other mornings we broadcasted live from local golf courses. Jordan loved to chase rabbits, so he waited until we were live on the air, then he would tear after a rabbit. To this day I'm not sure how he knew each time I was on the air. The only way I can reconcile this is that my voice somehow

changes when I go live, as opposed to all other times I'm off-air.
Jordan and I participated in station-sponsored back-to-school fairs,

 which were located at local malls. Dogs weren't allowed inside the malls, but mall management always issued us a special waiver so Jordan could attend. The first year Jordan was with me at a back-to-school fair, a woman approached us with a child in a stroller. Her child had an ice cream cone and before we knew

Back To School Fair Stealing Ice Cream 81405   it, Jordan nonchalantly leaned in and helped himself to the entire ice cream cone. Luckily, the woman had a good sense of humor and thought it was an absolutely riot. The kid started cracking up, too. No food was ever safe in a child's hand when Jordan was around.

Jordan's most famous on-air moment was one that continues to air on national television. We were doing a live broadcast from the Valley of Fire—located within a Native American reservation about forty-five miles northeast of Las Vegas—and the unexpected happened. While I was doing the weather live, Jordan stood behind me and hiked his leg on a bush and pissed right there for the viewers to see. The cameraman started laughing and I had no idea what was happening. When I turned around, and while I was still on-air, I saw what was so funny. I was so flustered I just said, "Okay!" and kept broadcasting. The segment was picked up by one those "Most Amazing Video" shows on NBC and continues to be a favorite to this day with the producers of the show.

One thing is for sure: outtakes may be the only thing you can count on with animals and kids on live television. And, whether he was fetching a shoe in the water or peeing on a bush, anything Jordan did on-air only served to further endear him in the hearts of our viewers.

Back of Car with Dead Battery, September 2004,
Back Home October 04, 2004

Snow Day, Mount Charleston, December 2004

CHAPTER 25

Strike One

As with most aging pets, Jordan had some serious health issues later on in life. Unfortunately, I was out of town during the two most serious. I've never forgiven myself for not being there for my boy during the times he needed me most.

During the last week of March 2005, my best buddy John and I went

on a five-day trip to Cancun, Mexico. We had a great time playing golf, lying by the pool and taking day trips. Unfortunately, the night before our trip home, I came down with what is known as Montezuma's Revenge and spent the final twenty-four hours bouncing between the bathroom and the bedroom. The four-hour flight back to Phoenix the following afternoon was one I'll never forget for a couple of reasons. I spent the entire flight praying I wouldn't get sick. Or worse yet, embarrass myself. Thankfully I didn't do either. And when I arrived in Phoenix for the connecting flight to Vegas, I learned some very scary news: Jordan was sick. My girlfriend Rosalind had been frantically trying to contact me.

When I arrived in Phoenix, something told me to call and check on Jordan. When I got Rosalind

Cancun Mexico
March 2005

on the phone I could tell immediately something was wrong. I asked her, "Is it Jordan."

"Yes."

"Is he dead?"

"No, but it's bad and you need to get home." The forty-five minute flight back to Las Vegas from Phoenix was the longest one I ever spent, not knowing what to expect when I got home to Jordan.

Before leaving for Cancun, despite Rosalind's offer to keep him at her home, I decided to board Jordan at his vet's office, Sahara Pines Animal Hospital. He was getting older and I felt they would give him the best care possible. Dr. Kristine Ziegler believed Jordan became stressed by my absence, and during his stay with them he stopped breathing. He had developed a condition called laryngeal paralysis, common among older dogs and certain breeds, including retrievers. Laryngeal paralysis develops when the muscles in the neck break down with age and they are no longer able to open and close the larynx. This is exactly what happened to Jordan. His larynx closed and he couldn't breathe. The condition doesn't happen overnight. Jordan had been showing signs of labored breathing. However, the trauma of him being alone, away from his dad apparently was too hard on him and his larynx closed altogether, shutting off his air supply.

Thankfully, Dr. Kristine was able to revive him and immediately called for a surgical consult. When the surgeon, Dr. Jeff Geels, arrived at Sahara Pines Animal Hospital for his consult, Dr. Kristine said to him, "This dog cannot die. And he cannot die on me." Dr. Kristine had been Jordan's vet for over seven years and she loved him dearly.

Jordan turned out to be a good surgical candidate. If performed successfully, the surgery would open his larynx allowing him to breathe properly. After the surgical consult, he was taken to the Animal Emergency Hospital for observation. That was where he was when I got home from Cancun that Sunday night in early April 2005.

Rosalind picked me up at the airport, and we raced over to the emergency hospital. When we got there, they immediately took me back to their observation area to see him. As I turned the corner to the observation area, I saw Jordan curled up in a kennel, attached to an IV. I couldn't believe how old and sad he looked. One of the techs took him out of his kennel and let me spend some time with him in one of the examination rooms. I sat on the floor of the room, placed his head in my lap, and cried in his fur like a baby. A short while later the vet on duty came in to check on us. I didn't even bother to try and compose myself. She looked down at me and said simply: "I know." With tears streaming down my face, I looked up at her and said: "I know he's going to die someday. I'm just not ready for him to die now."

A short while later I left to get some rest but got home and couldn't sleep. I decided Jordan needed something in his kennel to remind him of me. I grabbed one of my old Harley-Davidson T-shirts and raced back to the ER. They let me place the shirt in the kennel with him and I went out to the waiting area and fell asleep. I woke up about and hour later and went back to the observation area to check on him. Immediately, I noticed that the T-shirt I put in Jordan's kennel only an hour before was gone. I asked one of the techs if she knew where it was, and she told me that Jordan had "an accident" and they had to wash the shirt. I told her "that was no accident." As soon as I put my T-shirt in the kennel with him and went back out to the waiting area, he took a dump all over it. The old boy was sending me a message, loud and clear: "Dad, you were gone when I needed you most."

Although surgery is always risky, especially in older dogs, I thought it was in Jordan's best interest to go ahead with the operation. And while putting any older dog under a general anaesthesia was dangerous, Dr. Kristine made it clear to me that he'd probably not survive another collapse of his larynx.

Jordan's surgery was scheduled for the following Wednesday, April 6th at 2:00 p.m. at Dr. Ziegler's office. Rosalind came with me to the vet's office and Dr. Geels came out to the waiting area to explain the procedure, known as a "tie-back." He would make a small incision in the side of Jordan's neck, grab one side of the larynx, and "tie it" to the cartilage inside of Jordan's neck. That would mean Jordan would always have an open airway. Dr. Geels warned me that it would also cause a problem whereby food could accidentally get into Jordan's lungs, and Jordan would have to learn to "hack" it back up. Dr. Geels told us if the surgery was successful, given Jordan's general health at the time, there was no reason he couldn't live another two to three years. His words would turn out to be prophetic.

The surgery took just over an hour. While we were waiting, Rosalind decided I needed a little levity and decided to play a practical joke on me. She had been helping me remodel the kitchen of the home I purchased the previous year. The kitchen looked very dated and I wanted a more modern, yet homey look. One of the things I did was order granite counter tops, requiring the removal of the old, ugly porcelain white tile counters. The local trash people would not pick up the old counters so I was forced to dump them in big bins and trash cans in construction sites and behind local area businesses. Local city and county officials frown upon this practice. Rosalind kept warning me this was a shady practice and she decided to teach me a lesson and give me a laugh when I needed it the most.

While we were in the waiting room during Jordan's surgery, she reached into her purse and pulled out an envelope and handed it to me, saying: "I found this on your doorstep when you were in Cancun." The logo on the outside of the envelope looked like the official City of Las Vegas seal. I opened it up to find a very official-looking letter from some city sanitation official telling me that my fingerprints had been pulled off of a discarded countertop, illegally dumped. The letter went on to demand that I turn myself in immediately or face a bench warrant. As I felt the blood draining from my face, I turned to see Rosalind facing the other way trying to contain her laughter. Only then did I realize I'd been played, big time. She designed the envelope and wrote the letter. We laughed until we cried. It was just what I needed.

Jordan made it through surgery and he was allowed to come back home with me that following Friday. However, within an hour of getting him back home he had a seizure or minor stroke, later determined to have been caused by a reaction to his medication. As soon as I got him home, he crawled under my bed and fell asleep. I went in to check on him a short time later and realized his mouth was turning blue and his eyes had rolled back inside his head. Rosalind and I rolled Jordan onto an area rug, picked him up and loaded him into the back of my SUV. She drove as I cradled him in my arms. He was still breathing but each breath was very shallow and spaced far apart. Within a few miles of our home, Jordan started coming around and my tears of fear turned to tears of relief. Our vet's office had closed for the day, so we were instructed to take him to the emergency hospital. As soon as we got him there, they got him back on fluids and stabilized. He spent the rest of the night at the emergency room for observation. The following morning he was transported back over to Dr. Ziegler's office. I spent the night trying to sleep in the ER waiting room.

The next morning, Saturday, April 9, 2005, Jordan had been transported back to Dr. Kristine's office at Sahara Pines. When I went to visit him she told me that Jordan needed to go home. Puzzled, I asked her what she meant. Dr. Kristine told me he needed to be with me and in familiar surroundings. She said they couldn't do anything more for him except hope and pray he continued his recovery. Reluctantly, I loaded him into the back of our SUV. But, I was afraid to take him home. I had no idea what to expect. I had no idea what to do for him if he suffered another seizure or stroke. I also had absolute faith and trust in Dr. Kristine, so I did what she instructed.

We pulled out of the Sahara Pines Animal Hospital parking lot and headed home. After we'd gotten only a few miles from his vet's office, I looked into the rearview mirror and could see Jordan staring at me. At that moment I noticed something that had been gone for some time. The twinkle in my boy's eyes. It was as though a different dog was staring at me from the back of our SUV. That different dog was the Jordan that had been gone from my life for sometime, without me even realizing it. I was overcome with two immediate emotions: Jordan had been missing. And, Jordan was back. The light in his eyes that had slowly dimmed over time—without my realizing it—had returned.

I knew I had made the right decision by going ahead with the surgery. I looked at my own reflection in the rearview mirror and saw something in my own face that I had not seen for quite some time: A smile. My boy had turned a corner and was on the road to recovery. He had found his "lost light."

However, I knew the day would come when the light that found its way back to Jordan's eyes that Saturday morning, in April 2005 would leave him again, forever. On that day he would take the one and only journey he'd ever have to make on his own—to the Rainbow Bridge—to wait patiently for his dad.

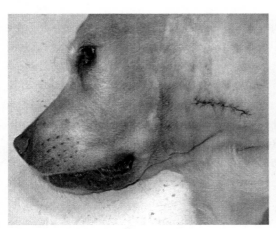

Jordan Post Surgery May 2005

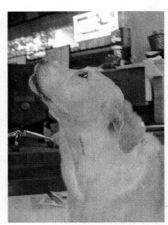

Jordan Post Surgery May 2005

THE RAINBOW BRIDGE POEM

When an animal dies that has been especially close to someone here, that pet goes to Rainbow Bridge. There are meadows and hills for all of our special friends so they can run and play together. There is plenty of food, water, and sunshine, and our friends are warm and comfortable.

All the animals that had been ill and old are restored to health and vigor. Those who were hurt or maimed are made whole and strong again, just as we remember them in our dreams of days and times gone by. The animals are happy and content, except for one small thing: they each miss someone very special to them, who had to be left behind.

They all run and play together, but the day comes when one suddenly stops and looks into the distance. His bright eyes are intent. His eager body quivers. Suddenly he begins to run from the group, flying over the green grass, his legs carrying him faster and faster.

You have been spotted, and when you and your special friend finally meet, you cling together in joyous reunion, never to be parted again. The happy kisses rain upon your face, your hands again caress the beloved head, and you look once more into the trusting eyes of your pet, so long gone from your life but never absent from your heart.

Then you cross Rainbow Bridge together . . .

Paul C. Dahm 1977©

Jordan Post Surgery May 2005

247

LIVE
broadcast with
Photographer
Erik Ho
Katrina
Fundraiser
2005

Collecting
Donations
for Katrina
Hurricane Pet
Victims 2005

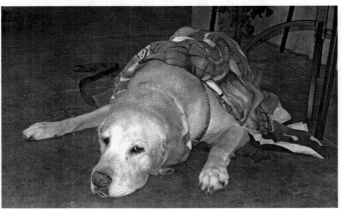

Montecito Revisited
July 2005

Fetching the Stick Santa Barbara Ca July 2005

*Taking Back the Beach
Santa Barbara Ca July 2005*

*Back Home at the Beach with Dad.
Photo courtesy of Rosalind Davis*

Pacific Ocean Swim Santa Barbara CA July 2005

In front of the Green Screen Summer 2005

On the Golf Course Spring 2005

CHAPTER 26

Strike Two

Jordan's second medical emergency occurred one year later in early June 2006. I'd gone to Mesquite, Nevada to play golf. On most occasions, I took Jordan to Mesquite with me. The hotel didn't allow pets, but we were allowed to stay in a room at the back of the property and Jordan could stay there with me. On this particular trip, the room became unavailable at the last minute. However, my golf tee-times were already booked and paid for so I felt I had little choice but to leave Jordan at home. By this time, he had fully recovered from surgery the previous year and seemed to be in good health.

My girlfriend Rosalind agreed to watch Jordan. On the final day of my trip she was called out of town on business and she had no choice but to drop Jordan off at my house. He was alone less than six hours. Sometime during those six hours, something happened to him. The best thing we can figure is he went outside to go to the bathroom in the pre-summer heat, got overheated, became disoriented and suffered a heat stroke.

When I got home Jordan was on the floor next to the door leading to the garage, almost completely unresponsive. He couldn't get up on his own and when I stood him up he couldn't walk. The floor was covered in his feces.

I rushed Jordan to Sahara Pines Animal Hospital and he was immediately taken back to be examined by Dr. Kristine Ziegler. I was allowed to wait for both of them in one of the other examination rooms. What seemed like an eternity went by. Finally, a vet technician brought Jordan in, and he stumbled over and lay on the floor by my side.

When Dr. Kristine came into the room she was crying. She said she thought whatever happened to Jordan was bad. She believed he had suffered some type of neurological "event," brought on by heat or maybe a brain tumor. She told me she had already made me the appointment and I was to take him immediately over to the Veterinary Neurological Center.

By the time we got to the neurological center and I got him out of our SUV, Jordan was able to walk again. Sort of. As the center's veterinarians watched him stumble toward them so they could get an initial impression of what might have happened to him, I commented that he was still able to run just a few days before. One of the vets looked up at me with a surprised expression on his face and said words I will never forget: "This dog could run?" I was crushed.

The tests they performed on Jordan proved to be inconclusive. However, the vets who examined him believed he did in fact have some type of neurological episode, like a mini-stroke. Or, a tumor was pressing on his brain, affecting his motor skills. Because Jordan was twelve years old they couldn't do anything for him. He was too old to be a good surgical candidate. Any surgery that could be performed would require putting him under general anaesthesia, and the doctors we're concerned that he wouldn't wake up once they put him under. I was told just to take him home and hope for the best. I thanked them and loaded Jordan in the back of our SUV and headed back home, feeling both defeated and broken-hearted.

Before this setback, Jordan could run almost as fast as a young puppy. But after this latest incident, the best he could do was trot. He had definitely lost a step and I knew in my heart that if we weren't close to the end, the end was almost certainly in sight.

To this day, I feel as though I had something to do with Jordan having that neurological episode. I feel it probably wouldn't have happened had he been with me instead of being left at home alone. I will carry that guilt around with me as long as I live.

High School Soccer Field Revisited
Fall 2006

Jordan gradually recovered from that episode and we tried to resume his normal activities as best we could. He continued to accompany me to work each day, still making his daily on-air appearances and still going with me, whenever he could when I did live broadcasts on location. He may have lost a step, but the viewers continued to love him more with each passing day and despite his old age, his popularity continued to grow. However, by this time the calls and e-mails had turned from joy and admiration to concern for his health and advancing years. We still went for our run—which was eventually reduced to a walk—at our favorite local high school soccer field.

By the end of 2006, he was doing as well as could be expected for a big dog approaching thirteen years of age and I thought he might be able to live another year or two. I was wrong.

Jordan and Friend LIVE Broadcast Winter 2006

At Home Fall 2006

School Visit March 1 2006

School Visit Spring 2006

School Visit Spring 2006

CHAPTER 27

Our Next-to-Last
Trip Together

Jordan and I traveled to Mammoth Lake Ski Resort in California in early January 2007, to attend a winter weather conference on global climate change. The trip served several functions. It gave Jordan and me the chance to spend another sixteen hours on the road together. I could do some long-overdue skiing, and I was going to learn more than I already knew about climate change from some of the top experts in their field. The journey was an eight-hour drive each way, giving me some much-

Road Trip to Mammoth Lakes Jan 2007

needed quality time with my boy. We arrived at the Mammoth Lakes Ski Resort area around noon on the Sunday prior to the first day of the conference and my Monday on-air reports back to the station. The only stops along the way were for gas, potty and photo breaks. The conference was scheduled to run through the following Wednesday and when I wasn't in conference lectures, my TV bosses wanted me to provide daily updates during my

Mammoth Lakes Ski Resort
Jan 2007

normal newscasts, live via satellite uplink.

Mammoth Lakes and Mammoth Lakes Ski Resort are located along Highway 395 in heart of the California Sierra Nevada Mountain Range. The base of the ski area is right about 7,900 feet and the skiing, both cross-country and Alpine, is some of the best in the world. My last trip to ski Mammoth was in 1990, while I was living and working in Santa Barbara, and I really looked forward to going back there, this time with Jordan.

Taking Jordan along meant we were able to stay at the only pet-friendly inn on the mountain, conveniently located at the base of the ski lifts. Everyone else attending the conference stayed downtown at the hotel where the conference was held. I was able to walk from our room directly to both the ski lifts and the main lodge, where I'd be doing my daily live updates.

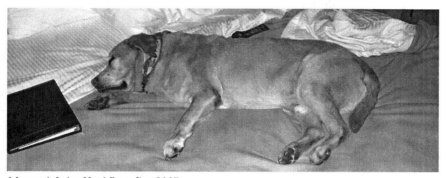

Mammoth Lakes Hotel Room Jan 2007

There were several of my on-air colleagues from TV stations around the west, and we coordinated our satellite interviews so they wouldn't conflict with one another. It was a blast hanging with other broadcasters I'd never met, all the while enjoying the ski area, majestic, tall trees and beautiful, fresh white snow as our scenic backdrop. Between the morning and noon broadcast, I would go back to our room to check on Jordan, take him outside to go potty and then head over to the ski lifts to get reacquainted with Alpine skiing. I'm not a great skier, but I sure do enjoy blasting down a mountain run, with the chill in the mountain air slapping my face with the

LIVE Broadcast from Mammoth Lakes Jan 2007

beautiful high-altitude scenery creating a sensory overload.

Jordan was great on this trip. He never had an accident in the hotel room. By now, accidents were becoming more common. Jordan was beginning to lose control of his bowels. He did take a dump in

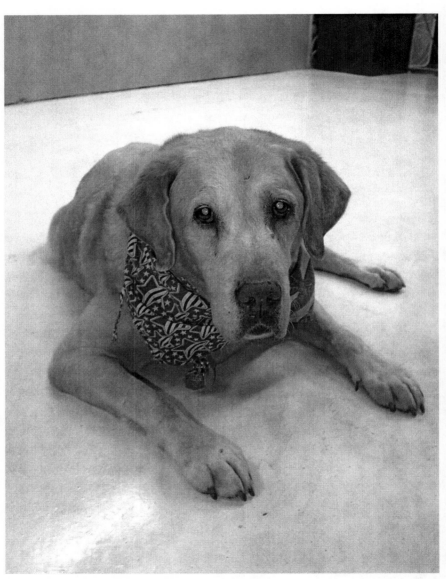

Jordan January 30, 2007, Birthday Morning

the hotel lobby one morning, but it was so early no one was around to see it and I quickly got it cleaned up.

By the time of our Mammoth Lakes trip, Jordan had been pooping in his sleep for several months. At first, I would get mad at him because I thought he was just being lazy and didn't want to go outside. Eventually, I realized that he was no longer able to control his bowels. I put fiber powder in his food, hoping it would help him control his bowels. It didn't. But it did make his poops hard as stone so they were easy to pick up and left no mess behind.

Jordan and I left the winter weather conference a few hours early on Wednesday afternoon because I had to be back at the television station the following morning. Jordan was waiting for me in the back of our SUV in the parking structure at the hotel. After leaving the conference, I got him out of the SUV and tried to get him to poop or pee before we hit the road. He just wandered around the parking structure, returning to the SUV for the ride home.

An hour north of Las Vegas, I knew Jordan must be getting close to the bowel-breaking point and decided it was time to stop. I pulled into an oversized gravel parking area just west U.S. 95, about an hour or so north of Las Vegas, I lifted Jordan out of the back of the SUV and placed him on the ground. It was pitch black outside and not a soul was in sight. After wandering around for only a few seconds, he started to squat and poop. Watching Jordan take a dump was like watching someone yawn. It was contagious, if you catch my drift. And, if you'd been there, you would've. Jordan and I shared a special moment that Wednesday night under clear skies and millions of stars. It was quite the bonding experience. I must have laughed for the next hour as we continued our drive home. We arrived back at our home in Las Vegas late that Wednesday night, without further incident.

We returned to work the following day and resumed our normal schedule: Jordan going with me to work each day; making his daily live on-air appearances. Our viewers continued to love him more with each passing day. Jordan no longer wandered the studio while I was on-air, and when the camera did pan over to him he just lay there next to me at the chroma key wall, usually sound asleep. I'm sure it was obvious to the viewers Jordan was really slowing down and they couldn't get enough of him. I'm also certain our viewers were beginning to sense that the end was drawing near.

Our television crew, having witnessed first-hand Jordan's physical deterioration, put together a special on-air video tribute to him. It aired on the morning of his thirteenth birthday, January 30, 2007. I put candles with the numbers "1" and "3" on top of a little beef "cake" I had made for him. I lit them and blew them out for him just as the newscast was about to end. It had become increasingly hard for me to contain my emotions about Jordan, even while I was on-air, and I didn't bother to wipe the tears from my face that January morning.

Jordan Right Eye signs of Horner Syndrome Spring 2007. Photo by Debbie Trevizo
Copyright 2007 Lucky Dog Magazine

CHAPTER 28

Strike Two and a Half

On a spring morning in 2007, I noticed that Jordan's right eye looked funny. It was as if it had somehow slanted back. It had. His vet, Dr. Kristine Ziegler examined him that morning and explained to me Jordan had developed Horner's Syndrome. It is a condition quite common in older dogs. Causes are varied, but they usually involve some type of neurological problem wherein the brain can no longer control the eye nerves and the eye actually does roll back into the socket. Dr. Kristine assured me that this was simply an aesthetic issue and was not causing Jordan any pain. However, it became painful for me during subsequent personal appearances. At the first appearance following the diagnosis, a young couple came up to greet Jordan and the wife said to the husband, "What's the matter with his eye?" He responded by saying: "He's just an old dog." It broke my heart. I immediately loaded Jordan into the back of our SUV and drove home.

There were days when the eye would appear to be better, but Dr. Kristine told me not to expect it to ever be normal again. Fortunately, the condition developed after the last of our school visits that year for Nevada Reading Week, and I was relieved that school kids would not be traumatized by his appearance. Once I got used to Jordan's new look, I came to find his appearance quite distinctive and it just made the old boy look that much sweeter to me.

School Visit March 2007

CHAPTER 29

One More Ocean Swim

On a Saturday morning, in late July 2007, Jordan and I went on what would turn out to be our last trip together. I knew that the end was drawing very near, and I promised my boy we would take one last trip to Santa Barbara together—to the beach where he romped, played and learned to swim as a puppy. It was a five-plus hour drive from Las Vegas to Santa Barbara and we left our house at 1:30 a.m. on that Saturday morning, pulling into the parking area of Santa Barbara's Arroyo State Beach just after sunrise. Memories of our daily trips to this beach during Jordan's youth came flooding back to me and I felt a lump in my chest knowing this would be his last trip back "home." The sea air was damp and the skies were gray with the morning coastal fog, further adding to my heavy heart and dampening my spirits.

Although it had been over two years since our last trip to the beach, Jordan immediately perked up when he got the first whiff of air and was up wagging his tail before we even pulled into the parking area of our old stomping grounds.

Jordan couldn't wait to get out of the SUV, and I quickly got our camera and got him leashed. He actually jumped from the back of the SUV, something he had stopped doing months before as I had gotten use to lifting him in and out of the car.

Despite all his excitement, Jordan's tired and weak back legs would not cooperate. Before we even got to the water, he lost the use of his left hind

Final Ocean Swim July 2007

leg, the one that had plagued him the most over the years. The moist sea air was just too much for his old joints. With his useless leg dragging behind, he eventually made it down to the water. I kept trying to help him, but he seemed to want to get to the water on his own. So I just stood back and watched. When he finally made it to the water, he sat there as the water and waves lapped over him. I knew he was probably in pain, but Jordan never appeared happier. I took some pictures of the waves splashing on him while tears rolled down my face. I knelt next to him, turned the camera around and took a few pictures of us together. One of those self-portraits greets me each day when I walk into our home. It hangs just above the hall that leads to our garage.

After less than thirty minutes at the beach where Jordan grew up—where we shared so many wonderful memories together—I knew it was time to leave. I had kept my promise to him. I slung one arm under his belly

Our Last Photo Together at the Beach In Santa Barbara July 2007

so he could walk to the showers near the parking lot. He collapsed right underneath the shower head. I rinsed the sand off him and a lady came by to ask if my dog was okay. I told her he was fine. I let her know he was just getting very old and I had just driven over five hours from Las Vegas so he could see the ocean one final time. With tears in her eyes she looked at me and said: "God bless you for doing that for your dog."

Jordan and I headed back to Las Vegas, but we first stopped at my mom's grave, at the Eternal Valley Cemetery along I-14 near Canyon Country, California. I have no problem admitting to being a mother's boy, and I know I inherited my love of animals from my mother, Eleanor. Any stray cat or dog we brought home as kids was welcomed immediately into our family. They were usually gone the following day, but she never stopped

Jordan at Mothers Grave July 2007

us from bringing stray dogs or cats home.

I had a childhood boxer named Duffy. He was my aunt and uncle's dog, but Duffy kind of adopted me. We shared the same birthday. When I would take naps, I'd use Duffy's tummy as my pillow. He'd stay still and wouldn't move until I woke up. He was also my protector.

One morning I was walking Duffy back to my aunt and uncle's and a German shepherd tried to attack me. Duffy kicked the dog's butt then chased it across two major intersections. He returned home unhurt later that afternoon. I hugged and thanked him for always looking out for me.

Duffy had to be euthanized when he was eight but my mother didn't tell me until she thought I was old enough to hear it. Whenever I asked about him, my mom would just tell me Duffy was visiting a neighbor or a family friend. Only years later would I learn that he had been put down at the age of eight, in 1963. My mom eventually gave me the sad news but by that time I'd already figured it out on my own.

In the late 1960s, when I was in my early teens, my sister brought home a Cockapoo puppy. She named the dog Morticia, after the Carolyn Jones character in *The Addams Family* television series. My sister lost interest in the puppy almost immediately, but my mom fell in love with her, and Morticia and my mom became inseparable. Morticia's name was eventually shortened to "Tish."

My mom loved Tish as much as she loved us kids. And in 1970, when we moved to Delano, California, Morticia moved with us.

Delano, a farming community in California's central valley, is probably best known as the home of Caesar Chavez, the founder and president of the United Farm Workers Labor Union. My mom had remarried in the summer of 1970, and we moved to Delano to live with my new stepfather, Miles. He managed a cotton gin just northwest of town.

The first year we were in Delano we lived in town in a mobile home park. The following year we moved out to the country where the cotton gin was, about fifteen miles outside of town in the middle of farming country. Soon after moving to the country, my mom and step dad adopted an Australian shepherd. The shepherd and Tish became fast friends. The dogs were not fenced in and were allowed to roam free. They'd wander up and down the roads and always came home at the end of the day when they got tired, smelling of cow dung or skunk.

In the fall of 1973, after I graduated from high school, I was hanging out with a friend in downtown Delano and my mom somehow tracked me down. When I called her back she was sobbing into the phone and her words to me were barely audible. I was finally able to make out that Tish had been hit and killed and was on the side of the road near the cotton gin. Mom said she needed me to "take care of Tish." I borrowed a shovel and drove out to the site where Tish had been killed. I dug a hole, buried her and made a crude, makeshift cross. This was a pretty traumatic event for a kid barely out of high school. My trauma was nothing compared to the grief and pain, both emotional and physical, that my mom would suffer.

Tish was hit by a truck that was on its way to our cotton gin. The truck driver went into the gin office and asked my mom if anyone there owned a dog. She asked the driver what the dog looked like and he said it was a "big black one." My mom told me later, at that very moment she felt a "snap" in the back of her neck. She was convinced that was the beginning of her medical problems.

My mother died three years later of brain cancer and the tumor that ended up taking her life was at the base of her brain, in the back of her neck. My mom was never the same after Tish was killed.

I am convinced that something physically happened to my mom the moment she found out Tish was killed. I am also convinced that her love of animals was one of the greatest gifts I inherited from her.

After arriving at the cemetery that July day in 2007, I spent a few minutes alone at my mother's headstone and then got Jordan out of the car and, being well away from the sea air, he was able to use his back leg once again and he walked right over to my mother's grave without direction or any prompting from me. I had him lay down next to my mom's grave marker and snapped off a few pictures. I was glad that Jordan got to spend a few minutes with my mom. She would've loved him as much as I did.

CHAPTER 30
He Jumped

On Saturday, July 28, 2007, our morning together started out as normal as it could by that point. Jordan was really having trouble getting around but he was still eating, so I fixed his breakfast and made myself a pot of coffee. I got dressed, backed the SUV out of the garage and parked it in the driveway. I opened the back lift-gate and went back inside to get Jordan. He loved to lay in back of the SUV with the lift-gate open so he could enjoy the sights and sounds of our neighborhood. To this day, I am convinced the back of our SUV was Jordan's favorite place on earth. I propped the back door leading to the garage open and opened the front door of the house so I could hear anything going on outside. Then I went back inside to finish up some work in my home office. Exactly what happened next is something I'll never really know for sure. But now I have a pretty good idea having over a year to think about it.

I was inside at my office desk, and had been working on my computer for about fifteen minutes when I thought I heard the sound of Jordan's dog tags "tinkling" in the hallway that lead to the garage, and the front of our house. I thought I was hearing things and continued working. Moments later, I heard the same sound and stopped, listening quietly. Jordan came stumbling around the corner from the hallway toward my office, which occupies the front room of our home. He was limping along at a snail's pace and I noticed the scab on top of his head from an old-age wart had broken. There was blood on the top of his head. He collapsed at my feet.

Morning He Jumped from back of SUV July 29, 2007

I cleaned up the top of his head and applied some medication. I let him lay there with me for a few more minutes before getting him back out to the car, for what would turn out to be his final run around the high school soccer field that he so loved much.

Until now, I've never told this story to anyone, even my best friend, John. For many months following that day I thought Jordan had fallen out of the back of the SUV. And that it was my fault. However, I've had a lot of time to think about that morning. I'm now convinced that Jordan did not fall that morning. He jumped. He wanted to be near his dad. I believe now that Jordan knew he was close to the end of his life. In those final days, he wanted to be by my side.

Jordan died the following Saturday morning, just two weeks after our final trip to the ocean. I will be forever grateful I made one last journey with him so he could spend some time in Santa Barbara, the place where he was born. His final days were the best I could make for him to ensure he was comfortable, happy and loved.

CHAPTER 31
Strike Three

Jordan's last day of work was on August 3, 2007. He hadn't eaten anything that morning and by that time he wasn't drinking much water. But he could still get up and move around with a little help, and I could tell he wanted to go with me to work.

When we got to the television station that morning, around 3:00 a.m., he seemed to be walking okay, but was getting noticeably shaky in his back legs. We clocked in—got into the studio—and I started researching the forecast for the next seven days. Jordan was content to lie by my side in the studio weather center.

Shortly after the newscast ended at 7:00 a.m., Jordan got up and hobbled over to the studio door, letting me know he wanted to go outside. He was still able to walk on his own and I thought we were in for another normal day. I was wrong.

A short time later, I went back outside to check on him. Jordan was in the doggy run, dragging his hind legs behind him. I ran inside, told everyone that Jordan was having some problems and I was taking him to the vet. I had put station management on notice that Jordan's days may be numbered and they no longer expected me to ask for permission if I had to take Jordan home or to the vet. I raced back outside, slung both arms under his belly and got him into the back of our SUV. I called the vet's office to let them know I was bringing Jordan in. I was told that Dr. Ziegler was off that Friday morning, but her husband, Dr. Daniel Ulichny, was on duty. That was fine with me. I knew him as well as Dr. Kristine and I trusted him with Jordan's care.

When we got to Sahara Pines Animal Hospital, Jordan and I were taken back to an exam room to wait for Dr. Dan. I sat there thinking this might be the last time we would ever be in this room together. I was wrong.

When Dr. Ulichny came into the exam room—after having a chance to look at Jordan—I asked him if "we were there yet." He told me Jordan was dehydrated and he wanted to keep him for the day to get some fluids in him. If he improved, he could go home. If he went home and he continued to get worse, Dr. Dan told me I would have to make the decision I never wanted to make. And, right before I left Jordan in his care, he told me that we could not continue down this path. Dr. Ulichny made it very clear to me that we may not have been "there" yet, but we were close.

I left Jordan in the care of Dr. Ulichny and the staff of Sahara Pines Animal Hospital, went out to our SUV and started crying. I called in to work and let them know I needed to take the rest of the day off. I returned a few calls from viewers and went home to rest, hope and pray.

When I got home, I was so exhausted I collapsed on the couch, immediately falling asleep. The phone woke me late that afternoon. It was almost 6:00 p.m. and I had been asleep for nearly eight hours. I answered the phone and Dr. Ulichny told me that Jordan was doing okay and I could come pick him up.

When I got to the vet's office I expected to see a significant improvement, but Jordan was unable to walk on his own and we had to use a towel as a sling to get him to the SUV. When we got home, I hoped and prayed that he might have a good night and he'd be feeling better by the following morning. I was wrong.

Jordan was not eating his normal food so I fixed him some tuna and water, and he wolfed it down. That briefly brightened my spirits. I was still very tired, so I grabbed a comforter, threw it down on the tile floor in our living room, curled up next to my old boy and fell asleep.

I woke up a few hours later and my clothes were soaking wet. I thought I'd knocked over a bottle of water. I looked around but didn't see an empty bottle. Then I smelled urine. Jordan had finally lost control of all his bodily functions and urinated all over our tile floor. I knew—then and there—the end had arrived.

I called Dr. Ziegler on her cell phone and told her I thought it was time. She told me to meet her at her office early the next morning at 7:30 a.m. before the office opened at 8:00 a.m. I told her it might be better if she came to our home. She told me she thought it best not to confuse Jordan, as she'd never treated him at our house. She also didn't want my final memory of him at home to be a sad one. I didn't think things could get any sadder, but I respected her advice and will be forever thankful I took it.

After ending the call with Dr. Ziegler, I curled back up next to my boy and had a serious talk with him. I told him that if he needed to leave, it would be okay with me and I would understand. I told him he was the best friend and son a dad could ask for and he would always be daddy's baby boy. Jordan's breathing suddenly became very shallow and his breaths seemed like they came an eternity apart. I thought he was going to die right there on the floor of our home in my arms. I hoped that would be the case as he would be relieving me of making that one final, gut-wrenching decision. Once again, I was wrong. His breathing soon became stronger and I knew that the final decision would be mine to make. Jordan's veterinarian of nine years, Dr. Kristine Ziegler, had warned me he wasn't going to let me off the hook that easy. She also told me that dogs rarely die in their sleep.

It was just after midnight and I knew I had only a few more hours with my best friend. I also knew it was time to try to make some amends. In our final hours together I started thinking back to the times when he was still young and I was too hard on him. I begged Jordan to forgive me if I ever was too hard on him, either emotionally or physically. I can

Jordan Last Night at Home 3AM August 04, 2007

only hope he somehow understood how bad I felt, and that I was finally apologizing to him after all those years. By this time, Jordan had become almost completely unresponsive to any outside stimulus, so I have no idea if my words were even getting through to him. But I needed to believe that God made him understand what I was trying to tell him.

A short while later I lifted my sweet boy off the floor, took him out to the pool and we had one last swim together. I hooked my arms around his body and walked him around the pool for a few last laps. Afterward, I lifted him onto the deck, toweled him off and helped him back inside. He collapsed on the fresh, dry towel I had placed on the floor for him. Then I

Jordan Last Photo at Home 630AM August 04, 2007

collapsed on the couch. Alone, depressed and exhausted. Too worried and upset to sleep, I just lay there, quietly sobbing, getting up every few minutes just to check on him.

Once, when I got up to check on him, I noticed Jordan was shivering. I went over to him, thinking he was cold from still being damp from our swim. I gently placed my hand on his tummy and his body was warm. When he looked up at me, I knew the reason he was shivering was not because he was cold. He was scared. I stroked his head and spoke words of comfort and support to him. After a while he stopped shivering and fell back asleep.

I tried so desperately hard in those last hours to keep my emotions in check, but I failed miserably. I knew I would have plenty of time for grief and emotion later, but somewhere in my heart and soul I never actually believed that Jordan would leave me. I had often said during interviews about him: "I don't remember what life was like before him. And, I can't imagine life without him."

Around 4:00 a.m. that Saturday morning, I made a pot of coffee and woke Jordan up to give him a few of his favorite treats. I noticed his eyes had stopped draining and there was none of the normal sleepy stuff in the corners of them. I thought he must have gotten dehydrated again so I tried to get him to drink some juice. He wouldn't.

I poured a cup of coffee, started the SUV and lifted Jordan in back for one last run at our favorite local high school, the same one we discovered during our first venture out in Las Vegas, in the summer of '96.

Last Self Portrait Together Back of SUV 430AM August 04, 2007

When we got to the high school soccer field, I lifted Jordan out of the back of the SUV and set him on the cool grass. He tried desperately to get up and go for his run, but the back third of his body had simply stopped working.

I reluctantly loaded him back in the SUV, grabbed my digital camera and took a final self-portrait of the two of us. I took a few other photos of him throughout the morning, as I wanted to remember our final day together.

We stopped by McDonald's on the way home and I bought Jordan a sausage McMuffin with egg. I figured diet was no longer an issue and a bit of comfort food wasn't going to hurt him. When I got home, I lifted the back lift gate of the SUV and gave Jordan his breakfast sandwich. To my surprise, he tore right through it. When he finished his breakfast, I lifted him out of the SUV and placed him gently on our front lawn so I could

Jordan and Gigi 7AM August 04, 2007

take a few more pictures.

At 6:30 a.m. on the final morning of Jordan's life, I loaded him up one last time in the back of our SUV and we headed off to the vet's office. As I was in no rush to get there, I decided to make a stop or two along the way.

I called Rosalind—now my ex-girlfriend—from my cell and told her we were coming by to say goodbye. When we got to her house she came out with her son, Elliott and their dog, Gigi. Rosalind told me she had no photos of Jordan and Gigi together so I got my camera while she lifted Gigi into the back of the SUV. I snapped off a picture of the two dogs side by side. Rosalind and Elliott were beginning to get pretty emotional, so I had them say a quick "goodbye." I got back into the SUV and drove off.

I was trying to put off the inevitable for as long as possible, so I decided to drive through our old townhouse complex and spent a few moments behind our old garage. I thought back on a September day in 2002, the day Jordan gave me a big "high four" when we arrived home from our first cross-country trip together.

I could think of no other places to stop. And I knew I was being selfish by stalling, so we continued on to Jordan's final destination: Sahara Pines Animal Hospital, to see Dr. Kristine one final time together. Jordan loved his vet and her staff, and I knew it was best that his final moments were going to be there with them. And his dad.

We arrived at Sahara Pines a bit early, so I lifted Jordan out of the back of our SUV and placed him on the grassy area in front of the hospital. I sat next to him and told him Dr. Kristine was going to make him feel better. I let him know that when we left Dr. Kristine's office we'd go for a long ride in the car, and then we'd go swimming in the ocean. I took a few more pictures of him and we talked some more while waiting for his doctor to arrive.

Dr. Ziegler pulled into the hospital parking lot right at 7:00 a.m. and immediately came over, gave us both a hug and told me she was going to

Jordan Last Picture Sahara Pines Animal Hospital 715AM August 04, 2007

go inside to get things ready. I could tell she was trying as hard as I was to hold things together.

Some of the best advice I've ever received was from Doug Duke, the executive director of the Nevada SPCA. During a conversation a few days earlier, Doug told me I might traumatize Jordan if I became too emotional during his final moments. He reminded me there would be plenty of time to grieve after Jordan was gone. So I spoke calmly and lovingly to my old boy and we shared a few more special moments together.

At 7:15 a.m., one of the vet technicians came out and lifted Jordan in his arms. He carried Jordan inside and lay him down on a soft blanket in the same examining room we'd been in less than twenty hours earlier. Jordan and I were on the examining room floor, surrounded by two other vet techs and Dr. Kristine, all who had come to know and love my boy. All three of them were crying uncontrollably. Hard as I tried to heed Doug Duke's advice and to keep it together, when I saw how upset everyone else in the room was, I lost it. I looked up at Dr. Kristine and said: "I don't think I can do this." She gave me a few moments to collect myself before beginning the procedure that would end my boy's pain, suffering and adventure on earth. She explained to me that Jordan would simply go to sleep and his heart would eventually stop beating. Then she hooked up the IV.

I mentioned earlier that Jordan had become dehydrated and his tear ducts had dried up. You have probably also been told that animals don't cry. Don't believe it for a minute. In those final quiet moments of Jordan's life he looked right into my eyes, and his eyes filled with tears. And, I knew exactly what he was thinking. My sweet, loving, kind old boy believed that after all those years, he was somehow letting me down. I leaned down, kissed his head and whispered into his ear, "You're the best, old man. Daddy loves you the most. You just go to sleep now and when you wake up we're gonna go for a really long ride in the car."

Dr. Ziegler had once told me that Jordan—like most Labs—had a very strong heart. That morning he proved it beyond a shadow of a doubt. Long after she thought he would have slipped away, holding the stethoscope to his chest, Dr. Kristine looked at me and said: "He's still here." And as tears rolled down her face she whispered to him, "Oh, Jordan."

At exactly 7:30 a.m., on the morning of August 4, 2007, Dr. Kristine Ziegler of the Sahara Pines Animal Hospital held the stethoscope closely to Jordan's side, looked up at me, and with tears still streaming down her face, said: "He's gone."

I looked down at my sleeping boy, gave him one last hug and kiss and stood up and gave Dr. Kristine a big hug. I told her how sorry I was that she was the one who had to end Jordan's life. She looked into my eyes and said words that I will remember until the day I die: "John, it was an honor and a privilege. And, I would not have had it any other way."

I thanked all the employees at the Sahara Pines Animal Hospital for their kindness and compassion over the years and walked outside to a beautiful, brilliant Las Vegas summer morning. I unlocked our SUV, got in and started the engine. And, for one final time, I drove away from my best friend and faithful companion, knowing he was already romping across grassy fields, meeting old friends and waiting for his daddy, just this side of Rainbow Bridge.

Jordan's Memorial Service, Dr Kristine Ziegler, Jordan's Eulogy, August 10, 2007.
Photos courtesy of John R. Tutora.

CHAPTER 32

The Memorial Service

Jordan's memorial service was held the following Friday, August 10, 2007 at 7:00 p.m. at the Craig Road Pet Cemetery in Las Vegas. Our television station aired a video tribute to him during each nightly newscast the week prior to the service. After each tribute aired, the anchors let our viewers know when and where the service was going to be held. And, despite temperatures still being over 100 degrees on the evening of the service, over 500 people attended. The cemetery owners told me it was the largest turn out for a memorial service there they'd ever seen. Those in attendance included many of my co-workers, newspaper and television reporters, police K-9 units and Jordan's loyal viewers. Motorcycle officers from the Las Vegas Metropolitan Police Department were out in the street directing traffic. I was overwhelmed by the number of people who came out that summer evening to pay a final tribute to their favorite yellow Labrador retriever.

By the end of the service, I was soaked with perspiration right through my shirt and dress suit. Not one person complained about the heat. In the days following the service, many of those in attendance e-mailed me to let me know Jordan's service ended just as the sun was setting over my shoulder. Setting figuratively and literally on such a remarkable life.

Just before I left my house for the service, with my best two-legged buddy John by my side, I got a call from Gail at the cemetery asking if I could bring one of Jordan's favorite red, white, and blue bandanas with me.

Jordan's Memorial Service, August 10, 2007. Photos courtesy of John R. Tutora.

I agreed, but I didn't understand why. When we arrived at the cemetery, I found out that Jordan was in the cemetery's beautiful little chapel in an open casket. Gail wanted to make sure Jordan was wearing his bandana one final time. Had I known beforehand they were planning an open casket service I'm sure I would've told them that was not what I wanted. I'm glad I didn't know until I got there. It gave me a chance to say a final "Goodbye." More importantly, it gave those who had never met Jordan a chance to do so as well.

Just before the service was about to begin, the pastor who was to officiate called to say he had been called away on an emergency. That meant I'd have to officiate the service myself—with no notes or preparation. Fortunately, I had lined up four speakers who did show. I grabbed a pen and paper and scribbled a few notes.

The memorial service was understandably emotional. I'd fall apart and then compose myself. However, each time I pulled it back together, I'd look out across a sea of crying faces and I'd break down all over again. I was saying goodbye to my best friend and it was the hardest thing I ever had to do. To give myself an occasional break, I'd call up one of my guest speakers. They included my friends, Snake Rock and Justin Cooper, Dr. Kristine Ziegler and Doug Duke of the Nevada SPCA. Each gave beautiful, even sometimes comical accounts of their relationship with Jordan. I don't think I would've ever made it through the service without their help.

After Jordan's memorial service ended, everyone in attendance formed a line so they could pass by his casket and pay their final respects. John and I slipped quietly through the crowd and drove home.

A link to the full video account of the service is available through our website: www.paws-across-america.com.

To this day, I'm still amazed and sometimes baffled by how people in our community became so attached to Jordan. The truth is—at the end of the day—he was just a dog. He never spoke a word, he didn't do anything fancy when he was on television, he wasn't outwardly affectionate and he wasn't the most intelligent dog in the world. And yet there was something about my sweet boy that stole the hearts of our viewers.

Dr. Ziegler set up a memorial fund for Jordan with the Nevada SPCA and they received over $30,000 in donations in his memory. Over 3,000 e-mails and 1,000 letters of condolence, came to the television station. With the help of my co-worker, Megan Monro, we answered every one of them. I receive letters and e-mails of condolence to this very day, many from people who've moved away from Las Vegas but heard the news of Jordan's passing from family and friends who are still here.

My co-workers would often tell me if they were having a bad day and they knew Jordan was out in the dog run, they would just go outside and spend time with him. They said just seeing him and having him come up to them with a smile on his face made them feel better.

I found comfort in spending time with Jordan as well. I would tell friends he was like "hours of free entertainment." He could look at me a certain way and I'd start laughing. And sometimes when he slept, I'd quietly curl up and sleep right by his side.

Many years ago when Jordan was young, we made a deal with each other: "Never grow old. Never get sick. And, never die." Each time I'd say those words, Jordan would lift up his paw and shake my hand. In his final days, when I knew he could no longer keep our deal, I stopped making him shake on it.

Jordan seemed to love knowing that he was making me happy. If I had a bad day, I would sit on the floor and tell him to come over and give daddy "huggies." He'd walk over to me and I would put my arms and legs around him. He'd rest his head on my shoulder and, as he got older he'd stay there as long as I needed him to. If I had a really bad day and I came home crying, he would let me lay my head on his neck and he wouldn't move until I was done. He wouldn't lick me or give me kisses, but he knew that I was upset and that I needed him. He was always there for me.

I think Jordan knew he was special because of the way people went out of their way to give him attention. He seemed to know when someone was going to take a picture of him or when he was on camera.

I think Jordan was special because he represented the unconditional love that our pets give us.

Many years ago, I read the following, anonymous quote: "A dog is the only living creature that loves you more than he loves himself." That was my Jordan. And, I'm sure that is your dog, too.

Jordan Memorial Hat and Sweatshirt, December 2007
Proceeds to NSPCA

Dr Kristine Ziegler with LJ September 01, 2007

Epilogue

Within days of Jordan's passing, viewers and prominent members of the community started calling station management, demanding they get me another dog. Some viewers even called threatening to bring a puppy down to the station to give me. It became a point of great concern and consternation for me. I wasn't ready for another pet. However, I started feeling as though such a personal decision might be torn from my grip.

One day while I was at work, a dear friend of mine, Jillian Springs of Springwood Labradors, in Pahrump e-mailed me a few pictures. She wrote: "Don't open the attachment unless you're ready for a new friend." Without even giving it a thought, I opened the attached picture only to see a young Jordan look-a-like staring right back at me. I faced a very difficult decision: Was I ready for a new dog? How would the community react to me getting one from a breeder and not a shelter or rescue group? And, while Jillian is the only breeder I've ever recommended to people who insist on getting a purebred Labrador retriever, had I been looking for a new companion at that time, I would've gotten a rescue. Or so I thought.

I explained to Jillian my concerns and she told me that my only obligation was to tell people the puppy was a gift from a friend, which was the truth. I told her I was going to really have to do some thinking about it.

That night it occurred to me that accepting her offer would be a very wise choice for a very important reason: This dog would be a public figure, a dog that would grow up on TV right in front of our viewers' eyes. And hopefully, they'd fall in love with him just like they fell in love with Jordan.

LJ Adoption Day September 01, 2007

JORDAN'S PAWS ACROSS AMERICA

LJ first Meeting August 25, 2007.
Photo courtesy of Jillian Springs.

Of greater importance: I had to know that my next dog would never have behavioral issues as I would presumably be taking him to see thousands of school kids over the coming years. I had to have a dog that would be as well-behaved as Jordan. But I needed someone's approval: Jordan's.

On my way in to work the following morning I had a long conversation with the old boy and told him what I was about to do, but only if he thought it was okay. I asked him to please give me some kind of "sign." At that very moment I looked down at the dash tray where my cell phone was laying face up, with Jordan's photo on the screen and the phone light flashed on and off, four consecutive times.

I knew at that moment what Jordan was telling me: "It's okay, Dad. My suffering ended when you sent me on to wait for you at Rainbow Bridge. It's time for some of your suffering to end, too. Don't worry, you won't be replacing me. You just need another friend." My sweet old boy had given me the answer I needed to hear.

A few weeks later, our SUV was broken into. Along with my billfold and stereo equipment, the thieves took my cell phone, the same one with Jordan's picture in its window. I never got it back.

A week from the following Saturday, September 1, 2007, I was united with my new little buddy, LJ. LJ stands for "Little Jordan" and I actually got the idea for his name from our TV station's owner. Shortly after Jordan

Unveling Jordan's Memorial at Craig Road Pet Cemetery August 04, 2008. Photo courtesy of Donna Stidham, Esq.

died, the owner of the station left me a voice mail telling me that he and his wife had heard that "poor old Jordan died and it made them sad." His voice message went on to say that he hoped someday I would "get another little Jordan."

The television audience took to my new friend immediately after I introduced him the following Monday morning, and has followed his development with incredible interest. In short, he's a hit with the Las Vegas TV viewing audience. I also have been told hundreds of times over the past year that viewers were heartbroken for me and so happy that I got a new friend.

I will tell you this: If you ever go through the loss of a pet, the decision to get a new one is one that you have to make on your own. Don't ever let anyone try to make it for you.

And yes, as a responsible pet owner, Dr. Kristine Ziegler neutered LJ at the appropriate age. And, though I was not prepared for raising another puppy, Jordan taught me valuable lessons about obedience and puppy training, LJ has turned out to be a wonderful companion. And, as I had the good sense to get him from a responsible AKC certified breeder, he has no physical or behavioral problems, and is absolutely wonderful with kids, just like Jordan. But LJ is not Jordan. He never will be. And that's just fine with me. However, I will admit it took some time to accept that fact. Once I did, it was easier to honor Jordan's memory without guilt, knowing there is nothing wrong with making new friends.

The most significant event that has happened to me in the past year, other than getting LJ, had to do with a permanent monument for Jordan. You see, the folks at Craig Road Pet Cemetery cremated Jordan and his ashes are contained in a beautiful cherrywood box that sits on our mantel. I did take

Spreading Jordan's Ashes, January 2008

LJ to Santa Barbara in January 2008 and I threw some of Jordan's ashes into the ocean where he had played as a pup. But most of Jordan remained at home with me. The problem was that his fans had nowhere to go to pay

tribute to him. The owners of the cemetery told me they would gladly set aside a special place near the entrance to the cemetery should I ever be able to get a memorial built because people were coming by weekly wanting to know, "Where's Jordan?"

Spreading Jordan's Ashes, January 2008

Jordan Memorial Night Fall 2008.

One year to the minute following Jordan's passing, a permanent monument was unveiled to a group of viewers, friends and reporters at the Craig Road Pet Cemetery. For a moment after the tarp was pulled away, the crowd went silent. That brief silence was followed by cheers, applause, and tears of joy. Jordan's memorial is the most magnificent piece of work I have ever seen. And, all of the labor and material was donated by pet-loving artisans in our community. I will be forever grateful for their acts of kindness and love. Because of their efforts, there will always be a special place for people to visit, and honor Jordan's memory.

At my request, a small opening was made in Jordan's memorial between the top and the base. Inside, I placed a sealed plastic bag. In that bag, for all of time, are the following: A card with a private message from his dad, a tuft of his hair, his ashes, and his favorite red, white, and blue bandana. And, one more item—his dog tag, should he ever become lost.

I visit him every day.

In Loving Memory
Jordan Fredericks
January 30, 1994 - August 4, 2007

John and LJ. Jordan's Memorial August 26, 2008. Photo courtesy of Donna Stidham, Esq.

Acknowledgements

Thank you, Donna, for all of your work on this project. Thanks also to Donna and Super Dave Stidham for personally overseeing the design, construction and placement of Jordan's beautiful permanent memorial at Craig Road Pet Cemetery in Las Vegas. And to all of those who donated their time, labor and materials in the building of the memorial.

To my book designer, Gwyn Kennedy Snider of GKS Creative. A huge "Thanks!" for making sure the book looks wonderful. And to Amy and Mary Frances of The Cadence Group for your outstanding job of editing my manuscript.

Many thanks to my best two-legged friend of forty-five years, John Tutora, who put up with all my stress during the final days of trying to get this book finished. Love you, buddy.

Thanks to the Art Institute of Las Vegas for designing all four of Jordan's Paws Across America calendars.

Thank you to Arlene Bell of AMB Web Design for managing our website all these years.

Huge thanks to Las Vegas Mayor, Oscar Goodman; my favorite comedian, Rita Rudner and to Roy of Siegfried and Roy for their testimonials.

The reference to "Lost Light" was from a novel by Michael Connelly.

Thanks also to my friends Toni and Robin. You helped me survive the days leading up to and after Jordan's passing. I'm forever in your debt.

A very special "Thank You" to the wonderful folks at the Craig Road Pet Cemetery for making available a very special place so that Jordan will forever have a place to call "home."

A million thanks to our viewers, who opened their hearts and homes to Jordan and me for all those wonderful years. Some of the proceeds from the sale of this book will help homeless pets.

Unless otherwise noted, the author took all of the photos for this book. For other photos, credit is not possible as the photos did not include credit information. If one of your photos ended up in this book without credit, I thank you and take responsibility for the omission.

All of the events described in this book actually took place. Events were either recreated from my memory or were taken from journal entries on my website, www.paws-across-america.com.

The only other source, for reference material was www.wikipedia. com

Finally, thanks to the best friend and son a man could ever hope for: my Jordan. You were there for me when I needed you the most. You're the best, old man. Daddy loves you the most. And, I miss you more with each passing day. Just know that it won't be long before we'll be back together again on that big, beautiful open road in the sky. For eternity. Then we're going to go for that really long ride in the car.

About the Authors

JOHN FREDERICKS is the former Chief Meteorologist for the NBC affiliate in Las Vegas, Nevada. His broadcast career has spanned over thirty years and he was recently inducted into the Nevada Broadcasters' Hall of Fame and was also recently named a recipient of the American Kennel Club's Community Achievement Award for his public education efforts throughout the Las Vegas metropolitan area. He serves on the Board of Directors of the Nevada SPCA. He is a four-time winner of the Electronic Media Awards "Best Local Weathercaster" and has been voted "Best Local Weathercaster" five of the last six years by the readers of the *Las Vegas Review Journal*. He lives with his new Labrador retriever companion, "LJ" (Little Jordan) in Las Vegas.

DONNA STIDHAM, ESQ. was born in New Jersey and moved to Las Vegas, Nevada when she was eight yeas old. She has lived in Las Vegas ever since. Donna has always loved animals but didn't get involved in the Las Vegas pet community until she was in law school. While in law school, Donna co-founded the student chapter of the Animal Legal Defense Fund. While working on a fundraising project with other students of the law school, Donna was introduced to the executive director of the Nevada SPCA, Las Vegas' only no-kill animal sanctuary that rescues all types of animals, not just the traditional dog and cat. That is when she realized there were so many animals that needed help. After law school, she started her own law firm specifically to help individuals not only plan for their lives and deaths but to make sure their pets were taken care of should the individual no longer be able to. Donna has had the privilege of working with the Nevada SPCA doing pro-bono legal work for the organization. www.stidhamlawoffice.com

Printed in the United States
143398LV00001BB/2/P

9 780982 176207